Cases on Supply Chain Management and Lessons Learned From COVID-19

Ana Paula Lopes
Polytechnic of Porto, Portugal

A volume in the Advances in
Logistics, Operations, and
Management Science (ALOMS) Book
Series

Published in the United States of America by
IGI Global
Business Science Reference (an imprint of IGI Global)
701 E. Chocolate Avenue
Hershey PA, USA 17033
Tel: 717-533-8845
Fax: 717-533-8661
E-mail: cust@igi-global.com
Web site: http://www.igi-global.com

Copyright © 2022 by IGI Global. All rights reserved. No part of this publication may be reproduced, stored or distributed in any form or by any means, electronic or mechanical, including photocopying, without written permission from the publisher.
Product or company names used in this set are for identification purposes only. Inclusion of the names of the products or companies does not indicate a claim of ownership by IGI Global of the trademark or registered trademark.

Library of Congress Cataloging-in-Publication Data

Names: Lopes, Ana Paula, 1967- editor.
Title: Cases on supply chain management and lessons learned from COVID-19 / Ana Paula Lopes, editor.
Description: Hershey, PA : Business Science Reference, [2022] | Includes bibliographical references and index. | Summary: "This book of contributed chapters allows researchers and academicians to exchange and share their experiences and results on all features of Logistics and Supply Chain Management, including theoretical and empirical research, case studies of important and fruitful applications in this field, leading to effective teaching and learning"-- Provided by publisher.
Identifiers: LCCN 2021035419 (print) | LCCN 2021035420 (ebook) | ISBN 9781799891406 (hardcover) | ISBN 9781799891413 (paperback) | ISBN 9781799891420 (ebook)
Subjects: LCSH: Business logistics. | Crisis management. | COVID-19 (Disease)--Economic aspects.
Classification: LCC HD38.5 .C2778 2022 (print) | LCC HD38.5 (ebook) | DDC 658.5--dc23
LC record available at https://lccn.loc.gov/2021035419
LC ebook record available at https://lccn.loc.gov/2021035420

This book is published in the IGI Global book series Advances in Logistics, Operations, and Management Science (ALOMS) (ISSN: 2327-350X; eISSN: 2327-3518)

British Cataloguing in Publication Data
A Cataloguing in Publication record for this book is available from the British Library.

All work contributed to this book is new, previously-unpublished material.
The views expressed in this book are those of the authors, but not necessarily of the publisher.

For electronic access to this publication, please contact: eresources@igi-global.com.

Advances in Logistics, Operations, and Management Science (ALOMS) Book Series

ISSN:2327-350X
EISSN:2327-3518

Editor-in-Chief: John Wang, Montclair State University, USA

MISSION

Operations research and management science continue to influence business processes, administration, and management information systems, particularly in covering the application methods for decision-making processes. New case studies and applications on management science, operations management, social sciences, and other behavioral sciences have been incorporated into business and organizations real-world objectives.

The **Advances in Logistics, Operations, and Management Science** (ALOMS) Book Series provides a collection of reference publications on the current trends, applications, theories, and practices in the management science field. Providing relevant and current research, this series and its individual publications would be useful for academics, researchers, scholars, and practitioners interested in improving decision making models and business functions.

COVERAGE

- Production Management
- Risk Management
- Decision analysis and decision support
- Operations Management
- Organizational Behavior
- Political Science
- Computing and information technologies
- Marketing engineering
- Services management
- Finance

IGI Global is currently accepting manuscripts for publication within this series. To submit a proposal for a volume in this series, please contact our Acquisition Editors at Acquisitions@igi-global.com or visit: http://www.igi-global.com/publish/.

The Advances in Logistics, Operations, and Management Science (ALOMS) Book Series (ISSN 2327-350X) is published by IGI Global, 701 E. Chocolate Avenue, Hershey, PA 17033-1240, USA, www.igi-global.com. This series is composed of titles available for purchase individually; each title is edited to be contextually exclusive from any other title within the series. For pricing and ordering information please visit http://www.igi-global.com/book-series/advances-logistics-operations-management-science/37170. Postmaster: Send all address changes to above address. © © 2022 IGI Global. All rights, including translation in other languages reserved by the publisher. No part of this series may be reproduced or used in any form or by any means – graphics, electronic, or mechanical, including photocopying, recording, taping, or information and retrieval systems – without written permission from the publisher, except for non commercial, educational use, including classroom teaching purposes. The views expressed in this series are those of the authors, but not necessarily of IGI Global.

Titles in this Series

For a list of additional titles in this series, please visit:
http://www.igi-global.com/book-series/advances-logistics-operations-management-science/37170

Key Factors and Use Cases of Servant Leadership Driving Organizational Performance
Maria Pressentin (International School of Management, France)
Business Science Reference • © 2022 • 368pp • H/C (ISBN: 9781799888208) • US $215.00

Handbook of Research on Innovative Management Using AI in Industry 5.0
Vikas Garg (Amity University, Greater Noida, India) and Richa Goel (Amity University, Noida, India)
Business Science Reference • © 2022 • 351pp • H/C (ISBN: 9781799884972) • US $295.00

Contemporary Challenges for Agile Project Management
Vannie Naidoo (University of Kwa-Zulu Natal, South Africa) and Rahul Verma (Delhi University, India)
Business Science Reference • © 2022 • 354pp • H/C (ISBN: 9781799878728) • US $225.00

Cases on Optimizing the Asset Management Process
Vicente González-Prida (University of Seville, Spain & National University of Distance Education, Spain) Carlos Alberto Parra Márquez (University of Seville, Spain) and Adolfo Crespo Márquez (University of Seville, Spain)
Business Science Reference • © 2022 • 457pp • H/C (ISBN: 9781799879435) • US $215.00

Handbook of Research on Current Trends in Asian Economics, Business, and Administration
Bülent Akkaya (Manisa Celal Bayar University, Turkey) Kittisak Jermsittiparsert (Henan University of Economics and Law, China) and Ayse Gunsel (Kocaeli University, Turkey)
Business Science Reference • © 2022 • 497pp • H/C (ISBN: 9781799884866) • US $295.00

Logistics and Supply Chain Management in the Globalized Business Era
Lincoln C. Wood (University of Otago, New Zealand) and Linh N.K. Duong (University of the West of England, Bristol, UK)
Business Science Reference • © 2022 • 413pp • H/C (ISBN: 9781799887096) • US $225.00

For an entire list of titles in this series, please visit:
http://www.igi-global.com/book-series/advances-logistics-operations-management-science/37170

701 East Chocolate Avenue, Hershey, PA 17033, USA
Tel: 717-533-8845 x100 • Fax: 717-533-8661
E-Mail: cust@igi-global.com • www.igi-global.com

Editorial Advisory Board

Emmanuel Adamides, *University of Patras, Greece*
Manuel Cruz, *Polytechnic of Porto, Portugal*
António Duarte, *Polytechnic Institute of Bragança, Portugal*
Yudi Fernando, *Universiti Malaysia Pahang, Malaysia*
Hugo Lam, *University of Liverpool, UK*
Stanley Lim, *University of San Diego, USA*
Xin Ma, *Monash University, Australia*
Farzad Mahmoodi, *Clarkson University, USA*
Maria Del Mar Muñoz Martos, *University of Malaga, Spain*
Robert Pellerin, *Polytechnique Montreal, Canada*
Ivan Russo, *University of Verona, Italy*
Doug Voss, *Central Arkansas University, USA*

Table of Contents

Preface xiii

Acknowledgment xxi

Introduction xxii

Chapter 1
Enablers and Barriers for the Transformation of Manufacturing After the COVID-19 Global Crisis 1
    Erdinç Koç, Bingol University, Turkey

Chapter 2
Critical Analysis of the Relocation Strategy of Production Between National Protectionist Policies, Global Supply, and Value Chains 21
    José G. Vargas-Hernández, Tecnológico Mario Molina, Unidad
        Zapopan, Mexico

Chapter 3
The Rating of Confusion in Supply Chain Dynamics in Food Business and Selecting the Most Ideal Capacity Strategy During COVID-19 39
    Selçuk Korucuk, Giresun University, Turkey
    Salih Memiş, Giresun University, Turkey
    Çağlar Karamaşa, Anadolu University, Turkey

Chapter 4
Insights From Supply Chain Disruptions in the COVID-19 Era: The Call for More Resilient Networks 62
    Türkan Müge Özbekler, Sinop University, Turkey

Chapter 5
Commercial Product Returns: Emerging Trends via Network Analysis............86
    Metehan Feridun Sorkun, Izmir University of Economics, Turkey

Chapter 6
Multicriteria Decision Support Model for Selection of Fiberglass Suppliers:
A Case Study in a Wind Industry Company..119
    Celina Rodrigues, Polytechnic of Porto, Portugal
    Ana Paula Lopes, Polytechnic of Porto, Portugal

Chapter 7
Practice of Green Supply Chain Management and Organization Performance
in the Manufacturing Industries of the Kathmandu Valley...............................146
    Seeprata Parajuli, Research Management Cell, Quest International
        College, Pokhara University, Nepal
    Ruby Shrestha, Quest International College, Pokhara University, Nepal
    Niranjan Devkota, Research Management Cell, Quest International
        College, Pokhara University, Nepal
    Sashi Rana Magar, Quest International College, Pokhara University,
        Nepal
    Sharad Rajbhandari, Quest International College, Pokhara University,
        Nepal
    Udaya Raj Poudel, Quest International College, Pokhara University,
        Nepal

Chapter 8
Rating Risk Factors Related to Dangerous Goods Transportation and
Selecting an Ideal Warehouse Location...164
    Çağlar Karamaşa, Anadolu University, Turkey
    Selçuk Korucuk, Giresun University, Turkey
    Ezgi Demir, Gebze Technical University, Turkey

Chapter 9
The Significant Impact of the COVID-19 Pandemic on Supply Chains.............185
    Ana Paula Lopes, Polytechnic of Porto, Portugal

Compilation of References 203

About the Contributors 233

Index 237

Detailed Table of Contents

Preface xiii

Acknowledgment xxi

Introduction xxii

Chapter 1
Enablers and Barriers for the Transformation of Manufacturing After the
COVID-19 Global Crisis 1
    Erdinç Koç, Bingol University, Turkey

It is obvious that COVID-19, which is one of the main agenda items of humanity, has an effect on global production facilities. It has been tried to create a roadmap for producers to overcome existing and similar crises with proactive solutions. The reflections of the global crisis on production are carefully examined in the study. The epidemic is not limited to a single country, but affects all parts of the world, leaving supply chains and manufacturers in a difficult situation. Just as the concept of the new normal for consumers has come to the fore, the necessity of adapting to the new norm by implementing certain technologies that have been emphasized in recent years is now more clearly felt for manufacturers. The pandemic process experienced and the difficulties and enablers that producers face/will face afterwards are explained in detail under the headings of human resource management, flexibility, sourcing, technology level, logistics.

Chapter 2
Critical Analysis of the Relocation Strategy of Production Between National
Protectionist Policies, Global Supply, and Value Chains 21
    *José G. Vargas-Hernández, Tecnológico Mario Molina, Unidad
        Zapopan, Mexico*

This chapter aims to critically analyze the implications that the national protectionist policies have on the global supply and value chains and the relocation of production.

The analysis is based on the assumptions that the global economy is facing the possibility of decoupling of many trade connections, and this trend favors deglobalization processes that have long been promoted by populism, nationalism, and economic protectionism. It is concluded that global supply, production, and value chains although being economically efficient are no longer any more secure under national protectionist policies, and therefore, the relocation of production processes is mainly due to the increase in the level of income and wages of the developing countries that are the destination and which reduce the advantages to relocate.

Chapter 3
The Rating of Confusion in Supply Chain Dynamics in Food Business and
Selecting the Most Ideal Capacity Strategy During COVID-19..........................39
Selçuk Korucuk, Giresun University, Turkey
Salih Memiş, Giresun University, Turkey
Çağlar Karamaşa, Anadolu University, Turkey

Supply chain dynamics are seen as important components that directly affect supply chain performance, business processes, management functions, and efficiency for businesses. Every company in the supply chain needs other businesses to achieve the desired level of supply accurately, with the least cost and in an effective manner. Therefore, supply chain dynamics are seen as important components in terms of increasing competitiveness, increasing business performance, avoiding problems in workflows, and ensuring customer satisfaction, and also play critical roles in the provision of necessary information, materials, and services and improvement of process management. Also, capacity and capacity development strategies have vital importance, and firms need to apply right strategies in order to achieve success.In this study, it is aimed to rank the confusion in the supply chain dynamics and select the most ideal capacity strategy for food establishments with 10 or more employees operating in Giresun province during the COVID-19 process via SWARA and WASPAS methods.

Chapter 4
Insights From Supply Chain Disruptions in the COVID-19 Era: The Call for
More Resilient Networks 62
Türkan Müge Özbekler, Sinop University, Turkey

The COVID-19 pandemic has created a devastating impact on supply chains. Especially, transportation disruptions, the slowdown in manufacturing, supply-demand imbalances, operational inefficiency in last-mile, and deficiencies in dealing with the crisis can be seen as main headings. This chapter aims to reveal the problems and learn lessons in these areas where significant risks are faced. During the COVID era, the need for resilient supply chains that are not affected by instantaneous changes has come to the fore. Accordingly, the second aim of the chapter is to offer solutions toward the short, medium, and long terms of the first-mile, production, and last-mile processes as enhancing the responsiveness of supply chains by the elements of supply chain resilience. This study is prepared as a review article in an exploratory approach through the supply chain literature and current practical examples. As a result of the study, digital-intensive business models, collaborative network design, and sustainability are highlighted as the main concepts to reach more resilient networks.

Chapter 5
Commercial Product Returns: Emerging Trends via Network Analysis..............86
Metehan Feridun Sorkun, Izmir University of Economics, Turkey

The increasing use of online shopping has escalated product returns and consequently the importance of their management. In parallel, the increasing scholarly interest on the subject is reflected in the number of publications. In such fast-growing research fields, mapping the whole research activity is useful in highlighting research areas that could provide a better knowledge accumulation in the field. With this aim, this chapter conducts co-citation and co-word analysis to identify future research directions. According to results, there is a need for future research to investigate 1) the consumer reaction when the service level received conflicts with the retailer environment (un)friendly operations, 2) the impacts of retailer return policies on their reverse logistics management, 3) the implementation difficulties of handling omni-channel returns in different organizational structures, and 4) the effectiveness of technological tools and applications used to avoid returns. This chapter also discusses the implications of COVID-19 on the commercial product returns research.

Chapter 6
Multicriteria Decision Support Model for Selection of Fiberglass Suppliers:
A Case Study in a Wind Industry Company 119
Celina Rodrigues, Polytechnic of Porto, Portugal
Ana Paula Lopes, Polytechnic of Porto, Portugal

This chapter presents a real case of a decision problem in supplier selection of one of the main raw materials of a wind blades industry. The study considered all currently qualified suppliers according to considerably rigorous standards and specifications and one in qualification process. It is a complex choice, given the strategic importance of the product and the multiplicity of criteria to be considered, both quantitative and qualitative. The strong competitiveness requires a special attention which concerns the supplier selection; not only the price matters; in fact, a day of stoppage due to failure in a delivery, for example, corresponds to high losses that would have justified the purchase from a supplier with a higher price but with no delivery failures. In order to contribute to the problem resolution, the methodologies PROMETHEE and AHP were applied, whose results allow the authors to stablish a ranking of the considered suppliers. The results will support the company on the selection of fiberglass suppliers and in some cases clarify where they can find the main trade-offs.

Chapter 7
Practice of Green Supply Chain Management and Organization Performance
in the Manufacturing Industries of the Kathmandu Valley 146
    Seeprata Parajuli, Research Management Cell, Quest International College, Pokhara University, Nepal
    Ruby Shrestha, Quest International College, Pokhara University, Nepal
    Niranjan Devkota, Research Management Cell, Quest International College, Pokhara University, Nepal
    Sashi Rana Magar, Quest International College, Pokhara University, Nepal
    Sharad Rajbhandari, Quest International College, Pokhara University, Nepal
    Udaya Raj Poudel, Quest International College, Pokhara University, Nepal

This chapter aims to analyze the practice of green supply chain management and organization performance in manufacturing industries of Kathmandu valley. This study uses descriptive research design. Two hundred and seven manufacturing industries in three industrial estates (Balaju, Bhaktapur, and Patan) of Kathmandu valley were taken as a sample for the study whereas all 245 operating industries were the population of the study. The findings revealed that 33.3% of industries are highly practicing green supply management chain whereas 23.7% and 19.6% are practicing it moderately and less, respectively. It was found that industries of all scale—large, medium, and low—are equally practicing green supply management chain to a greater extent. Thus, the study concludes that manufacturing industries ought to consider the systemic interaction between the internal and external facets of the application of the GSCM and to ensure that their respective operations are integrated in order to achieve improved environmental and organizational efficiency and consequently to achieve economic benefits.

Chapter 8
Rating Risk Factors Related to Dangerous Goods Transportation and
Selecting an Ideal Warehouse Location 164
    Çağlar Karamaşa, Anadolu University, Turkey
    Selçuk Korucuk, Giresun University, Turkey
    Ezgi Demir, Gebze Technical University, Turkey

Considering the environment and human life, the importance of dangerous goods transportation should be carefully considered. Preventing damages during this transportation, anticipating the dangers, and minimizing the risks are vital components for businesses, human life, and the environment. Therefore, reducing/minimizing risks in dangerous goods transportation is a critical element of vital importance. This chapter is aimed to rate the risk factors related to dangerous goods transportation and select the most ideal warehouse locations due to the their importance for human and environmental health. There are a number of factors for that purpose. There are six provinces in the Eastern Black Sea region having the strategic function and structure. According to the decision makers' views and judgments, three provinces are determined in terms of dangerous goods transportation. Picture fuzzy sets-based AHP-TOPSIS methodology was used to analyze the problem of dangerous goods transportation and the most ideal warehouse location selection.

Chapter 9
The Significant Impact of the COVID-19 Pandemic on Supply Chains............185
Ana Paula Lopes, Polytechnic of Porto, Portugal

As the COVID-19 pandemic has spread across the world, the existence of disruptions in demand and supply have become more severe, conducted by containment measures taken by countries and affecting different sectors around the world. Although businesses and workplaces are restarting activities in some countries, with containment measures gradually being lifted, overall consumer demand is expected to remain low, also determined by the loss of jobs and income. Therefore, the scale of the impact on supply chains exceeded anything most companies had anticipated. This study aims to understand how companies were affected and identify some lessons learned about their vulnerabilities and the possible ways to address them in the long term. On the other hand, it is intended to reveal some of the impacts of COVID-19 and make some practical suggestions that can help in political and operational decisions to strengthen and build additional resilience in supply chains in the future.

Compilation of References 203

About the Contributors 233

Index 237

Preface

In recent years, due to the increasingly aggressive market competition, it is essential to evaluate the role of logistics and supply chain management skills and applications for the success of any organization or business. The COVID-19 pandemic has affected every aspect of the modern world, and its impact is felt by all and revealed the fragility of the sustainability of economic organization, production, and supply chains globally. Particularly has had a large impact on businesses as they were forced to close and supply chains were disrupted.

Cases on Supply Chain Management and Lessons Learned From COVID-19 collects compelling case studies, theoretical and empirical research, experiences, and applications on numerous aspects of logistics and supply chain management. It not only focuses on industry and digital transformation and the critical nature of organizational agility, but also presents different methods, techniques, models, and competitive advantage prospects, providing an extremely relevant and current view of the subject matter. Covering topics such as green supply chain management, organizational performance, and supply chain disruptions, this book is the ideal reference source for managers, supply chain specialists, entrepreneurs, business professionals, consultants, researchers, academicians, educators, and students.

When the COVID-19 pandemic spread, it affected all sectors, with the impact felt stronger in some of these sectors than others. One of the most important factors contributing to this problem is supply chain disruption, although many innovations have recently emerged in the business world. The viability of the technology makes companies of all segments to invest so that their processes become more agile and competitive. Technological developments allow customer service to take place in real time and supply chain management can be done remotely and in a more transparent way.

Therefore, the COVID-19 pandemic led to a number of challenges across the supply chain. According to Lee (2021), the industry had to deal with some supply chain problems, like for instance:

- A lack of global resilience as they continue to break down in the face of multi-country interruptions;
- Inability to meet stakeholders' expectations for sustainability;
- A lack of flexibility, which tampers with the industry's demand to meet customer demands for personalization and customization;
- High costs of operations;
- Talent gaps across the supply chain, creating dependency on the human workforce;
- Over-reliance on legacy technologies.

The adverse effects of the breakdown on businesses might extend beyond 2021. However, there is great hope that the paint and coatings market will overcome the shock across the forecast period. After all, the situation is more of a result from an unprecedented event with drastic consequences than fundamental weakness in the market, industry or global economy.

The pandemic showed how the sustainability of the economic organization and of the production and supply chains that dominate the world is so weak and inadequate. So, fixing the problems caused by COVID-19 crisis requires a different way of thinking. In an attempt to solve these problems, a search has been launched in academic circles and country administrations for a global economic organization and supply chain that is much more operative and resilient to unfavourable developments like this. Supply chain issues require some degree of understanding as to how they affect people, buildings and logistics, but typically the situation only improves from the initial moment of disruption.

On the other hand, COVID-19 is a unique situation, and its impact has unfurled in successive waves; we still don't know if we're past all the worst of it or if there will be further setbacks. According Grant (2021), there has never been a disruption as critical, widespread and uncertain from a supply chain standpoint. To confuse the circumstances even more, it was well within our abilities to make it worse. If we opened manufacturing works too quickly or failed to take proper safety measures, the problem could escalate, which is unusual to the geopolitical problems we've had to contend with in the past.

In this post-pandemic restart, companies have to go back over their priorities and chart the best way forward (Rajah & Madduri, 2021). Companies need to consider which commerce strategies and infrastructures will be required to compete in the post pandemic environment. At the same time, they will have to deal with the uncertainty and volatility that continues. Companies are seeking to improve their supply chain resilience with flexibility and responsiveness. For instance, sourcing and manufacturing from China used to be the bedrock of global trade and is something that needs to be rethought. A large proportion of organizations are now exploring

Preface

alternatives to reduce their dependence on China and evaluating several sourcing and supply network strategies before proceeding with the transformation.

The target population for this book is researchers, teachers/faculty, academicians, educators, students, managers, supply chain specialists, entrepreneurs, business professionals and consultants. As the pandemic brought about an unusual situation for the world in particular for companies, the hope is that the narratives and information presented in this book could be useful for making future decisions regarding what supports researchers, students, decision makers, business people need and what concerns remain.

The result of this project was nine chapters based on several contexts authored by 18 authors hailing from four different countries: Mexico, Nepal, Portugal, and Turkey.

Chapter 1: Enablers and Barriers for the Transformation of Manufacturing After the COVID-19 Global Crisis

It is obvious that COVID-19, which is one of the main agenda items of humanity, has an effect on global production facilities. It has been tried to create a roadmap for producers to overcome existing and similar crises with proactive solutions. The reflections of the global crisis on production are carefully examined in the study. The epidemic is not limited to a single country, but affects all parts of the world, leaving supply chains and manufacturers in a difficult situation. Just as the concept of the new normal for consumers has come to the fore, the necessity of adapting to the new norm by implementing certain technologies that have been emphasized in recent years is now more clearly felt for manufacturers. The pandemic process experienced and the difficulties and enablers that producers face / will face afterwards; It is explained in detail under the headings of human resource management, flexibility, sourcing, technology level, logistics.

Chapter 2: Critical Analysis of the Relocation Strategy of Production Between National Protectionist Policies, Global Supply, and Value Chains

This paper aims to critically analyze the implications that the national protectionist policies have on the global supply and value chains and the relocation of production. The analysis is based on the assumptions that the global economy is facing the possibility of decoupling of many trade connections and this trend favors deglobalization processes have long been promoted by populism, nationalism, and economic protectionism. It is concluded that global supply, production and value chains although being economically efficient, are no longer any more secure under national protectionist policies and therefore, the relocation of production processes is mainly due to the increase in the level of income and wages of the developing countries that are the destination and which reduce the advantages to relocate.

Chapter 3: The Rating of Confusion in Supply Chain Dynamics in the Food Business and Selecting the Most Ideal Capacity Strategy During COVID-19

Supply chain dynamics are seen as important components that directly affect supply chain performance, business processes, management functions and efficiency for businesses. Every company in the supply chain needs other businesses to achieve the desired level of supply accurately, with the least cost and in an effective manner. Therefore, supply chain dynamics are seen as important components in terms of increasing competitiveness, increasing business performance, avoiding problems in workflows and ensuring customer satisfaction, and also play critical roles in the provision of necessary information, materials and services and improvement of process management. Also capacity and capacity development strategy have vital importance and firms need to apply right strategies in order to achieve success. In this study, it is aimed to rank the confusion in the supply chain dynamics and select the most ideal capacity strategy for food establishments with 10 or more employees operating in Giresun province during COVID-19 process via SWARA and WASPAS methods.

Chapter 4: Insights From Supply Chain Disruptions in the COVID-19 Era – The Call for More Resilient Networks

The COVID-19 pandemic has created a devastating impact on supply chains. Especially, transportation disruptions, the slowdown in manufacturing, supply-demand imbalances, operational inefficiency in last-mile, and deficiencies in dealing with the crisis can be seen as main headings. This chapter aims to reveal the problems and learn lessons in these areas where significant risks are faced. During the COVID-19 era, the need for resilient supply chains that are not affected by instantaneous changes has come to the fore. Accordingly, the second aim of the chapter is to offer solutions toward the short, medium, and long terms of the first-mile, production, and last-mile processes as enhancing the responsiveness of supply chains by the elements of supply chain resilience. This study is prepared as a review article in an exploratory approach through the supply chain literature and current practical examples. As a result of the study, digital-intensive business models, collaborative network design, and sustainability is highlighted as the main concepts to reach more resilient networks.

Preface

Chapter 5: Commercial Product Returns – Emerging Trends via Network Analysis

The increasing use of online shopping has escalated product returns, and consequently, the importance of their management. In parallel, the increasing scholarly interest on the subject is reflected in the number of publications. In such fast-growing research fields, mapping the whole research activity is useful in highlighting research areas that could provide a better knowledge accumulation in the field. With this aim, this chapter conducts co-citation and co-word analysis to identify future research directions. According to results, there is a need for future research to investigate i) the consumers' reaction when the service level received conflicts with the retailers' environment (un)friendly operations ii) the impacts of retailers' return policies on their reverse logistics management, iii) the implementation difficulties of handling omni-channel returns in different organizational structures, iv) the effectiveness of technological tools and applications used to avoid returns. This chapter also discusses the implications of covid-19 on the commercial product returns research.

Chapter 6: Multicriteria Decision Support Model for Selection of Fiberglass Suppliers – A Case Study in a Wind Industry Company

This paper presents a real case of a decision problem in supplier selection of one of the main raw materials of a wind blades industry. As a subsidiary company in a multinational group, it is subject to a limited group of suppliers previously qualified according to considerably rigorous standards and specifications. For the study were considered all currently qualified suppliers and one in qualification process. It is a complex choice, given the strategic importance of the product and the multiplicity of criteria to be considered, both quantitative and qualitative. The strong competitiveness, with other factories in the group, and with others outside the group, and with the COVID-19 pandemic, there are additional factors at play that are uniquely challenging, which require very special attention with regard to the supplier selection; not only the price matters, in fact, a day of stoppage due to failure in a delivery, for example, correspond to very high losses that would have justified the purchase from a supplier with a higher price, but with no delivery failures. Other factors, such as complexity of the import process or suppliers' lead time, will be considered as relevant criteria. In order to contribute to the resolution of the problem, the multicriteria decision support methodologies PROMETHEE and AHP were applied, whose results allow to stablish a ranking of the considered suppliers. Each supplier is evaluated against the set of established criteria, to which different weights are assigned depending on the perception of the decision maker.

In this study, the decision maker is from the financial department, but the criteria were decided together with procurement and production departments.

The results will support the company on the selection of two fiberglass supplier and in some cases will clarify where they can find the main trade-offs.

Chapter 7: Practice of Green Supply Chain Management and Organization Performance in the Manufacturing Industries of the Kathmandu Valley

Green supply chain management refers to whole sum of green purchasing, green manufacturing, green marketing and reverse logistics. This study aims to analyze practice of green supply chain management and organization performance in manufacturing industries of Kathmandu valley. This study uses descriptive research design. 207 manufacturing industries in three industrial estates (Balaju, Bhaktapur and Patan) of Kathmandu valley were taken as sample for the study whereas, all 245 operating industries were population of the study. The findings revealed that 33.3% industries are highly practicing green supply chain management whereas 23.7% and 19.6% are practicing it moderately and less respectively. On the positive notion it was found that industries of all scale large, medium and low are equally practicing green supply chain management to greater extent. Thus, the study concludes that Manufacturing industries ought to consider the systemic interaction between the internal and external facets of the application of the GSCM and to ensure that their respective operations are integrated in order to achieve improved environmental and organizational efficiency and consequently to achieve economic benefits. Overall aspects of GSCM implementation should be taken into account and that their respective activities should be combined in order to enhance environmental and operational effectiveness that further benefits overall business performance.

Chapter 8: Rating Risk Factors Related to Dangerous Goods Transportation and Selecting an Ideal Warehouse Location

The importance of dangerous goods transportation in our country as in the whole world; considering the environment and human life, it should be carefully considered. Preventing damages during this transportation, anticipating the dangers, and minimizing the risks are vital components for businesses, human life, and the environment. Therefore, reducing/minimizing risks in dangerous goods transportation is critical elements of vital importance. It is aimed to rate the risk factors related to dangerous goods transportation and select the most ideal warehouse location due to their importance for human and environment health in this study. There are a number of factors for that purpose. There are six provinces in Eastern Black Sea region with having the strategic function and structure. According to the decision makers' views and judgments three provinces are determined in terms of dangerous goods transportation. Picture fuzzy sets based AHP-TOPSIS methodology was used to analyze the problem of dangerous goods transportation and the most ideal warehouse location selection.

Chapter 9: The Significant Impact of the COVID-19 Pandemic on Supply Chains

As the COVID-19 pandemic has spread across the world, the existence of disruptions in demand and supply have become more severe, conducted by containment measures taken by countries and affecting different sectors around the world. Although businesses and workplaces are restarting activities in some countries, with containment measures gradually being lifted, overall consumer demand is expected to remain low, also determined by the loss of jobs and income. Therefore, the scale of the impact on Supply Chains exceeded anything most companies have anticipated.

This study aims to understand how companies were affected and identify some lessons learned about their vulnerabilities and the possible ways to address them in the long term. On the other hand, it is intended to reveal some of the impacts of COVID-19 and make some practical suggestions that can help in political and operational decisions to strengthen and build additional resilience in Supply Chains in the future.

CONCLUSION

While it is too early to assess and measure the full effect of COVID-19 on supply chains, this book is intended to provide information in ways that help supply chain managers better understand the interrelationship between these factors and the pandemic and drive the decision-making process of decision. With expert perspectives and research findings from academics, managers and entrepreneurs from many different countries, this book provides a significant guide to help decision makers, entrepreneurs, managers, professors, and organizational and government leaders to chart the way forward. Many at the moment are struggling to determine if employees should be required to work on premise or be allowed to work remotely.

The COVID-19 pandemic is adversely affecting, and is expected to continue to adversely affect, our operations and supply chains, and we have experienced and expect to continue to experience unpredictable reductions in demand for certain of our products.

Preface

While we expect the impacts of COVID-19 to have an adverse effect on our business, financial condition and results of operations, we are unable to predict with certainty the extent or nature of these impacts. The severity of the impact will depend on our ability to adjust to this uncertainty as well as a number of other factors, including, but not limited to, the duration and severity of the pandemic and the extent and severity of the impact on the Company's customers, disruptions and restrictions on availability of labor, as well as temporary disruptions to our supply chain, all of which are uncertain and cannot be predicted. The Company's future results of operations and liquidity could be adversely impacted by reduced revenues, delays in payments of outstanding receivable amounts beyond normal payment terms, supply chain disruptions and uncertain demand, and the impact of any initiatives or programs that the Company may undertake to address financial and operations challenges faced by its customers. (Corning, 2020)

This book explores a little bit of the impact of the COVID-19 pandemic on supply chains, discussing some of the causes of disruptions, related challenges, and the trend of the pandemic.

REFERENCES

Corning Inc. (2020). *Quarter 2 2020 Earnings Report.* Retrieved from: https://www.sec.gov/ix?doc=/Archives/edgar/data/24741/000002474120000055/glw-20200630x10q.htm

Grant, A. (2021). *Seven COVID-19 Lessons Learned in Supply Chain.* Jabil COVID-19 Report. Retrieved from: https://www.jabil.com/blog/covid-19-supply-chain-lessons.html

Lee, K. (2021). *Lessons Learned from COVID-19 About the Importance of Supply Chain Management.* Paint and Coating Market Reports. Retrieved from: https://www.pcimag.com/articles/109227-lessons-learned-from-covid-19-about-the-importance-of-supply-chain-management

Rajah, S., & Madduri, V. (2021). Lessons Learned: Requiem for COVID-19. *Supply Chain Management Review.* Retrieved from: https://www.scmr.com/article/lessons_learned_requiem_for_covid_19

Acknowledgment

The editor would like to acknowledge the help of all the people involved in this project and, more specifically, to the authors, editorial advisory board and reviewers that took part in the review process. Without their support, this book would not have become a reality.

First, the editor would like to thank each one of the authors for their contributions. My sincere gratitude goes to the chapter's authors who contributed their time and expertise to this book.

Second, the editor wishes to acknowledge the valuable contributions of the reviewers regarding the improvement of quality, coherence, and content presentation of chapters.

Most of the authors also served as referees; we highly appreciate their double task.

Ana Paula Lopes
Polytechnic of Porto, Portugal

Introduction

Supply chain disruptions started after the World Health Organization (WHO) declared the coronavirus disease outbreak to be global health emergency at the end of January 2020. Through the first half of 2020, the virus spread to almost all the countries in partial or total lockdown (McKenzie, 2020). This crisis affects the supply network both at source and destination, and its extreme effects on the supply chain can lead to interruption of the production process (Choudhury, 2020). Based on the data provided by the Institute of Supply Management, about 75% of companies reported interruptions in the supply chain, 80% expected some type of interruption in the near future, 62% reported delays in receiving goods and 53% of companies reported difficulties in obtaining information from China (McCrea, 2020). All over the world, organizations close stores, delete orders and suspend production. Many sectors have been suffered, in particular the supply chain sector, as employees in this sector are among the most vulnerable and are being affected by the pandemic (Kippenberg, 2020).

As the pandemic brought about an unusual situation for the world in particular for companies, the hope is that the chapters and information presented in this book could be useful for making future decisions regarding what supports researchers, students, decision makers, managers make better decisions regarding the current and future crises.

REFERENCES

Choudhury, A. (2020). *Quantzig. Analyzing the Impact of COVID-19 on the US Food Supply Chain*. E:\Conference paper\Papers\COVID19\LR\Analyzing the Impact of COVID-19 on the US Food Supply Chain.

Kippenberg, J. (2020). *COVID-19 puts millions of global supply chain workers at risk*. E:\Conference paper\Papers\COVID19\LR\COVID-19 Puts Millions of Global Supply Chain Workers at Risk

Introduction

McCrea, B. (2020). *Measuring COVID-19's Impact on the World's Supply Chains.* SourceToday. Retrieved from: https://www.sourcetoday.com/supply-chain-trends/article/21126824/measuring-covid19s-impact-on-the-worlds-supply-chains

McKenzie, B. (2020). *Beyond COVID-19: Supply chain resilience holds key to recovery.* Retrieved from https://www.bakermckenzie.com/en/newsroom/2020/04/global-supply-chains-under-huge-pressure-covid-19

Chapter 1
Enablers and Barriers for the Transformation of Manufacturing After the COVID-19 Global Crisis

Erdinç Koç
https://orcid.org/0000-0002-8209-5714
Bingol University, Turkey

EXECUTIVE SUMMARY

It is obvious that COVID-19, which is one of the main agenda items of humanity, has an effect on global production facilities. It has been tried to create a roadmap for producers to overcome existing and similar crises with proactive solutions. The reflections of the global crisis on production are carefully examined in the study. The epidemic is not limited to a single country, but affects all parts of the world, leaving supply chains and manufacturers in a difficult situation. Just as the concept of the new normal for consumers has come to the fore, the necessity of adapting to the new norm by implementing certain technologies that have been emphasized in recent years is now more clearly felt for manufacturers. The pandemic process experienced and the difficulties and enablers that producers face/will face afterwards are explained in detail under the headings of human resource management, flexibility, sourcing, technology level, logistics.

DOI: 10.4018/978-1-7998-9140-6.ch001

INTRODUCTION

It is claimed that the period of global recession that started in the pre-pandemic period was caused by the tension between China and the USA. This trade war between the world's two superpowers is the trigger of the stagnation in production. However, during this period, the recession in manufacturing remained limited. The manufacturing sector contributes 10-40% to most developed economies (Roberts, 2019). The ongoing upward trend in the service sector has enabled economies to absorb the contraction in the manufacturing sector.

On March 11, 2020, COVID-19 was declared a pandemic by the World Health Organization (WHO). With this declaration, governments, businesses, institutions and individuals began to predict what this process would bring them (Brannen, Ahmed, & Newton, 2020). The World Bank predicts that the world gross domestic product will decrease by 2%, developing countries 2.5% and developed countries 1.8% in 2020 due to the pandemic (Maliszewska, Mattoo, & Van Der Mensbrugghe, 2020). COVID-19 is spreading rapidly all over the world and manufacturers face significant operational challenges. Some companies appear to be temporarily closing manufacturing facilities in response to government restrictions and falling demand (Furtado et al., 2020). Global outbreaks are known to significantly reduce global economic production and increase unemployment (Tisdell, 2020). Volkswagen AG, Daimler AG and BMW AG produced 37% less production in March 2020 than in 2019. Rolls Royce, one of the important manufacturers in the aviation sector, announced that it will lay off 9000 people, and the automobile manufacturer McLaren, more than 1000 people due to the coronavirus. U.S. Bureau of Labor Statistics reports that, *"in the second quarter of 2020, productivity decreased 28.4 percent in durable goods manufacturing, reflecting a 58.1-percent decrease in output"*. According to the simulation of the global effects of the pandemic, the manufacturing industry will shrink by 3.61% in China, 2.45% in the United States, 2.77% in Japan, 3.98% in India and 3.13% worldwide (Maliszewska et al., 2020). In a study where predictions were shared with policy makers, it was stated that worldwide economic loss could be 10%, 24.8% or 37.3% according to different scenarios (Acemoglu et al., 2020).

The COVID-19 outbreak shook manufacturers unexpectedly and unprecedented. For the first time in the history of modern production, supply, demand and labor have been affected simultaneously on a global scale (Kroupenev, 2020). According to the 2020 third-quarter outlook survey of the National Association of Manufacturers (NAM), the expectations of companies to return to their pre-pandemic revenues are as follows. 17.6 percent of the companies stated that they currently have the income level before the pandemic. 6.9 percent of the companies are in the third quarter of 2020, 5.6 percent in the fourth quarter of 2020, 19.5 percent in the first half of 2021, 22.3 percent in the second half of 2021, 12.7 percent in the first half of 2022. half of them, 7.5 percent think they will have it in a longer period and 7.9 percent in an uncertain future.

ENABLERS AND BARRIERS

According to U.S. National Association of Manufacturers (NAM) (2018) survey, primary current business challenges are weaker domestic economy, attracting and retaining a quality workforce, rising health care/insurance costs, trade uncertainties, weaker global growth and slower export sales, increased raw material costs, unfavorable business climate (e.g., taxes, regulations), transportation and logistics costs, strengthened U.S. dollar relative to other currencies and challenges with access to capital. The focal points of the manufacturers before and after COVID-19 were different. The five essential requirements for long-term success achieved by the World Economic Forum (WEF) (2020) as a result of interviews with 400 senior executives in cooperation with Kearney are as follows:

1. Establishment of production and supply systems that can adapt to rapid changes in consumer behavior,
2. Development of agile production and supply systems with the use of advanced technologies,
3. Ensuring logistics coordination in global value chains,
4. Adopting new business and management methods to increase production resistance,
5. Establishing responsibility and cooperation between companies and authorities to tackle social and environmental challenges.

The effects of the barriers and enablers that occur with the COVID-19 virus on the manufacturing process can be divided into factors as in Figure1. These five factors are human resource management (HRM), flexibility, technology level, sourcing and logistics. The factors that barrier and enable transformation of each factor are explained in more detail below. These factors can be expanded for manufacturers operating in different sectors and sub-factors can be added. In creating the factors, the author has taken into account the most frequently recurring points in a small number of sources in the literature.

Figure 1. The effects of COVID-19 on the manufacturing sector

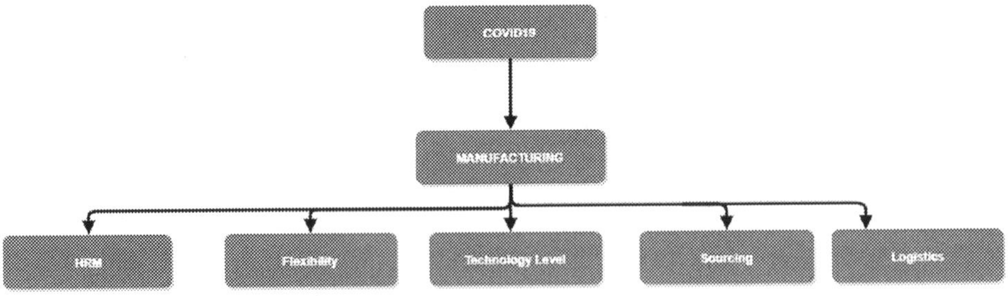

Human Resource Management

Workers' reluctance to work leads to a decrease in manpower due to the restriction decisions taken by governments and the rapid spread of the pandemic (S. Kumar, Raut, & Narwane, 2020). In addition, most of the operations performed in manufacturing facilities are not suitable for working from home. Manufacturers are trying to reduce the intensity of employees both within the factory and at the arrival stages of their employees with the shift-based working system that they apply when there is no closure. Although there are different predictions about how long the process will continue, a clear date is not yet known. Therefore, employees are expected to fulfill their activities within the new normal (Bonacini et al., 2021). Manufacturers also need to take precautions with a perspective that will prioritize employee health. Material elements such as advanced hygiene measures, additional personal protective equipment and physical distance, as well as intangible elements such as management and behavioral changes are some of the steps that businesses can develop to protect the health of their employees. It appears that some manufacturing facilities have developed an online survey that allows their employees to track their health and travel history. In this way, it is stated that it is easier for manufacturers to identify the person and the people they are in contact with in the case of any positive case. The companies in China providing consultancy services, in order to protect the mental health of the employees after the long quarantine process, can be shown as a good example practice (Furtado, Kolaja, Mueller, & Salguero, 2020).

In order to reduce the potential future impact of infections, companies need to develop team structures and working methods that can reduce the frequency of communication between employees. One way of doing this is that employees have workplaces that can be separated physically and socially, as shown in the figure below. In addition to such physical applications, applications such as taking control of the work done by the employee in each separated section, holding shift meetings online and differentiating shift break times for each workstation are some of the applications that will minimize the human contact in the production area.

Along with these applications, more advanced solutions such as location tracking mobile applications, machine vision algorithms and wearable technologies can also be used to establish a safe distance between employees in production processes. For example, an employee who cannot go to machine maintenance in a different manufacturing facility due to travel restrictions can have maintenance done through explanations and directions to another employee through augmented reality glasses. This maintenance can also increase machine efficiency by reducing machine downtime (Agrawal et al., 2020).

It is thought that the global epidemic period will accelerate the technological change of companies in the manufacturing sector through artificial intelligence and automation. Robots used in production systems can be used more to perform routine tasks that require workers to be close to each other (ILO, 2020). It is predicted that Industry 4.0 works, which gained speed before the pandemic process, will continue to increase. For example, demand forecasts performed with simple statistical methods used in traditional forecasting methods failed in the COVID-19 process., because traditional forecasting methods often create future projections based on previous period sales. On the other hand, autonomous methods, which have been used recently, do not only use data from the past. These methods use artificial intelligence and machine learning algorithms that use external data such as suppliers, customers, weather forecasters, economic indicators in the process (Agrawal et al., 2020).

Figure 2. Seperated workspace Source: Furtado et all., 2020

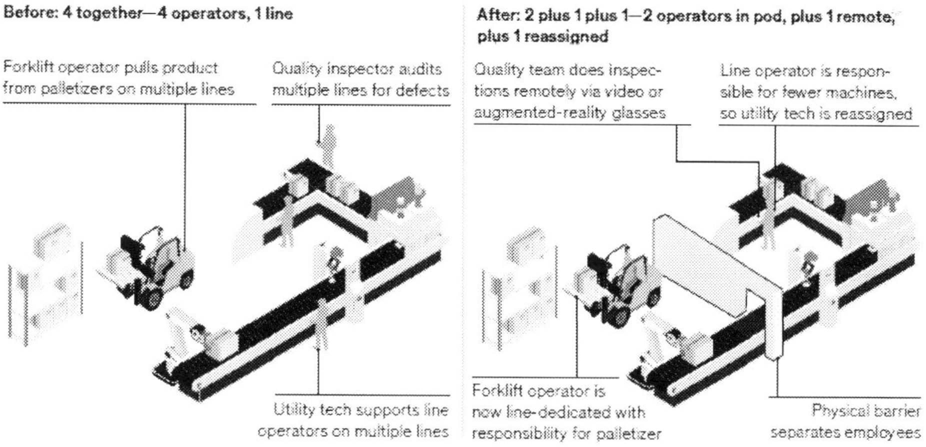

With COVID-19, global manufacturing leaders began to change the strategies they use in the management of employees and processes. It is stated that more than two-thirds of the managers have started to differentiate their workforce management methods and current approaches (Furtado et al. 2020). Similar rates are also seen in the automation and transformation speed in the sector.

Flexibility

It is known by the manufacturers that the product life cycle is getting shorter day by day. The globalization wave that started in the 90's is felt more and more every day. Lorenz's motto, *"The flapping of a butterfly in the Amazon forests can cause a storm to break out in the USA"* is frequently encountered in political, economic and social life. The effects of the Mortgage crisis (2008) in the USA on Europe and the spread of the COVID-19 virus to the world can be considered as examples. Transportation and ICT technologies developing with globalization change the product preferences of consumers. A young woman with a medium income level in Turkey, buying clothes from the Italian fashion designer with a shipping time may have it in a few days. In fact, this example clearly reveals the effect of globalization on consumers, but also shows its effect on production systems. That is to say, when we look at the last two centuries of production systems, it can be stated that they have drawn a full circle and returned to the point where it started, namely, individual customer focus in craft production. Personalized products, expressed in global production, act with the prediction that the focus of production is the individual customer (Koren, 2010). In addition, studies conducted in recent years show that even durable products used by consumers have shortened lifetime (Wieser et al.. 2015). In order to respond to the changing demand, manufacturers have been in an effort to transform their production systems into flexible production systems in the 1980s and into reconfigurable production systems in order to produce personalized products expressed in the 2000s.

Even in the pre-pandemic period, it was constantly recommended by theorists that producers should have flexible production systems in order to respond to rapid changes in consumer needs. Flexible production is briefly defined as the ability to restructure production resources to produce a new product (Sethi, 1990). Flexibility and automation are essential for flexible production systems (Browne & Dubois, 1984). Manufacturers with flexible machines, processes, handling systems, production and schedule only have the skills to respond to changes in market demand. The flexibility of manufacturers becomes more important in times of global crisis, such as COVID19. The inability of companies, which have traditional production systems, to respond to the demand of the market causes an increase in supply shortages. Manufacturers with flexible production systems, on the other hand, can quickly respond to the varying needs of consumers with their capabilities. The personal individualization paradigm of flexible production systems has turned into a global production concept that has been referred to with reconfigurable systems in recent years. With the use of IT and internet infrastructure, reconfigurable production systems have reached high responsiveness in the production of regionalized and personalized products.

Today, when the effects of the global epidemic are felt intensely, manufacturers feel the impact of flexible or reconfigurable production systems more clearly. For example, the patient transport vehicle based on the Hiace model, seen as a continuation of the "Kokoro Hakobu Project" started by Toyota in 2011, has been used in the transfer operations of COVID-19 patients since April 2020. Some of the technical features of the van are as follows: (1) the part where the driver and the front passenger are separated from the rear part of the van, and (2) the air at the rear is constantly tried to be taken out of the van thanks to the fan installed in the van. In this way, the air circulation in the van is prevented from passing into the front compartment of the van. In addition, Toyota has started to produce 70,000 pieces of medical face shields per month since April in order to support the efforts of healthcare professionals who are at the forefront of diagnosis and treatment of COVID-19 patients. Volkswagen Group, is known to produce thousands of visors, masks and medical devices using 3D printing technology during the epidemic period. GM, started to produce 30,000 ventilator devices in June, under a $ 489 million agreement with the U.S. Federal Government. Automotive manufacturers liken this to Ford's production of B-24 fighter jets, Chrysler tanks and GM's amphibians in the second world war.

Technology Level

COVID-19 has already accelerated some consumer trends such as online learning, working from home, video communication, consumer goods and service deliveries. It is not thought that the majority of consumers will be able to quit this habit after they gain it. This change in consumer tendencies shows itself similarly in the way of doing business. Especially during recession periods, the use of new technologies in the manufacturing sector accelerates job losses. The idea that jobs could be recovered after the recession did not come to life although new technologies continued to grow the job opportunities they created (ILO, 2020).

It can be seen that most of the practices presented as short-term solutions to global crises in history have been used for decades. Most things that seem normal now actually took different forms. Manufacturers who understand the new normal and act accordingly will gain a competitive advantage (Kroupenev, 2020). Industry 4.0, which has been on the world agenda since 2010, is the most important provider of the new normal in the field of production. Industry 4.0, in other words, the fourth industrial revolution, tries to meet the various personalized needs of people in a shorter time by using advanced production and information technologies (Javaid et al., 2020). Applications such as the Industrial Internet of Things (IIoT), which have become increasingly popular recently, should not be considered separate from Industry 4.0. IIoT prevents human to human communication and enables machine to machine communication. It is stated that smart production can be realized with the inclusion of Internet of Things applications in the industry and productivity will increase by using resources more effectively in the long term (Koç, 2020).

The inclusion of new generation applications such as artificial intelligence, 3D printing, data analysis, robots, cyber-physical systems in production technologies allows manufacturing to be carried out in separate places (A. Kumar, Luthra, Mangla, & Kazançoğlu, 2020). Brannen et al. (2020) state that production and investment will increase in robotics, additive manufacturing, internet of things, artificial intelligence and biotechnology in their future predictions. It can be stated that global production has just begun to adopt these concepts. However, these new technologies can help manufacturers to increase their supply chain transparency, accelerate product responsiveness, or develop the solutions needed to change their production economies. For example, Procter & Gamble has built a digital control tower where it can monitor every stage of the supply chain. In this way, they can monitor every stage from their own factories, as well as suppliers and distributors, from inventory levels to shipping processes, with a digital tower.

With the rapid spread of the COVID-19 virus, an increasing need for a ventilator has emerged worldwide. In this process, it is known that governments cooperate with companies to restructure factories and accelerate production in order to meet the demand for ventilators. The restructuring of factories allows manufacturers to increase the volume or produce a different product. However, in order for this to happen, the manufacturing process or the reconfiguration of the machines must be capable and adapted. This competence and compliance is measured by the ability of the machines to be easily and quickly integrated into the new product or product volume. In addition, the establishment of a highly automated production process enables the restructuring of the factory. Having a high level of automation within the factory allows to increase product volume, improve product quality, and save employees from repetitive tasks (Malik, Masood, & Kousar, 2020). For example, Kiva robots are used in loading and unloading operations in warehouses, helping manufacturers to manage their human resources more effectively (A. Kumar et al., 2020). The high level of automation causes manufacturers to face significant benefits as well as security risks. Cyber attacks in capital-intensive industries will be felt more intensely than labor-intensive industries in the manufacturing industry. It is clear that global outbreaks such as COVID-19 deeply affect labor-intensive sectors rather than capital-intensive sectors. For example, in 2019, unemployment and economic loss caused by COVID-19 can be observed in the Asia-Pacific region, which constitutes 75 percent of the total workers in this field in the world with approximately 65 million garment sector workers. It is known that approximately 85 percent of the factories in Bangladesh and 65 percent in Indonesia were closed for more than two weeks during this period. Closures of factories, order cancellations, supply chain bottlenecks and falling customer demand significantly affect ready-made clothing, which is one of the labor-intensive sectors in the manufacturing industry (Jackson & Judd, 2020). Decreases in customer demand were carefully monitored by manufacturers. The ready-to-wear industry with a low technology level has tried to adapt quickly to the production of products such as masks and medical gowns. However, the amount of demand for these products, which continue to be produced intensively, cannot be measured by the producers in a healthy way. The most important source of information that manufacturers use in creating production programs and schedules is demand forecasts. With the global epidemic period, traditional forecasting methods also lost their effectiveness. Instead of traditional forecasting methods, artificial intelligence and machine learning-based prediction methods, which take many data into account, started to be used.

Sourcing

The emergence of COVID-19 in China, the world's largest production and distribution center, inevitably affected the manufacturers that shaped the manufacturing process depending on China. Both the demand and supply side effects of the global epidemic period are felt more and more day by day. On the supply side, it is known that the ability of a significant portion of the manufacturers to continue their production depends on international suppliers. Especially, manufacturers using Chinese origin components in their products were significantly affected by the disruptions in the international supply chain (Tisdell, 2020). Closure decisions due to COVID-19 appear to have a direct impact on six industries (restaurant/bars, travel/transportation, entertainment, personal services, retailers and manufacturing). 20.4 percent of all employees in the USA work in these sectors and are directly affected by the process (Dey & Loewenstein, 2020).

It is known that the global supply chains of companies in the manufacturing industry such as automotive, electronics, and pharmaceutical industries extend to China. The closure of manufacturing facilities in China or the delay in production significantly affects the relevant industries in other regions (Cai & Luo, 2020). For example, Wuhan, the focal point of the COVID-19 outbreak, is an important center that produces automotive parts for global automotive manufacturers such as VW, GM, Hyundai and Toyota. In addition, factory closures that started with Wuhan in China and spread to Guangdong, Zhejiang and Jiangsu could ignite a global supply problem. China has an export volume of $ 2.4 Trillion according to 2018 World

Bank data. Of this amount, $ 41 billion consists of raw materials and $ 416 billion is composed of intermediate goods. The figures stated show that raw material and intermediate goods exports constitute approximately 20% of China's total exports. The disruption in China's export of raw materials and semi-finished products to almost all of the world may put many countries in a difficult situation. According to 2019 data, China has the highest share in the export of intermediate goods in the world with 9.65%.

The decrease in raw material or semi-finished product stocks arouses concern in manufacturers. The responsibility of their contracts or the cost of losing customers puts the business managers into an even more deadlock. Also, manufacturers' costs may increase due to overtime and accelerated freight costs. Although it is thought that managers can make a trade-off decision here, considering the continuity of the business, it is seen that managers do not have much room for action. Managers can only try to minimize their risks through cooperation agreements with different supply sources, namely suppliers. In a way, COVID-19 forces manufacturers to make their supply chains more resilient. The US-China tension experienced in the pre-pandemic period was actually another issue that brought this issue to the agenda of the manufacturers. In case of conflicts of interest between countries or in any global crisis, the manufacturers' ability to continue their operations depends on the resistance of the supply chains.

Logistics

Between the first quarter and the second quarter of 2020, the total volume of container and freight transportation in the world decreased by 5.8%. In the same period, the market volume of bulk cargo and Roll on/Roll off shrunk from 6.3% to 22.8%. COVID-19 caused 151 thousand cancellations in container and freight transportation between Europe and Asia. Considering that transoceanic transportation constitutes 90% of the global trade volume, the magnitude of the stated decreases can become more concrete. According to the data of December 2020, it is known that the weekly flight frequency worldwide has decreased by 40.5% compared to the previous year. The total container volume handled in Chinese ports decreased by around 10% in the first months of 2020 (Ian Twinn et al., 2020).

Maritime transport, which has a global load in the logistics sector, is being replaced by air transport, especially in expensive products such as electronic products. Considering the decreasing number of passengers in airline transportation, this situation has become attractive for airline operators. However, this alternative cannot be used by companies in the manufacturing sector, unfortunately. The necessity of considering the cost of the manufacturers also requires them to minimize the transportation costs of the raw materials or semi-products to be used in the manufacturing process. While this is the case in the international arena, manufacturers are faced with logistics problems within national borders. Logistics problems are encountered in the supply chain both between the supplier and the producer distributor/retailer.

At the beginning of the pandemic process, the supply shortage wave that started with China closing its manufacturing facilities affected Europe and the USA. Although more than a year has passed since the incident in Wuhan, the supply shortage still does not seem to be resolved. In addition to the cessation of manufacturing, the implementation of policies such as movement restrictions of people and goods, closing borders, and logistics restrictions are also among the factors that affect product supply (PwC, 2020). Accumulated workload, which is accepted as one of the important reasons As in the example of the automotive industry, even industries with low demand during the pandemic meet the demands received in the summer months when the pandemic is relatively less felt, with order delivery times lasting for months. One of the reasons that sectors such as automotive and electronics are more affected by the pandemic is their complex supply chain. In such a global crisis, it will not be easy to manage semi-products production distributed across different continents. In addition, the concern that the demands of distributors or retailers in the field of basic products will not be met, pushes their orders to increase in an unrealistic way. Naturally, the logistics planning process is also affected by this situation.

The concern that the global crisis will continue into an unpredictable future forces manufacturers to restructure their logistics processes. Manufacturers who produce semi-products for various reasons in different countries and even on continents need to cooperate with suppliers in nearby geographies in order to be less affected by the global crisis. In order to respond quickly to the demand of the market, producers should be able to use their resources outside the enterprise effectively as well as their internal resources. It is seen from the studies that supplier responsiveness has an effect on the agility of the manufacturer. Today, manufacturers no longer see suppliers as a business from which they purchase intermediate products, but as a business partner they include in new product development projects. For this reason, producers should use scientific methods when choosing their supplier and add semi-product producers with closer locations to the supplier pool, taking into account the logistical problems that may occur in times of crisis such as a global epidemic. This proposal also brings to mind the maxim of Markowitz, who is the architect of Modern Portfolio Theory, "Do not put all the eggs in the same basket". During the global epidemic, manufacturers who mostly supplied intermediate products from China in order to gain a cost advantage encountered supply problems. To overcome this situation, manufacturers can improve their supplier pool. In addition, it is known that long-term relationships with suppliers give producers a competitive advantage.

In the context of the above, it is known that many countries restructure their supply chain and many multinational companies restructure their outsourcing strategies. Thus, the impact of restriction decisions taken by governments will be felt as little as possible by countries and companies (Ian Twinn et al., 2020).

Data

Within the scope of this study, semi-structured interviews were held with five medium and large scale business managers operating in the manufacturing sector. Integrated textile, industrial machinery, furniture, construction chemicals and marble sectors were included in the research. Interviews made using qualitative research methods were conducted on online platforms due to the pandemic. Since researchers are asked to master the production process, four of the participants are in the position of production manager and one is in the position of factory manager. The opinions of the participants were tried to be taken with the interview form created within the scope of the sub-headings expressed in the theoretical background of the study. Each of the interviews lasted between 23-37 minutes and the total duration of all interviews was 145 minutes. The answers given by the participants from each sector to different questions are shared below. Thanks to the participants from different sectors, we have an opportunity to compare their responses.

The data obtained with the transcribed texts were subjected to descriptive and content analysis. The scope was tried to be enriched by including quotations in the descriptive analysis. In content analysis, a summary view is tried to be obtained by combining similar data under certain factors. While conducting the content analysis, the steps of Yıldırım and Şimşek (2005), "coding data, finding themes, organizing codes and themes, defining and interpreting findings" were followed. In the content analysis, first of all, the "coding made according to the concepts extracted from the data" approach was used and thus, the codes extracted directly from the data were used in the study. In the second step, the themes/factors were tried to be determined by considering the similarities and harmonies between the codes extracted from the data. While quantitative analysis deals with numbers, qualitative data is about meanings. The meanings, on the other hand, are obtained by using the words and sentences more clearly (Dey, 1993). In the third step, after determining the codes and themes, the findings were shared using clearer expressions. Considering the relationships between the findings, interpretations and conclusions were revealed.

Quotations from the interviewees made within the scope of descriptive analysis are expressed as ET for integrated textile, EM for industrial machine, F for furniture, CC for construction chemicals and M for marble. Some of the opinions received from the sector representatives under the five sub-factors are given below. In the content analysis part of the study, the inter-sectoral comparison was made, so the responses of the sector representatives for the sub-factor were not reported in this part.

RESULTS

The following question about the human resources practices implemented in the manufacturing sector during the pandemic process was asked to all five sector representatives. Part of the answer given by the integrated textile sector representative to the relevant question is given below.

1. How has the COVID-19 pandemic affected your human resource management applications in the manufacturing process? Do you plan to make a change in your human resources policies? What kind of applications have you developed in order to use your human resources more effectively in the new normal?

    IT- "With the beginning of the pandemic process, we started by developing hygiene standards and trying to reduce our employees' concerns about COVID-19. Arrangements were made in bus arrival and departure times in order to reduce the density of arrivals and departures to the workplace. In addition, the start and end times of shifts in different departments in facility have also been changed. The awareness level of our employees on the subject was tried to be increased with short informative seminars organized by our workplace doctor. If our employees or family members with whom they live with are diagnosed, they have been asked to immediately forward this to their responsible superiors. Employees' job charts and their positions within the company were reviewed. Thus, the separate working opportunities of close employees have been reviewed. Integrated textile facilities are factories that use intensive machinery due to the nature of the work performed. The fixed array of machines does not allow employees to work separately in some cases. For this reason, changing the in-plant design is not a suitable solution for the integrated textile industry. Alternating working or working from home system was introduced among our white-collar employees. Unfortunately, this has not been implemented for our blue collar employees. Although we express that the use of machinery is intense in the integrated textile sector, the machines we use are old machines. These old machines used unfortunately require more human resources to be used in the manufacturing process. Our facility, which has recently switched to the robot storage system, has saved both the space used and the human resources used in storage.

Realization of the aforementioned renewal in the manufacturing process will allow saving on human resources. However, tens of millions of dollars in return for this renewal is not at a level that can be met at the moment."

With the global epidemic period, the concept of flexibility has become one of the important agenda items of enterprises in the manufacturing sector. The question asked to five industry representatives regarding flexibility is as follows. The answer given by the industrial machinery sector representative to the question is below.

2. Do you think your manufacturing process is suitable for flexible production?

IM- "Our production process starts based on order (pull system). We often manufacture industrial machines needed in the food industry. The shock experienced in many sectors with the beginning of the pandemic process was also felt in our industry. However, the increase in demand for basic foodstuffs especially forced food producers to increase the supply. In this direction, our customers were asked for industrial machines that are rarely found in our product range. However, cancellations in customer orders require restructuring of the manufacturing process along with production scheduling. In some cases, it is requested to increase the orders without changing the deadline. In some cases, we have to plan our production process to produce two separate products in line with the demand. In order to meet the increasing demand for the production of the products in our product range, we include the employees who want to work overtime. In the order of products that are not included in our product range, it is evaluated whether production can be carried out with our existing machinery and equipment by taking into account the technical drawings. After the product design phase, the order that goes into the production process is mostly produced by using the machines in the enterprise. In some cases, some steps of production are outsourced."

The effect of the technology level of the manufacturers on the product range and production process has been explained in more detail above. In the interviews with the representatives of different sectors participating in the study, it was tried to learn the current technology levels and the targeted technology levels. In addition, the effectiveness of the current technology levels of manufacturing facilities in the COVID-19 process was investigated. The answer given by the furniture sector representative to the relevant question is shared below.

Enablers and Barriers for the Transformation of Manufacturing

3. Is the level of technology you have in production enough for you to adapt to COVID-19 or a similar global epidemic? Or can it be improved?

> F-"The technology level we have in our facility is competitive compared to our regional competitors. We see examples of the use of robots in the woodworking processes of furniture production, production line and storage processes in the world. In particular, we carefully monitor the contributions of Kuka robots to the manufacturing process. We are trying to increase the level of automation in our manufacturing process. However, most of our process is currently built on a labor-intensive manufacturing model. Considering our demand during the pandemic period, we thought that our current process would be responsive to this. However, periodic reductions in our human resources due to quarantine restrictions and illness caused accumulated workloads to occur. The idea of restructuring our manufacturing process stands before us as a discussion that has not been consensus yet. I don't think our budget is suitable for this renewal, which is worth millions of dollars."

Manufacturing facilities can survive as long as they can continue their production. The prerequisite for their continued production is to be able to supply raw materials or intermediate products. During the pandemic, cuts in supply resources deeply affect companies in the manufacturing sector. The sector-based evaluation of these deductions was made under this heading. The following question about raw material or intermediate supply was asked to five industry representatives. The answer given by the construction chemicals sector representative is given below.

4. During the pandemic process, did you experience interruptions in the supply of raw materials or intermediate goods? If your answer is yes, what solutions have you developed to overcome this?

> CC-We supply the raw materials of our products from the far east. Since we are both a manufacturer and a wholesaler, we keep stock in our inventory to meet the demand for several months. Our raw material stock ensured that the early stages of the process did not affect us. However, in the following months, our orders with a normal delivery period of 45 days started to reach us within 60-75 days. It was stated that the waiting times in different ports of our orders that reach us through ship transportation cause this. Naturally, this process led us to different suppliers from which we can supply raw materials. Other supplier alternatives for chemical raw materials are EU countries. We know that EU countries and Far East

countries are 2-3 times more costly than EU countries when compared in terms of raw material purchase prices. We did not choose this option, as these high-cost raw materials will increase the cost of the final product. Instead of this option, we increased the size of the order we placed in the Far East.

Another issue that is as important as raw material supply in the manufacturing sector is logistics activities. Uninterrupted and timely realization of upstream and downstream logistics activities allows manufacturers to avoid the bottleneck they encounter in the supply chain. During the pandemic process, general information on the functioning of logistics activities in the manufacturing sector was obtained from the sector representatives through the following question. The answer of the marble products manufacturer is shared below.

5. How has COVID-19 affected your logistics activities in the upstream or downstream supply chain?

M-In the marble sector, we produce intermediate products in line with the wishes of our customers. Our main customers are Vietnam, Hong Kong and Kuwait. We did not experience any interruption in our upstream logistics activities as we produce raw materials in our mines ourselves. However, the delays in ship shipping have greatly affected our order cycle. Namely; Our product, which reaches our customers in 20-30 days, takes 75 days to reach the end customer through the operations of our customers. As a result of the regulations introduced, our delivery time to the customer has reached 45-60 days. Although the bill of lading date seems important for us to charge the price of the product we sell, this situation extends the time for receiving orders again. In addition, we sell a significant part of our production after our customers mark them during factory visits. With the pandemic process, the arrivals of our customers decreased and this caused our sales to decrease by almost 50%.

The interviews made in the second part of the study were analyzed through the codes created. Nvivo program was used in the analysis phase. The answers of the sector representatives were analyzed through codes.

Figure 3. Barriers and enablers to transforming manufacturers in the global epidemic period

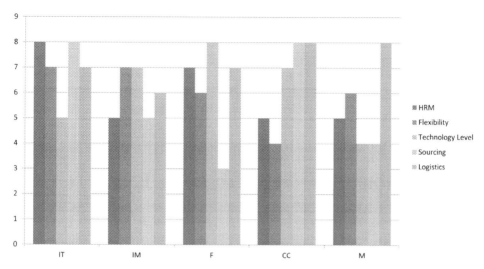

In the light of the findings obtained, human resources and raw material supply in the integrated textile sector, flexibility and technology level in the industrial machinery sector, technology level in the furniture sector, logistics and raw material supply in the construction chemicals sector, and the transformation of the elements expressed under the main headings of logistics in the production of marble products during and after COVID-19. It can be stated that those are the main barriers.

FUTURE RESEARCH DIRECTIONS

There are few studies in the literature that examine the COVID-19 production relationship. With the increase in the studies of different institutions and theorists on the subject, the literature will become even richer. New studies to be carried out in this context will be able to evaluate the effects of COVID-19 on production through different factors.

CONCLUSION

The manufacturing sector is one of the areas deeply affected by global crises and epidemics. As stated in the introduction of the study, although the pre-global epidemic period started for various reasons, the global epidemic period caused the manufacturing sector to cope with more difficulties. In the study, the difficulties faced by the manufacturing sector were examined under five main headings after the relevant literature review. Considering these sub-headings consisting of human resources management, flexibility, technology level, procurement and logistics, meetings were held with representatives of different sectors. The findings obtained were shared. When the findings are analyzed, the biggest challenge faced by the manufacturing sector during the global epidemic was expressed as the interruptions and delays in the logistics sector. The COVID-19 global epidemic era has brought about the necessity of a transformation in the manufacturing sector as well as in the service sector. The transformation to be experienced actually gave its first signals with the concept of Industry 4.0. However, realizing the expected transformation in both the supply chain and manufacturing process requires time and financial resources. It is inevitable for enterprises in the manufacturing sector to adapt to this transformation in order to ensure their continuity. Although there are obstacles to this transformation, there are also facilitators. Today, manufacturers feel more clearly how factors such as globalization, reduction in product lifetimes, COVID-19 affect their supply chain and manufacturing processes. Therefore, they need to raise their level of awareness and knowledge about the axioms that can be taken.

REFERENCES

Acemoglu, D., Chernozhukov, V., Werning, I., & Whinston, M. D. (2020). *Optimal Targeted Lockdowns in a Multi-Group SIR Model*. NBER Working Papers 27102, National Bureau of Economic Research, Inc.

Agrawal, M., Eloot, K., Mancini, M., & Patel, A. (2020). Industry 4.0: Reimagining manufacturing operations after COVID-19. *McKinsey Insights*, (July), 1–18.

Bonacini, L., Gallo, G., & Scicchitano, S. (2021). Working from home and income inequality: Risks of a 'new normal' with COVID-19. *Journal of Population Economics*, *34*(1), 303–360. doi:10.100700148-020-00800-7

Brannen, S., Ahmed, H., & Newton, H. (2020). *Covid-19 Reshapes the Future*. Center for Strategic and International Studies.

Browne, B. J., & Dubois, D. (1984). Classification of flexible manufacturing systems. *The FMS Magazine*, 114–117.

Cai, M., & Luo, J. (2020). Influence of COVID-19 on Manufacturing Industry and Corresponding Countermeasures from Supply Chain Perspective. *Journal of Shanghai Jiaotong University (Science)*, *25*(4), 409–416. doi:10.100712204-020-2206-z PMID:32834699

Dey, I. (1993). *Qualitative Data Analysis*. Routledge.

Dey, M., & Loewenstein, M. (2020). How many workers are employed in sectors directly affected by COVID-19 shutdowns, where do they work, and how much do they earn? *Monthly Labor Review*, (April), 1–19. doi:10.21916/mlr.2020.6

Furtado, V., Kolaja, T., Mueller, C., & Salguero, J. (2020, Apr.). Managing a manufacturing plant through the coronavirus crisis. *McKinsey & Company Insights*.

ILO. (2020). *The effects of COVID-19 on trade and global supply chains*. Research Brief.

Jackson, J. L., & Judd, J. (2020). *The Supply Chain Ripple Effect: How COVID-19 is affecting garment workers and factories in Asia and the Pacific*. Academic Press.

Javaid, M., Haleem, A., Vaishya, R., Bahl, S., Suman, R., & Vaish, A. (2020). Industry 4.0 technologies and their applications in fighting COVID-19 pandemic. *Diabetes & Metabolic Syndrome*, *14*(4), 419–422. doi:10.1016/j.dsx.2020.04.032 PMID:32344370

Koç, E. (2020). *Internet of Things (IoT) Applications for Enterprise Productivity*. IGI Global. doi:10.4018/978-1-7998-3175-4

Koren, Y. (2010). *The Global Manufacturing Revolution: Product-Process-Business Integration and Reconfigurable Systems*. John Wiley & Sons. doi:10.1002/9780470618813

Kroupenev, A. (2020). What Will Manufacturing's New Normal Be After COVID-19? *Industry Week*, 1–12.

Kumar, A., Luthra, S., Mangla, S. K., & Kazançoğlu, Y. (2020). COVID-19 impact on sustainable production and operations management. *Sustainable Operations and Computers*, *1*(July), 1–7. doi:10.1016/j.susoc.2020.06.001

Kumar, S., Raut, R. D., Narwane, V. S., & Narkhede, D. B. E. (2020). Applications of industry 4. 0 to overcome the COVID-19 operational challenges. *Diabetes & Metabolic Syndrome*, *14*(January), 1283–1289. doi:10.1016/j.dsx.2020.07.010 PMID:32755822

Malik, A. A., Masood, T., & Kousar, R. (2020). Reconfiguring and ramping-up ventilator production in the face of COVID-19: Can robots help? *Journal of Manufacturing Systems*, (June). Advance online publication. doi:10.1016/j.jmsy.2020.09.008 PMID:33082617

Maliszewska, M., Mattoo, A., & Van Der Mensbrugghe, D. (2020). *The Potential Impact of COVID-19 on GDP and Trade: A Preliminary Assessment*. World Bank Policy Research Working Paper.

National Association of Manufacturers. (2018). *NAM Manufacturers' Outlook Survey*. https://www.nam.org/wp-content/uploads/2019/05/NAM-Q4-2018-Manufacturers-Outlook-Survey.pdf

Roberts, M. (2020). *A global manufacturing recession*. https://www.cadtm.org/A-global-manufacturing-recession

Sethi, A. K., & Sethi, S. P. (1990). Flexibility in Manufacturing : A Survey. *International Journal of Flexible Manufacturing Systems, 2*(4), 289–328. doi:10.1007/BF00186471

Tisdell, C. A. (2020). Economic, social and political issues raised by the COVID-19 pandemic. *Economic Analysis and Policy, 68*, 17–28. doi:10.1016/j.eap.2020.08.002 PMID:32843816

Twinn, I., Qureshi, N., Conde, M. L., Guinea, C. G., Rojas, D. P., Luo, J., & Gupta, H. (2020). *The Impact of COVID-19 on Logistics*. International Finance Corporation (IFC).

U.S. Bureau of Labor Statistics. (2020). *Economic News Release*. https://www.bls.gov/news.release/archives/prod2_08142020.htm

Wieser, H., Tröger, N., & Hübner, R. (2015). The consumers' desired and expected product lifetimes. Plate Conference, 1-6.

World Economic Forum. (2020). *How to rebound stronger from Covid-19 Resilience in manufacturing and supply systems*. WEF White Paper. https://www3.weforum.org/docs/WEF_GVC_the_impact_of_COVID_19_Report.pdf

Yıldırım, A., & Şimşek, H. (2005). *Sosyal Bilimlerde Nitel Araştırma Yöntemleri*. Seçkin Yayıncılık.

Chapter 2
Critical Analysis of the Relocation Strategy of Production Between National Protectionist Policies, Global Supply, and Value Chains

José G. Vargas-Hernández
https://orcid.org/0000-0003-0938-4197
Tecnológico Mario Molina, Unidad Zapopan, Mexico

EXECUTIVE SUMMARY

This chapter aims to critically analyze the implications that the national protectionist policies have on the global supply and value chains and the relocation of production. The analysis is based on the assumptions that the global economy is facing the possibility of decoupling of many trade connections, and this trend favors deglobalization processes that have long been promoted by populism, nationalism, and economic protectionism. It is concluded that global supply, production, and value chains although being economically efficient are no longer any more secure under national protectionist policies, and therefore, the relocation of production processes is mainly due to the increase in the level of income and wages of the developing countries that are the destination and which reduce the advantages to relocate.

DOI: 10.4018/978-1-7998-9140-6.ch002

INTRODUCTION

This analysis shows expansive periods of free trade alternate with other periods in which protectionist measures and the relocation of production are part of a process that is called deglobalization and is characterized by a reduction in export growth that is compensated with increased consumption of the domestic market to defend national interests. Some developed economies have trade imbalances with negative effects on less developed countries.

The current environment of economic, social, political and health instability has intensified the increase in the economic costs of transaction and coordination of the subsidiaries of multinational companies located in other international host territories, making relocation processes unviable, for which they have initiated processes of repression or de-globalization to return its production to the countries of origin. This situation has meant stagnation, and in some cases a reversal in business strategy to deepen the globalization processes of companies.

The level of economic integration in globalization processes is well advanced, as it has been shown that when production in a province of China is paralyzed, the supply of inputs to other companies from other nations has affected, a situation of vulnerability that has motivated deglobalization as a response that makes relocation more profitable with the repatriation of factories.

This paper first makes a critical analysis of the national protectionist policies and its implications on the global supply and value chains and how these two factors determine the strategy of the relocation of production. Finally, it is offered a discussion on these issues.

NATIONAL PROTECTIONISM POLICY

Protectionism has returned, and it will be having to think about it if it is wanted to reap all the benefits and implement this reasoned "deglobalization" that it called for and that now seems inevitable (Sapir, 2016). The term deglobalization was coined by Sapir (2011) to refer to the protectionism of countries that have a similar level of development and economic growth limited by the commercial and financial dimensions of globalization than through outsourcing and relocation processes of large companies. groups of production centers. Deglobalization processes are characterized by the recovery of the sovereignty of nations, reduction of their interdependence, implementation of automatic and protectionist policies to reduce economic and commercial relations.

In a protectionist policy, countries increase restrictions on the free flow of trade, finance and people, reinforcing their national borders and are oriented towards deglobalization processes that threaten the internationalization of higher education, for example, which remains confined, although It is already advised to deepen the advancement of online education through platforms that reach all places, including the most remote places in the world. The concern about these changes is the depth in which they must occur to save and overcome the advances of globalization, so it can be considered that the advances will be different and different as it had been advancing before, although it is necessary that competition be promoted at the same time that cooperative and collaborative relationships are fostered.

Deglobalization is an inverse process to globalization that is manifested by the protectionist and regulatory economic and trade policies of the nation states as well as the trade wars that are carried out between the great economic and commercial powers. To protect national production, domestic markets increase tariff barriers with the intensification of trade wars between western and eastern markets. What the health crisis has done is accelerate the process.

The international competition on economic systems in the world economy is reduced to economic structures and enterprises mechanisms of macroeconomic players supported by the strengthen functions of the state to stabilize macroeconomics, protect intellectual property rights, to ensure legality and enforcement of contracts, infrastructure provision, and other micro economic policies to stablish incentives and mechanisms for corporate governance, stimulating research and development, investments in human development. Protectionist, nationalist and populist policies can be functional or dysfunctional depending on their correct design and implementation.

Some of the phenomena that disappointed the scope of the globalization economy were job insecurity and flexibility due to stagnant wages and rising unemployment. The far right has channeled discontent to promote protectionist measures. These situations have given rise to deglobalization processes through the implementation of protectionist economic policies. A greater presence of the State is necessary in the face of the challenges of economic growth, greater economic and social equality, social inclusion, environmental sustainability, protection of biodiversity and conservation of socio-ecosystems, the energetic and climate crisis, etc.

During the inter war era from 1914 to 1945, from the outbreak of World War I until the end of World War II, globalization processes were in retreat from the first time, after a period of increased economic integration from 1870 until 1914. After the First World War, protectionism and nationalism were on the rise as international institutions and organizations weakened, but the economic depression deepened. After the year 1918, with the rise of nationalism, international organizations were weakened, an economic depression arose that drove national states to protective economic models.

The abandonment of global economic integration is an option for nation states framed by a Keynesian scheme through the implementation of protectionist trade measures and maintaining democracy. These methods favored the economic growth of some developed countries that later embraced economic globalization (Rodrik 2000 and 2007; Steinberg, 2007, p. 45). The countries that remained with borders closed to trade through protectionist and nationalist measures were imposed asymmetric trade conditions, as was the case with the colonies. When these nations achieved their independence, they could already take off in their economic and social development.

After the Second World War, a system of international governance institutions was established with the programs of the Marshall Plan, the Bretton Woods institutions, the United Nations (UN) and the General Agreement on Customs Tariffs (GATT). During this period of globalization retreatment and economic dislocation led to reduced integration, the Great Depression and protectionism as the solution. After World War II, and until the 1980s, new global institutions for economic cooperation were created and developed to promote economic integration and enabling national economies to be opened to foreign markets. In 1989 the slow food movement was created to protect the consumption of local products, cultures, traditions and gastronomic customs perceived as healthier and safer. The movement aims to create awareness of decisions for food consumption and its origin.

During the international financial crisis of 2008 and 2009, the leaders of the most advanced economies managed adequately to avoid the trend of protectionist economic nationalism. The national state recovers functions that were taken from it and together with international institutions assume responsibilities to protect national economies and societies. In 2017, China promoted globalization as a mechanism for economic integration, generating wealth and multilateral cooperation, while the United States promoted trade protectionism. Protectionist trade policies used as an instrument for multilateral and bilateral negotiations do not always result in benefits for the country that promotes them, as has been recently demonstrated in the case of the United States, which has encountered strong resistance from the trend of economic globalization processes.

In 2018, many North American companies announced the relocation and transfer of their production plants back to the national territory. In 2019, the Kearney index detected a strategic trend in company production towards a greater weight of the "made in America" content of manufacturing production. In part this was achieved by the warning that if they wanted to receive the protection of the American legal system they should return the jobs. European countries grant aid through anti-crisis plans to their companies that disengage from tax havens.

Following North American policy, France encourages the repatriation of its companies while Japan favors its companies that return from China with incentives. Nation states have difficulty regulating the financialization that dominates the real economy and offshore strategies, as well as putting limits on the power of monopolies in the digital economy.

Critical Analysis of the Relocation Strategy

The unilateral discourses practiced by some powers attempt to control the world agenda of globalization processes through neo-protectionist mechanisms under the world economy revolving around a multipolarity. Geo-economics and geopolitical analyzes show a transition of leadership from the global economy to China. Now the United States plays the option of a more protectionist economy that drastically affects the economies that are more dependent on global trade. However, the slowdown in economic globalization began long before the pandemic, which has contributed to accelerating it by declining national economies.

The goal of the new United States government to eliminate the trade deficit through the implementation of protectionist and nationalist fiscal policies, and started a trade war against its trading partners, but above all with China, its main competitor, but which had repercussions worldwide, because it drastically reduced world trade. The elimination of the deficit simply to date, has not been achieved, but also worsened and deepened. The coronavirus health crisis imposed a truce on the trade war that paralyzes the negotiations of trade relations. However, the largest production of medical supplies is in China. With the health crisis, countries want to maintain their own economic activities and in proximity through protectionism. Consistent with this, multinational companies plan to repatriate in reshoring part of their international production.

The world economy faced threats in its globalization process long before the 2020 health crisis, such as the growing challenge of trade wars and the protectionism of the economies of different national states with the implementation of a tariff war. The health crisis is the result of negative externalities of an interconnected world in globalization processes that is perceived to be linked to physical security in identity and economic spheres, whose responsibility to protect against risks has fallen more on the nation state rather than on the international community.

The health crisis caused by the pandemic has accelerated the protectionist tendencies and the populist and nationalist policies of the nations and has caused tensions and trade wars in the face of the fall in international trade flows and foreign direct investment. The health crisis has accelerated and deepened this trend of economic deglobalization through protectionist actions, reduction of multilateral treaties, etc., with economic consequences that are legible, but uncertain and unpredictable.

The protectionist tensions that lead to a trade war constitute a reconsideration in the opposite direction to the progress of trade liberalization. This situation that arises unilaterally resists the continued opening of markets and international economies to position itself as a closed economy, erodes economic, commercial and political relations with its partners. In other words, the country that was the greatest promoter of economic globalization processes is now the greatest opponent of deepening economic, commercial and financial relations.

The liberalization of regulations of local financial markets that protected the host countries from foreign investments allows MNES to have access to local natural resources and get actively involved in local markets. As a consequence of this deregulation, the global FDI flows had increased regularly until 2000 and since then it had been falling until it reached a pick in 2007 (World Bank, 2016).

Now local governments try to implement different initiatives with protectionist measures against global markets since 2008, as ways to recover the economic growth of their economies, resulting in limitations to international trade. All these initiatives are strengthened to weaken the processes of economic globalization and cry out for deglobalization. After the subprime crisis, citizens demand to governments for protection of their own interests against the globalization interest through the redesign and implementation of more protective economic and financial liberalization policies.

The processes of economic globalization are being pressured by isolationist positions that seek to deepen the self-sufficiency of national states to protect local interests over global interests. These changes in perspective have implications and effects on the harmonious development of peoples. The national state recovers relevant functions in this process of deglobalization for the financial rescue in the face of the economic debacle of important economic actors and agents, such as multinational companies, financial institutions. The new scheme is configured with less market and more state with a geopolitical reconfiguration of national borders evidenced in a return to nationalist protectionism and more controls on cross-border financial transactions.

Factors such as technology-based automation, protectionist practices in national economies, rapid shipments and deliveries, among many other factors, contribute to the acceleration of the processes of slowing down or reversing globalization. Rather, the concern is diverted towards how profound these changes that are already occurring will be, but above all in the way they are going to be managed. These trends are driven by rising wages in countries that previously offered low labor cost advantages, as well as protectionism in local economies.

The restrictive and protectionist economic policy measures that materialize in the deglobalization processes are, among the most common, the increase in tariff rates, the establishment of phytosanitary measures, cross-border labor restrictions, limitations on foreign investment, control of movements immigration, trade wars, etc. As part of protectionist measures, importers raise their tariff barriers in response to the trade war.

Nation states are receding driven by protectionist trends due to falling global trade and investment flows driven by the health crisis. With the health crisis of the pandemic, the nation states enact protectionist, deglobalizing economic policy measures that reduce and retract the advance of globalization processes, such as, for example, the closure of the border to commercial exchange activities and nationalist control of migratory movements of the population. Nation states adopt nationalist, populist and protective economic policies in an attempt to recover their regulatory functions and fields of action in a gradual process of control of globalizing dynamics.

Trade protectionism is the relevant element of deglobalization for protecting the losers of globalization assuring gains though imposing high rates of industrial and trade protection and imposing manufacturing tariffs (Findlay and O'Rourke 2008, 401). Trade protectionism is a relevant action implemented in this deglobalization process. Deglobalization processes have repercussions that damage the economies that promote protectionist economic policies. The lack of leadership in the globalization processes makes it easier for each nation to reverse or at least slow down progress by adopting more protectionist measures.

National markets and economies are now less dependent on international markets and rely on the regulations of national economies to protect themselves. To exploit the advantages offered by the new environment, an emerging strategy has emerged that supports the resurgence of protection measures for national markets. The deglobalization of economic integration processes moves the center of gravity back from the market to the sustainable local market through a commercial policy and the use of fiscal, tariff and quota mechanisms to protect the national production of transnational companies. The uniformity and standardization of commercial regulations threaten regional and local development where the asymmetric is normal for self-protection.

Therefore, the protectionist attempt of an economy has a negative impact on national companies in such a way that the protectionist measures taken unilaterally by a country, damage the competitiveness of its companies and therefore its own economy. It is the same multinational companies that promote the relocation of production, distribution and consumption processes. Countries now attempt to relocate the production of goods within or near their national borders for the benefit of integrated regions through tariff protection measures.

The deglobalization process is supported by the promotion of protectionist measures and is characterized by export flows, investments, migratory movements and technological innovation that are reduced or diminished, are reflected in political and economic decisions to orient themselves to domestic demand with measures with tariffs, cross-border restrictions and limitations on investment and foreign labor.

Greater attention to domestic demand leads governments to reduce the growth of exports through direct or indirect protectionist measures. Countries alone are unlikely to oppose globalization given the omnipotence of global financial markets, so the alternative is to recur to the risks of trade wars more focused on national protectionisms. National governments grant tax incentives that benefit protectionism and populism for the repatriation of manufacturing plants and investments. Manufacturing employment is likely to decline while most forms of services employments are likely to be heavily protected from internationalization, therefore avoiding antiglobalization backlashes focus more on improving the quality and provision.

The same powers that before spread the gospel of open market and free trade are the same that now predicate protectionism and support deglobalization markets. It has been said that the global economic and financial elites pursue the creation of a world government by centralizing order and power by protecting from enemies through a surveillance system based on traceability.

Cultural globalization and an increase of human interactions has been the result of the economic, financial and trade exchanges, contributing to the different values, traditions, customs, habits, etc., are being shared among local communities and other communities in such a way that it is homogenizing a world's culture. Local culture requires protection to maintain its uniqueness at community level, environmental and development social movements and activists need the support of the nation state to defend society to defend and protect society from the destructive capacities of economic globalization and global market to exploit the human and natural resources.

GLOBAL SUPPLY, PRODUCTION AND VALUE CHAINS

Trade openness, economics, financial and commercial liberalization, information and communication technology innovations facilitated the special and operational expansion of transnational and multinational corporations which in turn, contributed to alter the exchange of resources flows and supply chains between intra and inter firm as well as to a global power redistribution. Economic globalization processes accelerated the flow of goods through global supply chains and global trade.

The development of ICTs and the emergence of the Internet accelerated the processes of globalization with world communication in real time, financial digitization and with the logistical development of supply and value chains, accelerated the scope of a global economy. Technological and scientific advances have intensified with economic globalization with the monopolistic emergence of digital companies that control the financialization of processes around global supply and value chains where BRICS countries have become the managers of changes in the global competitiveness (Rosales 2009: 77).

The value chains as well as the supply chains of the companies in a global economy scenario are distributed throughout the world. Mutinational and transnational corporations have established networks of supply chains, subcontractors and logistics around the world. The networking-based global economy is formed by chains developed by a large group of shadow enterprises that are connected for economic activities across the boundaries of countries and making meaningless the concept of distance and national borders.

In a competitive global market, the costs of the entire chain of supply, production and consumption spread worldwide should be the lowest (Bello, 2013). However, the globalization based on the economies of scale and scope due to location of production where is most efficient is over, while the concern is for the fragility of supply-chain diversification, because their processes rely each other to add their value.

The global production and distribution chains show the fragility of the high dependence on the processes of economic globalization to provide products and inputs to the economies that require them to continue their manufacturing processes. This failure in global production chains has exposed the weaknesses of national security and national industry, arguments that support protectionist positions, such as measures to guarantee supply in national markets. The national security policy acquires greater force by pressing for reversions in global production chains encouraged by supply decisions in local markets.

Starting in the 1990s, global production and value chains grew steadily. Since 2007, with the outbreak of the economic and financial crisis, the indicators of globalization processes show a trend of decrease in global production and supply chains, due to a drop in demand from international markets and not so much to the structural changes. Since the financial crisis of 2008-2009, world trade has failed to maintain the level of world GDP, due to the emergence of protectionist policies. Global economic, financial, health, and contingency crises such as natural disasters have a domino effect that has a greater impact on global production and value chains. The example is the tsunami in Japan in 2011 that affected global automobile production chains.

These stagnations in economic globalization processes have negative effects for the global economy due to the relocation of the production chain, although the reorientation may have some positive effects for certain national territories where some phases of this production chain can be carried out to take advantage of low labor costs. Reversing or slowing down the processes of economic globalization will mean changes in the practices and activities of multinational and transnational companies

In 2019 there is a high fragmentation of global supply chains, which is deepened by the 2020 health crisis. The ruptures of global supply chains produce a dislocation of production that produces in response the withdrawal of companies located abroad for The Coronavirus has paralyzed the growth of global trade, which contributes with more than 60% of the domestic product world gross. This situation has been called deglobalization, aggravated by the health crisis, which has made interconnections more difficult for commercial practices between different countries.

The current scenario of the health crisis has affected the complex global supply and value chains of intermediate goods, without being able to stop their fragmentation. This has shown that global supply chains are very vulnerable and complicated for companies to immediately redesign and redirect, which has accelerated deglobalization processes.

The critical situation of the health crisis has forced the space of global logistics and supply chains to be reduced to be replaced by shorter chains in such a way that the localities for the supply of raw materials and production of inputs or parts of a product must be shorter than the places where the final product is assembled. The health crisis has highlighted the limitations of global logistics and supply chains in sectors such as electronics, automotive, aeronautical, medical equipment, pharmaceutical products, textile industry, etc. The health crisis has broken global production chains.

The inability of the globalization processes to find a way out of the relocation of the production and supply chains, as well as the inability of the national industry in many countries to produce the required sanitary material, has complicated the economic scenario. The health crisis has exposed the dysfunctionality of global and multinational supply chains, placing excessively dependent companies at vulnerability. The health crisis has affected the global production chains of countries that are prone to international trade, although it is contradictory that it depends on corporate companies that originally relocated their production processes.

The dependence on imports of inputs for national production through supply chains, have been affected by the health crisis, so many nation-states have accelerated the processes of deglobalization by strengthening the production of inputs and operations in local spaces. Deglobalization processes imply having greater controls over commercial, financial, migration, travel flows, etc., which gives rise to retreats in the global supply and production chains.

Protecting and stimulating national food supply chains can help reduce the impact caused by the health crisis of the pandemic. Global supply and value chains have proven to be inoperative amid the health crisis. Multinational corporations transferred their productive operations to places where costs were lower, achieving supply through long global supply chains, which were suddenly interrupted during the Covid-19 health crisis, with serious threats to paralyze the production of certain essential products such as agro-food.

Deglobalization processes attempt to unlink local production from global supply chains to reorient production towards the internal market supported by movements in favor of food self-sufficiency and sovereignty based on domestic industrial and agricultural production, undertaken by economic policies and progressive commercials and not by right-wing nationalist governments that only serve the interests of the dominant ethnic and cultural group and displace minorities and immigrants.

With the emergence of the health crisis of the pandemic, countries have had to reconsider their supply chains and value of strategic productive activities, as in the case of food production. For this reason, strategic productive industries are a priority for national development, which is why they are considered to be maintained and strengthened with actions such as the development of local, flexible and fast supply chains of value chains.

Globalization undergoes profound changes with the crisis of the coronavirus pandemic and will not be as we knew it before in the modes of production, distribution and consumption and in the global production, supply and value chains. The dynamics of contemporary globalization processes have registered a strong interruption that calls into question the entire international economic system, disrupts global supply and value chains, as well as a slowdown in all economic sectors.

The continuity of the processes of economic globalization requires leading the mitigation of the negative impacts in the production and supply chains in the global economy based on the location in places where costs are lower. The priorities of the productive, distribution and consumption systems are changing their priorities through the location of supply chains as secure as possible rather than as economically as possible as was achieved during globalization. The economic efficiencies of globalization processes are being highly questioned with the dysfunctionality of global supply chains that lead to more protectionist economic and fiscal policies.

Deglobalization is a period of slowdown and decline in international economic, commercial, financial and people flows intensified by the coronavirus that has made companies rethink the risks of global supply chains that occur in remote locations. The economic phenomenon of deglobalization of the world economy is a period marked by a decline in commercial and financial flows, intensified by the coronavirus pandemic that has caused a rethinking of the risks of the global chain of supplies that come from geographically remote locations. Disruption of the supply chains of local companies' dependent on a global system generates economic losses.

With the interruption of global production and supply chains, and due to perceived risks, production and consumption turn to alternative sources of inputs, goods and services from local suppliers, passing the acquisition cost to second term Economic deglobalization, according to Witt (2019), assumes considering the strategic policies that affect the political sustainability of multinational companies, the dynamic organizations of value chain specializations and the national context in which these decisions about strategies, structures and behaviors. The breakdown of global supply chains has direct consequences on the profitability of many of these multinational companies.

The main causes that have given rise to the deglobalization processes, the slowdown in the growth of the global economy, the regression of global supply and value chains and the increase in protectionism of local economies against multilateral processes, to reduce the concerns about external dependence on essential supplies. The regression of global supply and value logistics chains go into regression processes for different causes, such as protectionism, wage increases and the level of income reduce the advantages of countries that were the destination of relocations. If production is less delocalized, flows in global supply and value chains are reduced, along with the investments that accompany them.

The interruption of global supply chains and therefore of value is a consequence of the trade wars started by countries with deficiencies in commercial and financial exchanges The Sino-US trade war is the landmark event for furthering the tendency of deglobalization with the disruption of the global supply chain and a declining global trade flows in value and volume.

The trade wars coupled with the risks of the coronavirus have caused the blockage of global supply chains and international supplies. They have been shortening their global supply and value chains for several years now, as a consequence of trade wars, through the relocation of their plants, production processes and the manufacture of their own components that came from distant locations and through the diversification of the origin of inputs and products. Companies around the world rethink their internationalization decisions as a reaction to dependence on global supply chains that distribute the production of products with the relocation of their plants and their production processes. This situation has shown the vulnerability of companies due to their excessive dependence on these chains.

Deglobalization manifests itself in changes in production systems based on the locations where production is most efficient, leading to many logistical mismatches in supply chains and value in trade connections. The creation of alternative supply chains modifies the rules of globalization processes. For the United States, the intensity of globalization shows vulnerabilities, such as in situations where national economies depend on a single country for the supply of goods, which leads to the blockage of supply chains.

Global supply chains are more complex in the production, distribution and consumption of products that have had to be interrupted or reduced due to the lack of provision of essential components. Globalization is transformed to be different than it was before the pandemic and it is possible that the modes of production, distribution and consumption are transformed due to changes in the global value, provision and supply chains.

Destructuring the networks in which currently major strategic activities are included in supply chains, production, management and distribution on global scale are organized and interconnected in real time on a sophisticated information and communication system. Companies are moving away from just-in-time production systems to more secure supply chains. The reduction of global supply and value chains negatively affects commercial, financial, investment and people flows. The deglobalization processes are pressing the global production, provision and value chains to change in organizational forms subject to local decisions.

Critical Analysis of the Relocation Strategy

Multinational companies are already reconsidering their logistics processes for the transport of goods that include socio-ecosystem concerns to try to shorten geographic distances and links in their global supply chains through the use and development of new technologies that reduce the costs and risks of production, increase quality and respond more quickly to market demand. Multinational companies reconfigure global value chains to strengthen themselves in the face of shocks.

National economies are bounded together in globalization through the supply chains to achieve manufacturing efficiency and better prices in international trade. The flow of international business activities is retracted as global supply and supply chains are reconfigured, prioritizing production over economic efficiency. Business organizations are assessing the location of global supply chains relocating their production elsewhere, which is a globalization trend of natural churn and premises. International trade replicates its operations while reconfiguring its supply chains sacrificing economic efficiencies in exchange for greater security in the provision of its inputs. International trade is territorially withdrawn to the national through the reconfiguration of its production chains and supply, leading to importers raising tariff barriers.

Populist and nationalist nation states have taken up this message, supported by political parties and social organizations to promote actions to deglobalize the economy that attempt to dismantle globalization through withdrawals of global value chains, repatriation of investments and strategic relocation of Business.

Global supply chains are relocated, which implies the reorganization of production, distribution and commercialization activities, reinforced with government policies, especially in sectors considered of national security. Returning plants to the country of origin can be more expensive, but in the current conditions of interrupted global supply chains, it turns out to be more productive and competitive due to savings in logistics risks, transportation, tariffs, etc. The reduction of dependence on the provision of supplies from other geographically distant locations through global chains of manufactured inputs has led to relocation or reshoring trends. Not only are the production sites relocated close to the markets, but also innovation, design, logistics, distribution and marketing activities, etc.

New technologies advance innovations in automation, robotization, artificial intelligence, internet of things, etc., which tend to replace the more routine and cheap labor, which implies that global supply and value chains reduce their importance with a localized and robotic production.

The deglobalization trend converted into regional trade agreements allows economies to be fully integrated and to take advantage of regional and local value chains. From the crisis that economic globalization is going through, companies that have less global supply chains, more regional and therefore shorter with respect to assembly or marketing lines, will emerge strengthened, not necessarily from lower cost suppliers and with minimal inventory levels, which confirms deglobalization. The interruptions of the global supply chains forced people and companies to look for alternative local or regional sources of supply, even though they were more expensive.

The less advanced economies have seen their global value chains reduced with premature processes of deindustrialization, lower economic growth, a commodity boom that has given rise to the Dutch disease phenomenon, non-redistributive and regressive fiscal reforms with an increase in income levels of poverty and inequality. Countries are backtracking in their globalization advances and trying to avoid the continuity of outsourced production chains to maintain strategic productive activities internally or as regionally as possible, with more flexible and faster local value chains.

The blockade of global supply chains represents the opportunity for Mexico to be the beneficiary due to its proximity to the North American market, as has been the case in the automotive, electronics and aeronautical sectors. Without the supplies produced in Mexico by these industrial sectors, the manufacturing of finished products is interrupted. Deglobalization and the T-MEC favor the rapid integration of the sectors of the electrical, automotive, medical equipment, aeronautical, pharmaceutical, aeronautical industries, etc. to the supply chains of North American companies. Complementation among the member countries of the T-MEC facilitates regional integration processes and solves the problem of supply and logistics chains.

Risk assessment focuses on disturbances in production processes mainly due to supply chains of inputs that come from geographically distant locations, or other phenomena such as natural disasters, wars, etc. One of the risks that are run with deglobalization is derived from geopolitical and geoeconomic uncertainty and its impact on investments with repercussions on production levels for global supply chains, exports and market volatility. Companies have reacted to the perception of risks through a strategy of geographic diversification of sources of supply and production that can affect global trade as production is relocated in the country itself.

The inability of the globalization processes to find a way out of the relocation of the production and supply chains, as well as the inability of the national industry in many countries to produce the required sanitary material, has complicated the economic scenario.

RELOCATION OF PRODUCTION

In a free market system under the invisible hand, companies continue to track the location of their production, distribution and consumption systems through offshoring or relocation decisions that mean benefits and cost efficiency. Tensions and trade wars accelerated the de-globalization processes under the premise of relocating the production and supply of resources from sources as close as possible, which confirms the trend towards open regionalism.

The processes of economic and financial de-globalization propose that local economies should be reoriented in short circuits towards production for local consumption, avoiding the relocation of companies that generate competition because they look for places where labor costs are lower, production standards and ecological are less restrictive, etc. On the other hand, foreign direct investment movements facilitate the relocation of production systems in global factories, taking advantage of the advantages offered by other national economies in cheap labor, more direct transport systems, the privatization of public companies, etc. The relocation of production that is manifested in the flows of direct foreign investment (Grunwald, and Flamm, 1985).

The relocation of production processes is mainly due to the increase in the level of income and wages of the developing countries that are the destination and which reduce the advantages to relocate. Delocalized production of companies motivated by lower production costs, are returning to a closer place through relocation or reshoring processes. Discontent over the growing impoverishment of the working middle classes in the most developed countries, the precariousness of employment and labor benefits, and the loss of employment, due to the relocation and flight of companies to locations where labor costs are lower. The advantages for relocating production, distribution and consumption systems have been reduced due to an increase in the income and living standards of workers in the countries that were the destination of these relocations.

There are several reasons that are making the processes of economic globalization dysfunctional to the growth and development of some countries, such as the loss of their political and economic sovereignty, growth in unemployment due to the relocation of production and the increase in automated systems and robotization, which also reduces relocations.

Companies have reacted to the perception of risks through a strategy of geographic diversification of sources of supply and production that can affect global trade as production is relocated in the country itself. Extraterritoriality characterizes economic globalization (Palomares 2006: 30) because of the capacity that transnational companies have to relocate production with geographic fragmentation. In such a way, this trend of regional proximity of production occurs, pointing to a relocation of production processes in countries that belong to the same economic region. The processes of regionalization of production is a trend in proximity to consumer markets that ensures the supply of resources, goods and services in places to consumer markets to respond quickly and flexibly to demand through customization or product customization.

With globalization, companies become more dependent on the places from which the inputs and products necessary for production are provided, so national states are now offering incentives to their companies to return operations that they had relocated in other countries. The continuity of the processes of economic globalization currently marks a break in the breakdown of international economic relations that, although it attempts to relocate production, the competition for the attraction of talent, technology and more advanced production capacity.

Relocation as a strategy of deglobalization processes has as immediate consequences the increase in labor costs due to differentials between nations, but also to the health crisis, with a tendency to reduce economic inequality. Another trend that accelerates as a result of relocation is robotization, which in times of pandemic is positive because it reduces the risks of contagion by eliminating or reducing face-to-face contacts. Another trend is the increase and consolidation of teleworking, with many implications for people's movements and the market for office space, parking lots, etc.

The increase in e-commerce is a trend that increases more with relocation and the health crisis of the pandemic. Pandemics have shown the risks that the globalized economy has under the logic of relocation of production to take advantage of lower costs that are then marketed in other regions of the world without establishing the pertinent health controls.

DISCUSSION

The post-pandemic world economy tends to be less globalized as it is rejected by national governments and populations to protect their national economies. The processes of economic globalization are deepening instead of a gradual process of deglobalization, under the argument of the principle of sovereignty with economic policies and measures that show a tendency towards a nationalist, protectionist and populist retreat. The actions of national states and international organizations promoting globalization processes such as regional integration treaties for free trade tend to weaken the sovereignty of the states. This is somewhat paradoxical in its contradictory processes due to its origin of globalized localisms that have contributed to strengthening hierarchies and inequalities both between nations and between individuals, the creation of victims who lack the protection of the state subject to their localities or forced to abandon them.

The world order that has prevailed since the Second World War has been considered under the conception of linear processes of irreversible economic globalization and has undergone structural changes in the last ten years that require reconfiguration. This reconfiguration has been called a deglobalization stage and corresponds to a regression of global integration processes in the form of retractions in world trade and international financial investments carried out through nationalist, populist and protectionist policies.

The movement of trade protectionism as a retreat from the processes of economic globalization with the renegotiation of trade agreements and trade wars was initiated by the United States. The trade war declared by the United States against China tries to weaken its strategic position in economic growth, cooperation, trade, finance, etc. The phenomenon of deglobalization is a popular political cause motivated by protectionist and reindustrializing economic forces.

The nation states face great challenges to guarantee the protection of the minimum welfare of the citizens. Another consequence of the reversal of the global integration of production processes is the increase in costs and therefore consumer prices, which results in a drop in welfare. From an ethical perspective, deglobalization processes should give higher priority to values over interests, cooperative relationships over competition, and community welfare over efficiency. From this same perspective, real economic thinking strengthens the values of social solidarity, justice, equity and community to subordinate the action of the market.

Local economies must exercise fiscal and economic policy mechanisms for the protection of their own production, distribution and consumption systems, as well as their socio-ecosystems from the subsidized importation of large transnational corporations that establish subsidized and artificial prices. A viable alternative as a sample is the emergence of large self-centered spaces that are constituted as poles of economic, political, social, cultural and civilization power.

The new nationalist and protectionist sentiments that drive the decisions of the n countries have a high impact on migrant workers who seek better economic conditions and greater well-being for their families. Nation states can prevent the flight of endogenous technological talent to other economies by creating institutional and instrumental frameworks for the establishment and protection of competitive advantages through reindustrialization processes.

REFERENCES

Bello, W. (2013). *Capitalism's Last Stand? Deglobalization in the Age of Austerity*. Zed Books. doi:10.5040/9781350218895

Findlay, R., & O'Rourke, K. (2008). *Power and Plenty: Trade, War, and the World Economy in the Second Millennium*. Princeton University Press.

Grunwald, J., & Flamm, K. (1985). The global factory: Foreign assembly in international trade, Brookings Institution. *Washington D., C*, 1985.

Palomares, G. (2006). *Relaciones internacionales en el siglo XXI*. Tecnos.

Rodrik, D. (2000). How far will international economic integration go? *Journal of Economic Perspective*, *14*(1), 177-186.

Rodrik, D. (2007). *One Economics Many Recipes, Globalization, Institutions and Economic Growth*. Princeton University Press. doi:10.1515/9781400829354

Sapir, J. (2011). *La demondialisation*. Seuil.

Sapir, J. (2016). Jacques Sapir: Donald Trump, président de la démondialisation? *Le Figaro*. Available on web: https://www.lefigaro.fr/vox/monde/2016/11/10/31002-20161110ARTFIG00233-jacques-sapir-donald-trump-president-de-la-demondialisation.php

Steinberg, F. (2005). *Cooperación y Conflicto en el Sistema Comercial Multilateral: La Organización Mundial de Comercio como Institución de Gobernanza Económica Global* (Tesis Doctoral). Presentada en el Departamento de Análisis Económico: Teoría Económica e Historia Económica de la Facultada de Ciencias Económicas y Empresariales de la Universidad Autónoma de Madrid, España.

World Bank. (2016). *World Bank Data*. http://data.worldbank.org/?display=default

KEY TERMS AND DEFINITIONS

Deglobalization: The slow-down or reverse of globalization. A political project opposed to neoliberal globalization. In the first definition, the term describes how global flows of trade, investment, and migration can decline.

Global Supply Chain: It is the set of activities, facilities and means of distribution throughout the world necessary to carry out the entire sales process of a product. This is, from the search for raw materials, their subsequent transformation and even the manufacture, transport, and delivery to the final consumer anywhere in the world.

Production Chain: It is a system made up of people and companies related to each other, by a succession of production operations.

Protectionism: Is a commercial policy established by a government that aims to protect the national industry against foreign competition with the application of tariffs or any other type of import restriction.

Relocation of Production: The international displacement of a productive structure.

Value Chains: It is a theoretical model that graphs and allows to describe the activities of an organization to generate value to the end customer and to it.

Chapter 3
The Rating of Confusion in Supply Chain Dynamics in Food Business and Selecting the Most Ideal Capacity Strategy During COVID-19

Selçuk Korucuk
Giresun University, Turkey

Salih Memiş
Giresun University, Turkey

Çağlar Karamaşa
Anadolu University, Turkey

EXECUTIVE SUMMARY

Supply chain dynamics are seen as important components that directly affect supply chain performance, business processes, management functions, and efficiency for businesses. Every company in the supply chain needs other businesses to achieve the desired level of supply accurately, with the least cost and in an effective manner. Therefore, supply chain dynamics are seen as important components in terms of increasing competitiveness, increasing business performance, avoiding problems in workflows, and ensuring customer satisfaction, and also play critical roles in the provision of necessary information, materials, and services and improvement of process management. Also, capacity and capacity development strategies have vital importance, and firms need to apply right strategies in order to achieve success. In this study, it is aimed to rank the confusion in the supply chain dynamics and select the most ideal capacity strategy for food establishments with 10 or more employees operating in Giresun province during the COVID-19 process via SWARA and WASPAS methods.

DOI: 10.4018/978-1-7998-9140-6.ch003

INTRODUCTION

Nowadays firms tend to cooperate in order to meet the customers' dynamic changing and extraordinary requirements. Because it is impossible for firms to compete successfully in complex environment per se. Therefore firms utilize supply chain cooperation for using customers' resources and knowledge to the end with respect to avoiding complexity.Firms aware the importance of supply chain management on the behalf of obtaining the sustainable competitive superiority. Supply chain management incorporates the systems connecting supplier, producer, distributor and retailer via the network of transportation, finance and information. Both the level of operational productivity and customer satisfaction have increased by operating supply chain management function efficiently. The sustainability of this function can be made via regular performance analyses, controls and improvements. Elements of time, speed and quality have an increasing pressure on manufacturers in order to be competitive in global market. Thus competition can be measured via supply chain performance and amendments can be proposed for solving available supply chain problems (Korucuk et al., 2021).

Supply chain management essentially incorporates various dynamics and can be defined as establishing a common business managemeny system containing all marketing, informatics, finance and distribution processes beyond a typical logistic optimization. Furthermore that means creating improvable structure forming chain and affecting each other instead of integrating logistical infrastructures. The most important change requiring second dynamic is the impossibility of competing individually in today's environment in terms of parent companies (Memiş & Korucuk, 2018).

Supply chain management needs to have dynamic structure according to the changing and developing conditions. In this point it is important for firms to create supply chain dynamics with respect to determined strategic plan.

The dynamics of supply chains can be addressed under the headings of product quality (meeting customer needs and requirements), level of customer service (availing the product in the required quantity and time), and time to market (faster access to new products) (Chen & Paulraj, 2004). According to another view, the focus in supply chain management has evolved from the order-winning quotation into a winning business in the market (Christopher & Towill, 2001). This is because the dynamics in the supply chains should be able to quickly respond to the increasing fluctuations in the environmental conditions and the unpredictable market changes on the basis of volume and diversity while maintaining a cost advantage. Looking at marketing, in many industry branches, on a global scale, we find that all business processes currently depend on supply chains, networks, and dynamics. Each business or business unit is working on an independent structure within the supply chain management in order to meet product demands and obtain information. This independence transforms the resources under their control into autonomous agencies that they offer to subsequent businesses (Lin et al., 2006).

One of the amendments in supply chain dynamics according to the emerged conditions within the frame of strategic planning is to establish capacity plannings. Strategic business plans need to be made with respect to determined optimal capacity level for firms.

According to Hatinoglu (2014), once an enterprise starts production, the average unit costs decrease up to a certain production volume. The biggest factor here is the increase in the number of products to which the fixed costs are distributed, and thus the decrease in the fixed cost per unit. In addition, as the production batches grow, machine setup and preparation times will decrease, and productivity will increase. This positive development of increasing returns to scale also known as economies of scale continues until a certain point (Adabalı, 2020).

The costs start to increase after the optimal capacity point. This arising complexity is caused by factors like programming difficulties; supply difficulties; loss of effectiveness in management, communication, and control; negative impact on workforce morale; exaggerated use of overtime; interference with maintenance programs; increased failure frequencies among others that cause increased costs and reduced productivity. The advantages of economies of scale are lost with movement away from the optimal capacity level (Bulut, 2004).

There is a decrease in average costs until the size of the enterprise reaches the optimum level. Any expansion after the optimum size, where the costs are at their lowest, is accompanied by an increase in average costs. As such, businesses whose sizes have surpassed their optimum will have difficulty in competing with those operating at their optimum as they will have to work at higher costs than those of optimum size. The determination of the optimal capacity, therefore, can be considered as one of the vital indicators for the sustainability of the enterprise both in the sense of reducing costs and in ensuring customer satisfaction and increasing competitiveness.

Determined capacity level needs to be followed in parallel with firms' growth. In this context three main strategy are proposed for capacity increase time related to constant growth (Kobu, 2017):

Capacity Lead Strategy: Capacity is increased with the thought that demand growth. This aggressive strategy is being used to gain customers from competitors and promote in rapidly growing market.

Capacity Decline Strategy: Capacity is growed with documented demand increasing. This conservative strategy provides more investment returns but having risk of customer lose in process. It is substantially used in standard products, cost and low competition based industries. Strategy considers the regaining customers from competitors after capacity expansion.

Average Capacity Strategy: Capacity is being increased in order to coincide with expected average demand. Managers can sell at least some additional output via this average strategy.

Supply chain dynamics can be considered as essential components for increasing competitive power, business performance and customer satisfaction and play critical role for providing required knowledge, equipment and service.

In terms of capacity management, the main difference between the food supply chain from other supply chains is the expectation that it will create a flexible supply chain network that meets the most basic needs of consumers. In this sense, the food supply chain needs to be sustainable, flexible, and highly competitive. Especially, healthy and sustainable food procurement have gained importance with the COVID-19 pandemia.

Because demand towards food sector has increased with irrevocable expenses during quarantine process. Business models for food sector and supply chain have changed especially with precautions taken in pandemia process and change in customer behaviours. It is crucial to examine the facing problems and developed strategies in food sector due to having forward and backward connections in supply chain dynamics. By this way the strength of sector toward future can be handled. Additionally capacity strategies as important elements in supply chain dynamics need to be formed according to the conditions in pandemia process.

According to the literature review there is not found any study that aims to analyze confusion happened in supply chain dynamics related to food enterprises. From this point the purpose of study is to rate the confusion happened in food enterprises containing 10 and more employees and select the most ideal capacity strategy in Covid 19 process via integrated SWARA-WASPAS methodology. Remaining parts of the study can be summarized as follows. Studies related to supply chain dynamics are presented under the literature review part. Steps of the SWARA and WASPAS are explained in methodology section. Case study is mentioned in the application part. Finally conclusion and future suggestions are presented in the last part.

The complexity in the supply chain is defined as the detailed and dynamic complexity exhibited by the products, processes, and relationships that make up a supply chain (Bozarth et al., 2009). The supply chain complexity can arise from within the enterprise (internal production complexity), relationships with upstream partners (suppliers), relationships with downstream partners (customers), and from inadequacies in the decision-making process (Ustasüleyman & Perçin, 2014).

According to studies by Bozarth et al. (2009), Serdarasan (2013), Perona and Miragliotta (2004), Vachon and Klassen (2002), Milgate (2001), Gerschberger et al.

(2012), Manuj and Sahin (2011), and Blome et al. (2013), supply chain complexity is made up of by four components: upward complexity, internal production complexity, downstream complexity, and inadequacy in the decision-making process.

We then talk of supply chain risk management which can be defined as the implementation of strategies for the management of daily and extraordinary risks that occur throughout the supply chain (Wieland & Wallenburg, 2012). In another definition, supply chain risk management is the management of risks through cooperation and coordination with members of the supply chain in a way that ensures profitability and continuity throughout the supply chain (Blos et al., 2009).

Supply chain risk management is the control of performance measures that enable early detection disruptions and uncertainties that may arise in the supply chain of enterprises and that may cause a decrease in the profitability of the chain, as well as the decision-making and correction processes in the chain in line with these measures (Giannakis & Louis, 2011).

Risk management is considered as one of the main objectives for businesses operating internationally (Briggs, 2010). This is because, often, in the globalizing economy, businesses that deliver products and services to the same customer, such as manufacturers, suppliers, and distributors face the same set of difficulties.

While the risk management process is generally related to the risks that concern the organization, supply chain risk management is related to the risks affecting the supply chain as a whole. Supply chain risks are concerned with all kinds of risks related to the flow of products, materials, and information from the first supplier to the end-user (Jüttner et al., 2003).

Agile supply chain management and supply chain flexibility are considered important components in ensuring business performance and increasing competitiveness. Agile supply chain can be defined as the ability to read the wishes of the end customer and respond to their needs. Agile supply chain considers both flexibility and the ability to operate with an eye on consumer demand (Lyons & Ma'aram, 2014). In another definition, agile supply chain is defined as the ability to effectively integrate the relationships in the supply chains so as to create effective change against internal and external uncertainties in an environment that contains internal and/or critical business partners. (Fayezi et al., 2017).

Agile supply chain is expected to be both market-sensitive and market-driven. Simply put, the agile supply chain must have the ability to read and respond to market demands. One of the most important features of the agile supply chain is its focus on "speed and flexibility". An agile supply chain also enables the development of some activities other than "core capabilities". It uses information technologies intensively in the development of activities and follows global outsourcing policies (Banerjee, 2016).

Different types of uncertainty and variations in demand reveal the need for different capabilities for effective and efficient organizational responses. These capabilities can be tied to strategic agility and flexibility. The supply chain literature emphasizes the role of business partners with respect to flexibility and the importance of inter-organizational systems and relationships in providing and developing flexibility in the supply chain. Supply, production, distribution, information systems, and purchasing are considered as the organizational functions of flexibility (Fayezi et al., 2017).

In the literature, it is noted that businesses with high levels of agility are able to develop the skills of their suppliers in a way that provides greater customer satisfaction. Businesses with a lower level of agility focus on the internal framework of the organization and are mostly concerned with the management of technological problems (Power et al., 2001; Fayezi et al., 2017).

The flexibility of the supply chain is a feature that businesses that establish a supply chain try to achieve in order to adapt to the changes in the market and to prevent the disruptions in the chain from causing the system to crash. In supply chain structures where materials are sequentially moving from one side to the other, all "partners" in the chain must be flexible to respond to change. This view has influenced the supply chain measurement literature and the concept of "flexibility to meet specific customer needs" has become an important strategic performance measure (Gunasekaran et al., 2001; Lummus et al., 2005; Sadler, 2007). In addition, in order to coordinate supply chains in the form of production networks, it is necessary to examine the flexibility and relationships of system components and evaluate their effects on the overall system performance (Garavelli, 2003).

METHODOLOGY

Multi-criteria decision making (MCDM) can be defined as the selection process made by the decision-maker using at least two criteria within a set of a countably finite or uncountable number of options. Many methods have been developed for MCDM. These methods have some advantages over each other and one of the problems that the decision-maker may encounter when faced with a problem that requires MCDM is to determine the appropriate method. While determining the most appropriate method, the decision-maker should look at the nature of the problem and the characteristics of the process. In multi-criteria, all problems have more than one criterion. Relevant criteria are determined in each problem set. Although there are hundreds of factors to be considered for the decision, the decision-maker should only accept the most important ones as criteria (Ersöz & Kabak, 2010).

MCDM is expressed as the process of assigning values to alternatives by evaluating many criteria together. Multi-criteria decision-making approaches are divided into two; multi-qualified decision making and multi-objective decision making. An approach is considered a multi-qualified decision making if it is based on the evaluation of alternatives and selection of the best by assigning scores to several features. The multi-objective decision making problem is concerned with choosing the best alternative based on conflicting objectives. In both problem types, there are one or more decision-makers. This study discusses the problem of multi-qualified decision-making (Phua & Minowa, 2005).

The methods developed for criterion weighting in the literature are divided into three categories; subjective, objective, and integrated (Wang & Luo, 2010). In subjective methods, the evaluation criteria are weighted based on the preferences and judgments of the decision-makers. Decision-makers and practitioners cannot easily weight the criteria because it requires experience in practice and directly affects the analysis results. In addition, the weights obtained do not have an economic meaning, they only help to model the decision problem (Opricovic & Tzeng, 2007).

In order to minimize the effects of subjective weighting, some objective weighting techniques have been developed by researchers in the literature. The common point of these methods is to weight the criteria using only the available data and using mathematical programming techniques without resorting to the subjective judgments of the decision-makers. In the integrated models, which is another weighting approach in the literature, weighting is made using both the judgments of the decision-makers and the numerical data of the decision matrix in an integrated way (Çakır & Perçin, 2013).

According to Keeney (1992), multi-criteria decision-making techniques consist of three steps: determining the relevant criteria and alternatives; determining the effects of these criteria on the alternatives, and the numerical measurements of the relative importance of the criteria; a numerical evaluation process to determine the order of each alternative. The main purpose of multi-criteria decision-making problems is to identify the best alternative that provides the highest level of satisfaction in terms of all relevant criteria (Chatterjee & Chakraborty, 2012).

The SWARA method allows decision-makers to choose their own priorities, taking into account the current environmental and economic situations. Another important aspect of this method is the role of experts considered as the decision-makers (Zolfani & Saparauskas, 2013). From the literature, the SWARA method is seen to have been used in solving many problems including dispute resolution, architect selection, the selection of optimal mechanical ventilation alternative, supplier selection, product design, machine part selection, energy sustainability assessment indicators, personnel selection, investment prioritization, selection of the region where solar power plants will be installed, supplier clustering and ranking, sales branch selection, assessment of regional landslide hazard, R&D project selection, and the selection of mining engineer candidates to be recruited (Çakır & Karabıyık, 2017).

As a new method, WASPAS uses both methods together and has been proposed as the most appropriate MCDM method that is accuracy-based or confirmation oriented. The purpose of this method is to increase the ranking accuracy (Zavadskas et al., 2013a). The alternatives are ranked according to the value of the combined optimality criterion calculated from the results of these two models. The method can control the consistency in the alternative rankings by performing a sensitivity analysis within its own operation (Chakraborty & Zavadskas, 2014). Studies that have used the WASPAS method have applied it in areas such as the selection of the most appropriate manufacturing process, development of the best outsourcing strategy, site selection, and contractor selection (Akçakanat et al., 2017).

Due to the reasons mentioned above, SWARA and WASPAS methods were preferred in the study.

SWARA and WASPAS as MCDM methods are used for detecting the importance levels of confusion happened in supply chain dynamics and select the most ideal strategy for firms having corporate identity in Giresun province during Covid 19 process.

MCDM methods consider and evaluate objective and subjective factors apart from statistical analysis techniques within the framework of expert's opinions as single or group (Korucuk, 2021).

Steps of the SWARA and WASPAS methods that are used for evaluating criteria related to confusion happened in supply chain dynamics and selecting the most ideal capacity strategy are presented under this part.

SWARA Method

SWARA that is used for solving uncertainties in evaluating criteria and alternatives via linguistic expressions, is one of the mostly used MCDM methods recently (Korucuk,2019). The main advantage of this method is that in some problems priorities are determined according to the policies of companies or countries and there aren't any needs for rank criteria evaluation (Kouchaksaraei et al., 2015). In this context steps of SWARA method can be summarized as below (Ruzgys et al., 2014 ve Stanujkic et al., 2015):

Step 1: Sorting criteria: The criteria are sorted in descending order according to their expected significances. Geometric mean is applied for group decision making process.

Step 2: Determining the relative importance of each criterion: Starting from the second criterion, the decision maker explains the relative importance of criterion j in relation to the previous (j-1) criterion, for each particular criterion. According to Kersuliene et al. (2010), this ratio is called the Comparative importance of average value, s_j.

Table 1. Obtaining the general ranking

Criteria	DM_1	DM_2	DM_3	DM_4	DM_5	Geometric Means
C_1	4	5	5	6	5	4,956
C_2	3	4	4	3	4	3,565
C_3	2	1	1	2	3	1,644
C_4	1	6	3	4	1	2,352
C_5	5	2	6	8	6	4,919
C_6	8	7	8	9	2	6,044
C_7	7	9	7	7	8	7,560
C_8	9	8	9	5	9	7,816
C_9	6	3	2	1	7	3,022

Step 3: Detecting the coefficient of k_j: The coefficient k_j is determined according to Eq.(1):

$$kj = \begin{cases} 1 & j=1 \\ sj+1 & j>1 \end{cases}, \qquad (1)$$

Table 2. K_j calculations for decision maker 1 and decision maker 2

		Decision Maker 1		Decision Maker 2	
	General ranking	s_j	k_j	s_j	k_j
C_3		-	-	-	-
C_4		0,05	1,05	0,10	1,10
C_9		0,15	1,15	0,15	1,15
C_2		0,20	1,20	0,15	1,15
C_5		0,10	1,10	0,05	1,05
C_1		0,10	1,10	0,20	1,20
C_6		0,15	1,15	0,20	1,20
C_7		0,05	1,05	0,15	1,15
C_8		0,20	1,20	0,10	1,10

Step 4: Calculating the coefficient of *qj*: The coefficient of *qj* is computed according to Eq. (2):

$$q = \begin{cases} 1 & j = 1 \\ \dfrac{qj - 1}{kj} & j > 1 \end{cases}, \qquad (2)$$

Table 3. Q_j calculations for decision maker 1 and decision maker 2

	General ranking	Decision Maker 1			Decision Maker 2		
		s_j	k_j	q_j	s_j	k_j	q_j
C_3		-	-	1,00	-	-	1,00
C_4		0,05	1,05	0,952	0,10	1,10	0,909
C_9		0,15	1,15	0,828	0,15	1,15	0,790
C_2		0,20	1,20	0,690	0,15	1,15	0,687
C_5		0,10	1,10	0,627	0,05	1,05	0,654
C_1		0,10	1,10	0,570	0,20	1,20	0,545
C_6		0,15	1,15	0,496	0,20	1,20	0,454
C_7		0,05	1,05	0,472	0,15	1,15	0,395
C_8		0,20	1,20	0,393	0,10	1,10	0,359

Step 5: Determining the relative weights of criteria: Relative weights of criteria are determined by using Eq.(3):

$$wj = \frac{qj}{\sum_{k=1}^{n} qk} \qquad (3)$$

where w_j denotes the relative weight of criterion j.

Table 4. W_j values calculation and ranking

Criteria	Arithmetic means	Geometric means
C_1	0,110	0,110
C_2	0,124	0,124
C_3	0,158	0,158
C_4	0,132	0,132
C_5	0,106	0,106
C_6	0,090	0,090
C_7	0,079	0,079
C_8	0,076	0,076
C_9	0,125	0,125

WASPAS Method

This method, developed by Chakraborty and Zavadskas in 2012, is a MCDM approach that combines the results of WSM (Weighted Sum Model) and WPM (Weighted Product Model), and also it is one of the methods that increase the accuracy of ranking (Zavadskas, et al., 2013b). Steps of WASPAS method can be summarized as follows:

Step 1: Forming decision matrix and normalized decision matrix: Chakraborty et al., (2015), in order to analyze this method in the study of the decision matrix must be created first. In order to normalize the decision matrix, the following Eq. (4) and Eq. (5) are used. Decision matrix and normalized decision matrix are formed as Table 5 and Table 6 respectively.

Table 5. Decision matrix for WASPAS method

Alternatives	C_1 Max.	C_2 Min.	C_3 Min.	C_4 Min.	C_5 Max.	C_6 Max.	C_7 Min.	C_8 Max.	C_9 Max.
A_1	2,44949	2,82843	1,41421	3,22371	1,31608	2,21336	2,51487	3,63424	4,37345
A_2	4,47214	1,73205	3,46410	1,86121	4,64159	3,56521	2,21336	3,08616	3,51948
A_3	2,62074	3,30193	2,71081	2,91951	3,46410	3,36587	2,63215	2,94168	3,72792

$$-xij = \frac{-xij}{maksi - xij} \quad (4),$$

$$-xij = \frac{\min i - xij}{-xij} \quad (5),$$

Although the criteria are desired to be maximum and minimum, Table 6 was obtained by using Eqs. (4) and (5).

Table 6. Normalized decision matrix

Criteria Weights	0,110	0,124	0,158	0,132	0,106	0,090	0,079	0,076	0,125
Alternatives	C_1 Max.	C_2 Min.	C_3 Min.	C_4 Min.	C_5 Max.	C_6 Max.	C_7 Min.	C_8 Max.	C_9 Max.
A_1	0,5477	0,6124	1	0,5774	0,2835	0,6208	0,8801	1	1
A_2	1	1	0,4082	1	1	1	1	0,8492	0,8047
A_3	0,5860	0,5246	0,5217	0,0639	0,7463	0,9441	0,8409	0,8094	0,8524

Step 2: Computing the total relative significance value for each alternative via Weighted Sum Model (WSM): Zavadskas et al., (2013b), the total relative significance value for each alternative, primarily the Weighted Sum Model of Eq. (6) and the total relative value for each alternative to the Weighted Product Model is calculated with the help of Eq. (7).

$$Q_i^{(1)} = \sum_{j=1}^{n} w_j r_{ij} \quad (6)$$

Table 7 is created by using Eq.(6) and presented as below:

Table 7. Calculated total relative significance values for each alternative via Weighted Sum Model (WSM)

Alternatives	C_1	C_2	C_3	C_4	C_5	C_6	C_7	C_8	C_9	$Q^{(1)}$
A_1	0,0602	0,0759	0,158	0,0762	0,0301	0,0559	0,0695	0,076	0,125	0,7248
A_2	0,110	0,124	0,0645	0,132	0,106	0,090	0,079	0,0645	0,1006	0,8706
A_3	0,0645	0,0651	0,0824	0,0084	0,0791	0,0850	0,0664	0,0615	0,1066	0,6173

The Rating of Confusion in Supply Chain Dynamics

$$Q_i^{(2)} = \prod_{j=1}^{n} r_{ij}^{wj} \qquad (7)$$

Table 8 is created by using Eq.(7) and presented as below:

Table 8. Calculated total relative values for each alternative via Weighted Product Model (WPM)

Alternatives	C_1	C_2	C_3	C_4	C_5	C_6	C_7	C_8	C_9	$Q^{(2)}$
A_1	0,9354	0,9410	1	0,9301	0,8750	0,9580	0,9899	1	1	0,6793
A_2	1	1	0,8680	1	1	1	1	0,9877	0,9732	0,8344
A_3	0,9434	0,9231	0,9023	0,6956	0,9695	0,9948	0,9864	0,9841	0,9802	0,5016

Step 3: Determining relative and total importance levels for each alternative: Šaparauskas et al. (2011), in their study, calculated the combined optimality value for each alternative. This value obtained by using Eq. (8) is calculated by taking into consideration the Weighted Sum Model and Weighted Product Model results.

$$Q_i = \lambda Q_i^{(1)} + (1-\lambda)Q_i^{(2)} = \lambda \sum_{j=1}^{n} -xij\ w_j + (1-\lambda)\prod_{j=1}^{n}(xij)^{wj},\ \lambda = 0,0,1,\ldots,1 \quad (8),$$

Table 9 is formed by taking Eq. (8) into the consideration and shown as below:

Table 9. Total importance levels for alternatives

Alternatives	$Q^{(1)}$	$Q^{(2)}$	$Q^{(i)}$
A_1	0,7248	0,6793	0,702
A_2	0,8706	0,8344	0,853
A_3	0,6173	0,5016	0,560

APPLICATION

In this study it is aimed to determine confusion happened in supply chain dynamics and select the most ideal capacity strategy selection for hazelnut enterprises having corporate identity in Giresun province during Covid 19 process. Firstly criteria and alternatives related to confusion happened in supply chain dynamics and capacity strategies for hazelnut enterprises are determined according to depth literature review and expert opinions. Following that while criteria are prioritized with SWARA method, alternatives are ranked by using WASPAS method.

Criteria for study are determined by total of 5 experts (2 academician, 3 hazelnut enterprises' managers) and literature review (Krajewski et al., 2016) and given as Table 10:

Table 10. Decision criteria

Criteria	Mark
Technical changes	C_1
Intrabusiness supply deficiency	C_2
Late deliveries	C_3
Information errors	C_4
Volume change	C_5
Protecting the values of goods and services	C_6
Order accumulation	C_7
Promotions for goods and services	C_8
New goods and services displaying	C_9

Alternatives for study are determined by expert opinions and literature review (Kobu, 2017; Şenses, 2019) and given as Table 11:

Table 11. Alternatives

Alternatives	Mark
Capacity lead strategy	A_1
Capacity decline strategy	A_2
Average capacity strategy	A_3

Criteria Weighting

Criteria are evaluated within SWARA method by forming pairwise comparison survey. Total of five experts are responded to survey and obtained weight values are presented as Table 12.

Table 12. Criteria weight values

	C_1	C_2	C_3	C_4	C_5	C_6	C_7	C_8	C_9
Weight	0,110	0,124	0,158	0,132	0,106	0,090	0,079	0,076	0,125
Rank	5	4	1	2	6	7	8	9	3

According to the Table 12 while the most important criterion was found as late deliveries (C_3) for confusion happened in supply chain dynamics for hazelnut enterprises during Covid 19 process, the least important criterion was obtained as promotions for goods and services (C_8). Remaining criteria are ranked as $C_4 > C_9 > C_2 > C_1 > C_5 > C_6 > C_7$ respectively.

Alternative Ranking

Alternatives are ranked within WASPAS method by considering the criteria weights obtained via SWARA method. Respondents give points to each alternative ranging from 1-5 (1-the worst, 5-the best) in terms of criteria. Alternative ranking is given as Table 13.

Table 13. Alternative ranking

Alternatives	$Q^{(1)}$	$Q^{(2)}$	$Q^{(i)}$	Ranking
A_1	0,7248	0,6793	0,702	2
A_2	0,8706	0,8344	0,853	1
A_3	0,6173	0,5016	0,560	3

According to the Table 13 the most ideal capacity strategy was found as capacity decline strategy (A_2) and ranking of strategies are $A_2>A_1>A_3$ respectively.

CONCLUSION

Nowadays firms need to focus on supply chain and supply chain management due to the increased importance of competitive environment and rapidly changing market structure. They can remain by creating and applying efficient supply chain structure and network. In this context, one of the main problems firms face can be considered as confusion happened in supply chain dynamics which has vital importance. Because product realization process can be possible with efficient supply chain management. From this viewpoint confusion happened in supply chain dynamics have critical importance for all firms.

Capacity planning is long term strategic decision that forms the total resources' level. Firms' strategic capacity decisions affect the conditions of product delivery time, customer responsiveness, operating expenses and their fulfillment ability. At that point making strategic capacity plans have gained importance for food enterprises especially during Covid 19 pandemia.

In this context, it was found that the most effective factors for the confusion happened in the supply chain dynamics in hazelnut enterprises are "Late Deliveries" and "Information Errors", respectively. The resulting outcome is consistent with those of Özçakar and Demir, (2011), Zhou et al. (2011), Supeekit et al.(2016), and Korucuk, (2018).

Other important criteria are stated as " New goods and services displaying", "Intrabusiness supply deficiency", "Technical changes" and "Protecting the values of goods and services". On the other hand the least important supply chain dynamics factors have been determined as "Promotions for goods and services" and "Order Accumulation", respectively. The results obtained resemble those by Sellitto et al. (2015), Arashpour et al. (2017), and Jaśkowski et al. (2018).

According to the alternative ranking, the most ideal capacity strategy for hazelnut enterprises having corporate identity during Covid 19 process was found as capacity decline strategy. The results are similar to those obtained by Anupindi and Jiang (2008), but not to the study of Goyal and Netessine (2007). Other alternatives are ranked as capacity leaad strategy and average capacity strategy respectively. The results obtained are consistent with the studies of Fazlietal et al. (2018) and Lim and Srai (2018).

According to the authors' knowledge there is not sufficient study related to confusion happened in supply chain dynamics and capacity strategy selection in literature so that shows the novelty and originality of this study. But a complete discussion and comparison with other studies are not possible due to lack of studies related to that. So this can be considered as one constraint of the study. The number of expert does not increase due to the Covid 19 pandemia and that can be considered as another constraint. Besides conclusions obtained from SWARA and WASPAS methods can be changed due to differentiation in expert group.

A review of the literature also reveals that there is no study on supply chain dynamics and the selection of the most ideal capacity, making it an area that can be considered for comparison from different perspectives. The fact that there is no other study that has used the method followed in this research adds to the unique value of the study.

The data for this study was collected by interviewing expert groups. However, due to the pandemic and time constraints, the number of experts considered was limited. This notwithstanding, the results of the study determined that the outcomes of the interviews supported the expectations of the decision-makers.

Due to the uncertain nature of human decisions, expectations, and judgments and the diffculties in clearly quantifying them, modeling the real situation is also very difficult and complex. Due to this complexity, future studies could use fuzzy MCDM methods and statistical analysis to compare the results.

In the study, people who were thought to be experts in the subject were interviewed, but due to time constraints, the research was only conducted in Giresun Province of Turkey. A similar study covering more provinces could provide a comparative discussion of the priority of supply chain dynamics in the food sector among provinces. The problem considered in this study could also be expanded to include consumers so as to determine the priority of supply chain dynamics from the perspective of the consumers as well.

For future studies application are can be differentiated apart from hazelnut enterprises. Also various hybrid MCDM techniques can be applied in different environments (fuzzy, intuitionistic, neutrosophic, hesitant, Pythagorean, etc.).

REFERENCES

Adabalı, M. M. (2020). Konya İlinde Faaliyet Gösteren 4 ve 5 Yıldızlı Otel İşletmelerinde Kapasite Yönetimi Stratejilerinin Belirlenmesi ve Bir Uygulama. *International Journal of Arts and Social Studies*, 3(4), 34–49.

Akçakanat, Ö., Eren, H., Aksoy, E., & Ömürbek, V. (2017). Bankacılık Sektöründe Entropi Ve Waspas Yöntemleri İle Performans Değerlendirmesi. *Süleyman Demirel Üniversitesi İktisadi ve İdari Bilimler Fakültesi Dergisi*, 22(2), 285–300.

Anupindi, R., & Jiang, L. (2008). Capacity investment under postponement strategies, market competition, and demand uncertainty. *Management Science*, 54(11), 1876–1890. doi:10.1287/mnsc.1080.0940

Arashpour, M., Bai, Y., Aranda-mena, G., Bab-Hadiashar, A., Hosseini, R., & Kalutara, P. (2017). Optimizing decisions in advanced manufacturing of prefabricated products: Theorizing supply chain configurations in off-site construction. *Journal of Automation in Construction*, 84, 146–153. doi:10.1016/j.autcon.2017.08.032

Banerjee, A. (2016). Agile Supply Chain Mangement. In Handbook of Research on Strategic Supply Chain Management in the Retail Industry (pp. 55-152). IGI Global.

Blome, C., Schoenherr, T., & Eckstein, D. (2013). The impact of knowledge transfer and complexity on supply chain flexibility: A knowledge-based view. *International Journal of Production Economics*, 147, 307–316. doi:10.1016/j.ijpe.2013.02.028

Blos, M. F., Mohammed Quaddus, H. M. W., & Watanabe, K. (2009). Supply Chain Risk Management (SCRM): A Case Study on the Automotive and Electronic Industries in Brazil. *Supply Chain Management*, 14(4), 247–252. doi:10.1108/13598540910970072

Bozarth, C. C., Donald, P. W., Barbara, B. F., & Flynn, E. J. (2009). The impact of Supply Chain Complexity on manufacturing plant performance. *Journal of Operations Management*, 27(1), 78–93. doi:10.1016/j.jom.2008.07.003

Briggs, C. A. (2010). *Risk Assessment in the Up Stream Crude Oil Supply Chain: Leveraging Analytic Hierarchy Process* (Unpublished Ph.D. thesis). North Dakota University.

Bulut, Z. A. (2004). İşletmeler Açısından Kapasite Planlaması ve Kapasite Planlamasına Etki Eden Faktörler. *Mevzuat Dergisi*, 7(80), 1–13.

Çakır, E. & Kutlu Karabıyık, B. (n.d.). Bütünleşik SWARA - COPRAS Yöntemi Kullanarak Bulut Depolama Hizmet Sağlayıcılarının Değerlendirilmesi. *Bilişim Teknolojileri Dergisi*, 10, 417-434 .

Çakır, S., & Perçin, S. (2013). Çok Kriterli Karar Verme Teknikleriyle Lojistik Firmalarında Performans Ölçümü. *Ege Akademik Bakış*, *13*(4), 449–459. doi:10.21121/eab.2013418079

Chakraborty, S., Bhattacharyya, O., Zavadskas, E. K., & Antucheviciene, J. (2015). Application of WASPAS Method as an Optimization Tool in Non-Traditional Machining Processes. *Information Technology and Control*, *44*(1), 77–88.

Chakraborty, S., & Zavadskas, E. K. (2014). Applications of WASPAS Method in Manufacturing Decision Making. *Informatica (Vilnius)*, *25*(1), 1–20. doi:10.15388/Informatica.2014.01

Chatterjee, P., & Chakraborty, S. (2012). Material Selection Using Preferential Ranking Methods. *Materials & Design*, *35*, 384–393. doi:10.1016/j.matdes.2011.09.027

Chen, J. I., & Paulraj, A. (2004). Towards A Theory Of Supply Chain Management: The Constructs And Measurements. *Journal of Operations Management*, *22*(2), 119–150. doi:10.1016/j.jom.2003.12.007

Christopher, M., & Towill, D. R. (2001). An Integrated Model for The Design of Agile Supply Chains. *International Journal of Physical Distribution & Logistics Management*, *31*(4), 235–246. doi:10.1108/09600030110394914

Ersöz, F., & Kabak, M. (2010). Savunma Sanayi Uygulamalarında Çok Kriterli Karar Verme Yöntemlerinin Literatür Araştırması. *Savunma Bilimleri Dergisi*, *9*(1), 97–125.

Fayezi, S., Zutshi, A., & O'Loughlin, A. (2017). Understanding and Devolopment of Supply Chain Agillity and Flexibility A Structured Literature Review. *International Journal of Management Reviews*, *19*(4), 379–407. doi:10.1111/ijmr.12096

Fazli, A., Sayedi, A., & Shulman, J. D. (2018). The effects of autoscaling in cloud computing. *Manage.Scence*, *64*(11), 5149–5163. doi:10.1287/mnsc.2017.2891

Garavelli, A. C. (2003). Flexibility Configurations for the Supply Chain Management. *International Journal of Production Economics*, *85*(2), 141–153. doi:10.1016/S0925-5273(03)00106-3

Gerschberger, M., Nowitzki, C. E., & Kummer, S. (2012). A model to determine complexity in supply networks. *Journal of Manufacturing Technology Management*, *23*(8), 1015–1037. doi:10.1108/17410381211276853

Giannakis, M., & Louis, M. (2010). A multi-agent based framework for supply chain risk management. *Journal of Purchasing and Supply Management*, *17*(1), 23–31. doi:10.1016/j.pursup.2010.05.001

Goyal, M., & Netessine, S. (2007). Strategic technology choice and capacity investment under demand uncertainty. *Management Science, 53*(2), 192–207. doi:10.1287/mnsc.1060.0611

Gunasekaran, A., Patel, C., & Tirtirogu, E. (2001). Performance Measures and Metrics in A Supply Chain Environment. *International Journal of Operations & Production Management, 21*(1/2), 71–87. doi:10.1108/01443570110358468

Jaśkowski, P., Sobotka, A., & Czarnigowska, A. (2018). Decision model for planning material supply channels in construction. *Automation in Construction, 98*(15), 773–787. doi:10.1016/j.autcon.2018.02.026

Jüttner, U., Peck, H., & Christopher, M. (2003). Supply Chain Risk Management: Outlining an Agenda for Future Research. *International Journal of Logistics: Research and Applications, 6*(4), 197–210. doi:10.1080/13675560310001627016

Keršuliene, V., Zavadskas, E. K., & Turskis, Z. (2010). Selection of Rational Dispute Resolution Method by Applying New Step-Wise Weight Assessment Ratio Analysis (SWARA). *Journal of Business Economics and Management, 11*(2), 243–258. doi:10.3846/jbem.2010.12

Kobu, B. (2017). Üretim Yönetimi. İstanbul: Beta Basım Yayım Dağıtım A.Ş.

Korucuk, S. (2018). ÇKKV Yöntemleri İle İmalat İşletmelerinde TZY Performans Faktörlerinin Önem Derecelerinin Belirlenmesi ve En İdeal Rekabet Stratejisi Seçimi: Ordu İli Örneği. *Dokuz Eylül Üniversitesi İktisadi ve İdari Bilimler Fakültesi Dergisi, 33*(2), 569–593. doi:10.24988/deuiibf.2018332782

Korucuk, S. (2021). Ordu Ve Giresun İllerinde Kentsel Lojistik Performans Unsurlarına Yönelik Karşılaştırmalı Bir Analiz. *Dicle Üniversitesi Sosyal Bilimler Enstitüsü Dergisi, 13*(26), 141–155.

Korucuk, S., & Memiş, S. (2018). Tedarik Zinciri Yönetimindeki Risk Faktörlerinin AHP ile Ölçülmesi: Erzurum İli Örneği. *Bitlis Eren Üniversitesi Sosyal Bilimler Dergisi, 7*(2), 1036–1051.

Korucuk, S., Memiş, S., & Karamaşa, Ç. (2021). *Gıda İşletmelerinde Tedarik Zinciri Dinamiklerinde Meydana Gelen Karışıklıkların Derecelendirilmesi: Giresun İli Örneği.* International Academician Studies Congress 2021 Spring, Mersin.

Kouchaksaraeı, R. H., Zolfanı, S. H., & Golabchı, M. (2015). Glasshouse Locating Based On SWARA-COPRAS Approach. *International Journal of Strategic Property Management, 19*(2), 111–122. doi:10.3846/1648715X.2015.1004565

Krajewski, L. J., Malhotra, M. K. & Ritzman, L. P. (2016). *Operations Management Processes and Supply Chains.* Pearson.

Lim, S. F. W. T., & Srai, J. S. (2018). Examining the anatomy of last-mile distribution in e-commerce omnichannel retailing: A supply network configuration approach. *International Journal of Operations & Production Management, 38*(9), 1735–1764. doi:10.1108/IJOPM-12-2016-0733

Lin, C. T., Chiu, H., Chu, P. Y., & Lou, P. (2006). Agility Index In The Supply Chain. *International Journal of Production Economics, 100*(2), 285–289. doi:10.1016/j.ijpe.2004.11.013

Lummus, R. R., Vokurka, R. J., & Duclos, L. K. (2005). Delphi Study on Supply Chain Flexibility. *International Journal of Production Research, 43*(13), 2687–2708. doi:10.1080/00207540500056102

Lyons, A. C., & Ma'aram, A. (2014). An Examination of Multi-tier Supply Chain Strategy Alignment in the Food Industry. *International Journal of Production Research, 52*(7), 1911–1925. doi:10.1080/00207543.2013.787172

Manuj, I., & Şahin, F. (2011). A model of supply chain and supply chain decision-making complexity. *International Journal of Physical Distribution & Logistics Management, 41*(5), 511–549. doi:10.1108/09600031111138844

Milgate, M. (2001). Supply chain complexity and delivery performance: An international exploratory study. *Supply Chain Management, 6*(3), 106–118. doi:10.1108/13598540110399110

Opricovic, S., & Tzeng, G. H. (2007). Extended VIKOR Method in Comparison with Outranking Methods. *European Journal of Operational Research, 178*(2), 514–529. doi:10.1016/j.ejor.2006.01.020

Özçakar, N., & Demir, H. (2011). Bulanık TOPSIS Yöntemiyle Tedarikçi Seçimi. *Yönetim Dergisi., 69*, 25–44.

Perona, M., & Miragliotta, G. (2004). Complexity management and supply chain performance assessment: A field study and a conceptual framework. *International Journal of Production Economics, 90*(1), 103–115. doi:10.1016/S0925-5273(02)00482-6

Phua, M. H., & Minowa, M. (2005). A GIS-Based Multi-Criteria Decision Making Approach To Forest Conservation Planning At A Landscape Scale: A Case Study In The Kinabalu Area, Sabah, Malaysia. *Landscape and Urban Planning, 71*(2-4), 207–222. doi:10.1016/j.landurbplan.2004.03.004

Power, D. J., Sohal, A. S., & Rahman, S. U. (2001). Criticial Success Factors In Agile Supply Chain Management – Emprical Study. *International Journal of Physical Distribution & Logistics Management, 31*(4), 247–265. doi:10.1108/09600030110394923

Ruzgys, A., Volvačiovas, R., Ignatavičius, Č., & Turskis, Z. (2014). *Integrated Evaluation of External Wall Insulation in Residential Buildings Using SWARA-TODIM MCDM*. Academic Press.

Sadler, I. (2007). *Logistics and Supply Chain Integration*. Sage Publications Ltd.

Šaparauskas, J., Zavadskas, E. K., & Turskis, Z. (2011). Selection of Facade's Alternatives of Commercial and Public Buildings Based on Multiple Criteria. *International Journal of Strategic Property Management, 15*(2), 189203. doi:10.3846/1648715X.2011.586532

Sellitto, M. A., Pereira, G. M., Borchardt, M., Da Silva, R. I., & Viegas, C. V. (2015). A SCOR-based model for supply chain performance measurement: Application in the footwear industry. *International Journal of Production Research, 53*(16), 4917–4926. doi:10.1080/00207543.2015.1005251

Şenses, O. (2019). *İşletme Açısından Kapasite*. http://disticaret.besikduzumyo.trabzon.edu.tr/Files/ ckFiles/disticaret-besikduzumyo-trabzon-edu-tr/Orhan%20%C5%9Eenses/Genel%20%C4%B0%C5%9Fletme/ b%C3%B6l%C3%BCm%207-%20%C4%B0%C5%9ELETMELER%20A%C3%87ISINDAN%20%20KAPAS%C4%B0TE%20pdf.pdf

Serdarasan, S. (2013). A review of supply chain complexity drivers. *Computers & Industrial Engineering, 66*(3), 533–540. doi:10.1016/j.cie.2012.12.008

Stanujkic, D., Karabasevic, D., & Zavadskas, E. K. (2015). A Framework For The Selection of A Packaging Design Based on The SWARA Method, *Inzinerine Ekonomika-. The Engineering Economist, 26*(2), 181–187.

Supeekit, T., Somboonwiwat, T., & Kritchanchai, D. (2016). DEMATEL-modified ANP to evaluate internal hospital supply chain performance. *Computers & Industrial Engineering, 102*, 318–330. doi:10.1016/j.cie.2016.07.019

Ustasüleyman, T., & Perçin, S. (2015). Tedarik Zinciri Karmaşıklığının İşletme Performansına Etkisinin Belirlenmesine Yönelik Yapısal Model Önerisi. *Global Journal of Economics and Business Studies, 3*(6), 1–12.

Vachon, S., & Klassen, R. D. (2002). An Exploratory Investigation of the Effects of Supply Chain Complexity on Delivery Performance. *IEEE Transactions on Engineering Management, 49*(3), 218–230. doi:10.1109/TEM.2002.803387

Wang, Y. M., & Luo, Y. (2010). Integration of Correlations with Standard Deviations for Determining Attribute Weights in Multiple Attribute Decision Making. *Mathematical and Computer Modelling, 51*(1-2), 1–12. doi:10.1016/j.mcm.2009.07.016

Wieland, A., & Wallenburg, C. M. (2012). Dealing With Supply Chain Risks: Linking Risk Management Practices and Strategies to Performance. *International Journal of Physical Distribution & Logistics Management, 42*(10), 887–905. doi:10.1108/09600031211281411

Zavadskas, E. K., Antucheviciene, J., Saparauskas, J., & Turskis, Z. (2013a). MCDM Methods WASPAS and MULTIMOORA: Verification Of Robustness Of Methods When Assessing Alternative Solutions. *Economic Computation and Economic Cybernetics Studies and Research, 47*(2), 1–5.

Zavadskas, E. K., Antucheviciene, J., Šaparauskas, J., & Turskis, Z. (2013b). Multi-Criteria Assessment of Facades' Alternatives: Peculiarities of Ranking Methodology. *Procedia Engineering, 57*, 107–112. doi:10.1016/j.proeng.2013.04.016

Zhou, H., Benton, W. C. Jr, Schilling, D. A., & Milligan, G. W. (2011). Supply chain integration and the SCOR model. *Journal of Business Logistics, 32*(4), 332–344. doi:10.1111/j.0000-0000.2011.01029.x

Chapter 4
Insights From Supply Chain Disruptions in the COVID-19 Era:
The Call for More Resilient Networks

Türkan Müge Özbekler
https://orcid.org/0000-0003-1127-4325
Sinop University, Turkey

EXECUTIVE SUMMARY

The COVID-19 pandemic has created a devastating impact on supply chains. Especially, transportation disruptions, the slowdown in manufacturing, supply-demand imbalances, operational inefficiency in last-mile, and deficiencies in dealing with the crisis can be seen as main headings. This chapter aims to reveal the problems and learn lessons in these areas where significant risks are faced. During the COVID era, the need for resilient supply chains that are not affected by instantaneous changes has come to the fore. Accordingly, the second aim of the chapter is to offer solutions toward the short, medium, and long terms of the first-mile, production, and last-mile processes as enhancing the responsiveness of supply chains by the elements of supply chain resilience. This study is prepared as a review article in an exploratory approach through the supply chain literature and current practical examples. As a result of the study, digital-intensive business models, collaborative network design, and sustainability are highlighted as the main concepts to reach more resilient networks.

DOI: 10.4018/978-1-7998-9140-6.ch004

INTRODUCTION

Modern Supply chains consist of a highly complex ecosystem and play a vital role in regulating operations as a whole at the right time, in the right quantity, and cost-effectively. Competitive pressures in almost all industries and globalization of markets are forcing organizations to strive for comprehensive supply chains that can operate worldwide, making supply chains more vulnerable to risks. The Covid-19 pandemic, as a socio-economic reality affecting the whole world, has created a devastating impact on supply chains. According to the report by Dun and Bradstreet (2020), Wuhan city of China, where the outbreak occurred, has one or more direct suppliers of 51,000 companies worldwide and at least 5 million collaborators indirectly. Mainly, China's significant share in intermediate product supply has caused supply chain disruptions in 94% of Fortune 1000 companies with a low-cost global supply chain structure (Fortune, 2020). Rather than creating a limited risk for companies doing business with China, the epidemic has brought the whole world to face various commercial and logistical risks. In this context, significant disruptions were experienced in maintaining product, information, and money flows from raw material procurement to the delivery of finished products. Due to the Covid-19 pandemic, risk has emerged beyond previous crisis scenarios in almost all areas, especially on food and health supply chains. This process pointed to the most significant deterioration in recent years, with " simultaneous supply chain disruptions in many global chains."

There are a wide variety of risks in supply chain processes. For example, market changes, scarcity of resources, financial risk, information sharing failure, demand uncertainty, and pandemic disruption are significant dangers in the supply chain mechanism (Dohale et al., 2021). The risk management approach in the supply chain requires an ecosystem insight with the fact that different layers may pose multiple risks, and all members in the chain may be affected by this situation (Fan and Stevenson, 2018). Juttner et al. (2003) defined supply chain risk management as "implementing appropriate strategies with a coordinated approach among supply chain members to identify potential sources of risk and reduce supply chain vulnerability." Supply chain risk management links the issue of risk with the probability of disruptive events (Heckmann et al., 2015) and the business impact of disruptions (Brindley, 2004). Implementing effective risk management throughout the chain is critical to risk mitigation, preparedness, better responsiveness, greater flexibility, and reduction in the severity of risks.

Table 1. A review of various supply chain risk management strategies

Supply Chain Risk Management Strategies	Description	Source	Strategy Type Proactive	Strategy Type Reactive
Postponement	Reducing incurring cost by delaying the actual commitment of resources (e.g. form postponement and time postponement)	Um and Han (2020)		X
Speculation	Enabling the movement of goods to forward inventories to gain economies of scale (e.g. limiting the number of stock outs)	Um and Han (2020)	X	
Avoidance	Avoiding activities and processes which are considered unacceptable (e.g. avoiding investment in an unstable region)	Um and Han (2020)	X	
Visibility and Transparency	Enhancing the information flow across the supply chain actors to improve visibility	Dohale et al. (2021)	X	X
Collaboration	Creating collective processes across supply chain partners having shared vision and commitment	Dohale et al. (2021)		X
Flexibility	Developing the ability to efficient and agile respond or adapt to the occurrence of any disruption	Dohale et al. (2021)		X
Multiple sourcing	Enabling business sustainability by working with alternative suppliers	Dohale et al. (2021)		X
Redundancy	Keeping some resources in reserve to be used in case of a disruption (e.g. having safety stocks toward demand variations)	Dohale et al. (2021)	X	X

There are various strategies to minimize the effects of any disruption in supply chain management. These strategies are also known as supply chain risk mitigation strategies. They have been developed to make an effective response in case of a disruption, taking into account the short-term and long-term benefits of the supply chain. Supply chain risk management strategies in the literature are not only limited to the strategies presented in Table 1. There are also many different traditional risk management strategies; e.g. risk assessment, vulnerability analysis and continuity planning (Scholten et al., 2014). When the supply chain risk management literature is examined, it is seen that these strategies are examined under two prime categories, viz., (1) proactive (ex-ante risk state) (2) reactive (post risk state). While proactive strategies involve pre-evaluation of possible risks and planning accordingly, reactive strategies mean evaluating the situation, taking appropriate decisions, and taking action after the occurrence of the risk (Dohale et al., 2021). In most cases, reactive strategies lead to high severity in supply chain processes as they do not immediately act on the risk. In addition, most traditional proactive strategies offer 'guess and adapt' approaches to maintaining existing performance requiring risk identification and quantification.

The Covid-19, which has reached a scalable size from a small impact area, contains many unknowns that make it challenging to react correctly to the effects on the supply chain. In other disruptions, traditional mitigation strategies would ensure normalization; however, the targeted improvements could not be seen with the strategies for effective management in the disruptions that occurred in the pandemic conditions. Situations involving uncertainty, such as a pandemic, require adapting to uncertainties and enabling a supply chain to reconstitute itself (Scholten et al., 2019). Resilience strategy is appropriate in such cases that suggest all risks cannot be prevented and need the capability to react to, cope with, adapt to, or withstand unforeseeable disruptions (Um and Han, 2020). Resilience is a proactive and holistic approach based on improving traditional risk management strategies to provide sustainability in supply chains and reduce potential costs due to disruptions. Without requiring any risk identification, it provides "shock absorption" between stages of the supply chain thanks to the adaptive capability (Scholten et. al., 2014).

The disruptions caused by the Covid-19 pandemic within the network structure from the inbound to the outbound processes of the supply chain are quite remarkable in some areas. These headings can be seen as; disruptions in transportation, the slowdown in manufacturing and services, supply-demand imbalances, operational inefficiency in outbound logistics, and deficiencies in dealing with the crisis. The risks arising in all these areas are characterized by simultaneous sustainability problems in supply, demand, and logistics processes (Ivanov, 2020). The first aim of this study is to reveal the problems and learn lessons in these areas where significant risks are faced due to disruptions in the supply chain. It has been found essential to understand the supply chain disruptions correctly, reduce their effects with fast and effective responses, and make a wake-up call that will implement the necessary transformations of global supply chain strategies for the future.

Within the scope of proactive strategies for disruptions that may occur in different supply chain processes, a transformation to a more resilient supply chain design is required by considering backup suppliers and warehouses, different transportation alternatives, new technologies, inventory and capacity improvements, and innovative business models. In this respect, the second purpose of the study is to offer solutions through the short, medium, and long term towards the disruptions on the inbound logistics (supplier-manufacturer), production (manufacturer) and outbound logistics (retailer-customer). The study starts with summary information about the impact of Covid-19 on the main processes of the supply chain. Later, the headings of the supply chain resilience and resilient solutions toward supply chain disruptions follow this section. Finally, directions for future research and conclusion sections are discussed.

THE IMPACT OF COVID-19 ON THE SUPPLY CHAINS

Although the intensity of research on the effects of the epidemic on humanitarian logistics has attracted attention recently (Farahani et al., 2020), there is still a need to develop field studies to analyze its effects on supply chains from an economic perspective. Previous studies have highlighted the negative impact of epidemics such as SARS and Ebola on global logistics, especially for the airline industry (Chou et al., 2004), disruptions in supply chain flows (BSI, 2014), and operational inadequacies of supply chains during and after the crisis (Calnan et al., 2018). Contrary to Covid-19, none of these outbreaks have affected the whole world simultaneously, so there has not been such a break in supply chains.

The impacts of Covid-19 have been examined by various researchers within the scope of different processes of the supply chain, starting from the procurement process to the outbound logistics delivery (see; Shokrani et al., 2020; Xu et al., 2020; Ivanov and Dolgui, 2021). In this context, the areas examined can be seen as demand and supply management, production management, transportation and logistics management, relationship management, supply chain-wide impact, financial management, and sustainability management (Chowdhury et al., 2021). In order to highlight the impact of Covid-19 on supply chain processes, this study focuses on disruptions in transportation, the slowdown in production and services, supply-demand imbalances, operational inefficiency in outbound logistics, and deficiencies in dealing with the crisis.

Disruptions in Transportation

Since the Covid-19 virus can live even on inanimate objects and spread rapidly through physical contact, governments have implemented measures that almost completely restrict people and goods at the borders of the country. This situation has caused significant disruptions and inefficiencies in transportation, which is vital for ensuring flow in supply chains (Chiaramonti and Maniatis, 2020). The prominent issues in the disruptions experienced according to different transportation modes are as follows:

Air transport is one of the modes most affected by the obstacles brought by the pandemic. In Europe, passenger air traffic fell by 90%, and with the limitation of the airfreight capacity between China and Europe, the original capacity used up to 40% (Tardivo et al., 2021). Partial load mostly carried on passenger aircraft, has increased the demand for cargo aircraft due to cancelled passenger flights (UTIKAD, 2020). Although the costs are more affordable when transporting the cargo is shared with the passenger, this situation has caused relatively high freight costs. Also, air cargo capacities are uncertain in terms of matching with the existing demand.

Insights From Supply Chain Disruptions in the COVID-19 Era

The pandemic also affected the maritime cargo transport closely. Shipowners' reduction in sea voyages to China has damaged container traffic around the world. Hence, the decrease in imports from the Far East led to a shortage of empty containers for loading export goods. Globally, 1.9 million TEU volume was lost in the first two months of 2020 due to frequent delays or cancellations of liner lines as well as blank sailing of ships (Uta Logistics Magazine, 2020).

In international road transport, the controls and restrictions applied at border crossings have caused significant delays in freight flow. The closing of the Brenner pass, for example, generated queues up to 90 km in length on the Italian side of the border (Tardivo et al., 2021). According to COVID-19 Impact on the Road Transport Industry report published by International Road Transport Union (IRU), global losses for the goods road transport sector are expected to reach 347 billion USD in 2021. Although this is around half of the losses suffered by the sector in previous year, liquidity shortages remain the most serious challenge for goods transport operators (IRU, 2021).

Among all modes of transport, rail transport was the least affected by the epidemic. The fact that physical contact in shipments is less than other modes of transport has enabled countries to continue operations with more flexible measures. For example, contrary to other transport modes, trans-Eurasian rail is, in fact, experiencing a growth period. As a result of the lack of viable transport modes during COVID-19 crisis, trans-Eurasian rail lines became a reliable choice and economical option for companies that need to receive and send goods (Tardivo et al., 2021).

The Slowdown in Manufacturing and Services

Many sectors globally, especially tourism, travel, transportation, logistics, accommodation, restaurant, consumer products, electronics, retail, pharmaceutical, and health sectors, have been influenced by the Covid-19 epidemic. In this sense, as economic activities stagnated in 2020, there was a sharp decline in world trade growth of about 8 percent (United Nations, 2021). The significant decrease in production rates in sectors with restrictions due to the epidemic also led to inefficient use of capacity in other input-producing sectors. Moreover, the decrease in the workers' incomes, which are directly affected by the epidemic, also reduced the demand for the rest of the products (Taymaz, 2020).

According to the report published by the Food and Agriculture Organization (FAO) (2020), increasing the measures to ensure the appropriate health standards towards sustainability in food supply chains under pandemic conditions requires high financial budgets. The report also reveals that the measures affecting the free movement of people cause a shortage in the seasonal labor market. This situation affects global food market prices by causing agricultural production to slow down or even come to a standstill.

The National Association of Manufacturers (NAM), the largest manufacturing association in the United States, surveyed to reveal the economic and operational impacts of COVID-19 on manufacturers (NAM, 2020). Results of the survey highlighted that 78.3% of manufacturers anticipate a financial impact, 53.1% of manufacturers anticipate a change in operations, and 35.5% of manufacturers face supply chain disruptions. According to the report published by Turkey's Purchasing Managers Index (PMI) (2020), it is stated that while firms have a general reluctance to hold stocks due to the current uncertainty, new stock purchasing levels have decreased for most sectors. It can be said that this decrease is mainly related to the general price increases in input costs and that the effect of these price fluctuations is reflected in the final consumer through the price levels of the products sold by the producers.

Supply-Demand Imbalances

While the pandemic period refers to a peak period when the demand is more intense than ever, it is seen that there are problems related to flexibility in the supply chains of the companies, namely adapting to this situation. During the pandemic process, the demand for some product groups in the retail sector, especially hygiene products, cleaning materials, dry food, and personal care products, has reached 4-5 times the average level (KMPG Turkey, 2020). For the past few years, companies have statistically followed safety stock practices throughout the supply chain to reduce inventory and balance demand and supply variability. However, most companies were caught off-guard without a stock strategy for the disruptions caused by the outbreak and could not respond to the demands with the required supply levels.

As there were deficiencies in predicting customer-side demands during the pandemic process, disruptions have occurred in the sustainability of supply chain operations (Hobbs, 2020). The Bullwhip Effect, which indicates exponential deterioration from the last link of the supply chain, causes the entire supply chain to become cumbersome as a result of increasing fluctuations in inventory in response to changes in customer demand and makes it difficult to optimize in terms of costs. With the pandemic, this situation has become even more evident due to the lack of real-time monitoring of the entire supply chain and visibility of stocks throughout the supply chain. For example, the increase in demand for toilet paper due to panic buying and hoarding in the United States has led to the depletion of stocks, although people do not need more toilet paper than before. This will lead to a significant decline in demand after the pandemic, and demand fluctuations will be costly for supply chains.

Operational Inefficiency in Outbound Logistics

With Covid-19, there is a period in which a large volume of shopping from physical stores shifts to online platforms, and even people who have not experienced online shopping before request products and services from these platforms. Within the scope of the 'stay at home, stay healthy' policy, cargo companies have undertaken an essential task in delivering online shopping to customers' doorsteps. In addition, a hygienic shipping and distribution process has come to the fore among customers' expectations, and contactless delivery methods have gained importance in terms of social distance.

In the work intensity of this outbound logistics process, there were problems in the continuity of operations due to both vehicle and workforce capacity problems (Darchambeau, 2020). In particular, the need for central distribution centers covering all operational areas and micro-fulfillment centers in the final distribution leg has emerged (MMH, 2020). In this respect, the distribution network in the final delivery process needs to be reconfigured in a flexible structure that will respond to current and potential capacity increases.

Deficiencies in Dealing with the Crisis

In an effective supply chain risk management approach, crises foreseen or existing should be resolved proactively rather than reactively. It has been observed that operations for product and service flow within most sectors, including global and integrated supply chains, do not have a professional crisis management plan for instant response to the situation. In this sense, updating the supply chain priorities in demand, supply, stock, and final distribution and adapting to the existing situation is needed. Hence, to not disrupt operations, it is necessary to increase the resilience of both labor resources and distribution channels.

Amazon, a world giant in online retail, has tried to support its logistics operation to meet the online demand from people staying at home. Although the company stated that it had increased its order capacity by more than 60% due to the pandemic, it has not been able to deliver the orders made by customers for convenience products and fresh foods on time. Amazon, which bought Whole Foods, which is an organic food retailer and has 500 stores, has transformed these physical stores into dark stores called Dark Stores as a new strategy. The company struggles with the crisis by using these online order distribution centers that only employees use to receive and package products (Wells, 2020).

SUPPLY CHAIN RESILIENCE

Resilience in supply chains refers to the capacity to withstand, recover and adapt to disruptions, fluctuations or changes, even 'to move into a new and more desirable state after disruptions' (Christopher and Peck, 2004). This requires a "detailed understanding of the risk environment, identifying the areas impacted by risks, and strengthening the components that help confront these risks" (Van der Vegt et al., 2015). Although a considerable amount of literature has been published on supply chain resilience, far too little attention has been paid to empirical researches to understand how resilience can be created in supply chains (Fiksel et al., 2015). Scholten et al. (2019) explained the importance of the situation in their study as "We know little about what constitutes supply chain resilience beyond high-level generic supply chain strategies." Therefore, there is a need to take risk management in supply chains to the "next level" by gathering new information and analytical tools for more resilient networks.

The most emphasized elements of a supply chain resilience in the literature are volume (capacity), reliability, flexibility, collaboration, speed and visibility (Tukamuhabwa et al., 2015; Ribeiro and Barbosa-Povoa, 2018). While volume refers to the ability to respond to disruptions through investments in capital and capacity, such as safety stocks, backup suppliers, or warehousing (Rice and Caniato, 2003), flexibility refers to the use of flexible processes for shipping and fulfilling orders and maintaining operations in the face of existing changes (Ali et al., 2017). Reliability refers to the ability of a supply chain network to perform as planned and make it sustainable (Adenso-Diaz et al., 2012). In addition, collaboration refers to the level of shared information and decisions between two or more members of the supply chain (Scholten and Schilder, 2015). Moreover, While the element of speed covers the ability to react quickly to changes (Christopher and Peck, 2004), visibility concerns the extent to which supply chain participants can access their operations or share information during the crisis (Wieland and Wallenburg, 2013). Strategies developed with these perspectives in the literature are called supply chain risk mitigation strategies (Chang et al., 2015), which can be defined as actions aimed at reducing the likelihood of risks occurring in the supply chain and the severity of their adverse effects.

Solutions developed for disruptions in the supply chain based on supply chain resilience can be examined from different studies. First of all, Vanpoucke and Ellis (2020) tried to understand managers' personality traits and their role that help increase resilience in business through risk perceptions and decision-making approaches on an individual and team basis. This study provides insight into all teams' attribute and effective decision-making structure, including regular management teams responding to "everyday" problems and emergency teams responding to crises and unforeseen threats.

Secondly, Polyviou et al. (2019) examined supply chain resilience structures at the organizational level based on four case studies of manufacturing organizations. The study, which focuses specifically on medium-sized firms, draws attention to the fact that these firms do not have the resources, scale, or impact on developing capabilities that can compete and increase resilience in the same way as large firms. In addition, it is emphasized that businesses in this structure can have the power to adapt to changes by increasing the interaction between the teams in their organizations. Finally, Sá et al. (2019) investigated how supply chains in two different industries, consisting of three or more members, prepare for, respond to, and normalize disruptions based on supply chain network structure. The researchers examined each member's contribution to chain resilience and found that firms implement isolated solutions at the organizational level rather than devising strategies to build overall supply chain resilience.

In the light of the studies in the literature, it is seen that some mathematical-based analyzes and models are mainly used to increase the flexibility of the supply chain with new designs after disruptions in the supply chain. Ivanov et al. (2014) adopted a reactive approach in their studies and aimed to adapt the supply chain processes and structures to the situation in the presence of unexpected events. In this sense, researchers have adopted a unique approach that centers the flow of activities at the top of the production chain to formulate the multi-node distribution (re)planning problem and planned the supply chain with the linear programming model. In the study of Rafiei et al. (2013), a comprehensive model was developed for the existence of multiple products and long-term failures, and a priority-based genetic algorithm was used to solve the model. Sawik (2013) developed a scenario-based and stochastic programming model based on specific parameters to integrate supplier selection, order quantity allocation, and customer order planning in the presence of risks arising from disruptions in the supply chain.

Schmitt and Singh (2012) carried out a quantitative estimation of the risk of disruption to production and supply capacities in a multi-stage supply chain using discrete-event system simulation. Vahdani et al. (2011) applied fuzzy program evaluation and review techniques to calculate the completion time of supply chain operations in case of severe disruption. Zhu et al. (2016) developed a model that proposes a solution to the disruptions in the chain through the collaboration of manufacturers, logistics service providers, and retailers, which are the layers in the supply chain, using dynamic system simulation. In addition to these, Swierczek (2020) examined supply chain risks under four headings as demand-sourced, supply-driven, process-driven, and control-driven, and the data were analyzed using PLS-SEM. In the study, demand planning activities were considered the source of the significant disruptions that cause operational risks in the supply chain.

Given the studies reviewed, most highlight factors such as capacity and resilience to manage disruptions in the supply chain at the organizational level. In contrast, some refer to collective efforts, such as collaboration, to improve the performance of the entire supply chain (Stone and Rahimifard, 2018). According to Stone and Rahimifard (2018), it should not be forgotten that the supply chain is a holistic ecosystem, and solutions at all levels must generate strategies by considering the whole system.

RESILIENT SOLUTIONS TOWARD SUPPLY CHAIN DISRUPTIONS

During the Covid-19 era, the need for resilient supply chains that are not affected by instantaneous changes has come to the fore. Accordingly, this part of the chapter offers solutions toward the short, medium, and long terms of the inbound logistics, production, and outbound logistics processes as enhancing the responsiveness of supply chains by the elements of supply chain resilience.

Table 2. Suggested resilient solutions for supply chain processes

	Inbound Logistics Process	Production Process	Outbound Logistics Process	Integrated Supply Chain
Short Term (Operational Plans)	Directing product flows using alternative suppliers and safety stocks. Shifting operations from globalization to localization Real-time tracking	Reallocating resources and changing production plans Optimum management of all resources (human, nature, financial, machinery/equipment, land) Budget revisions and updating sales forecasts Effective planning of workforce capacity Renegotiating agreements with stakeholders Real-time tracking	Reallocating resources and evaluating transportation alternatives Giving importance to hygiene practices in distribution channels Implementing contactless delivery practices Increasing workforce capacity Leveraging crowdsourcing Technologies Real-time tracking	Holistic redesign of inbound logistics, production and outbound logistics processes
Medium Term (Tactical Plans)	Monitoring changes and proactively warning other stakeholders	Increasing the use of technology Implementing new business models Reviewing growth opportunities	Optimizing inventory management and leveraging micro depots Providing effective customer relationship management	
Long Term (Strategic Plans)	Segmenting suppliers according to their risk of experiencing disruptions Optimizing inventory management with technology Collaboration	Segmentation of production issues according to the risks of experiencing disruptions Flexible production capacity management Collaboration	Redesigning the design of distribution channels within the framework of speed and low cost Leveraging new technologies in the distribution process Increasing flexibility for operational capabilities Collaboration	**Supply Chain Resilience**

More specific approaches and solutions in the design of resilient supply chains proposed in the study can be stated as follows:

- Along with the disruptions experienced during the pandemic process, the need for more cost-effective, sustainable, and fast solutions came to the fore in the outbound logistics process. In this sense, central distribution facility structures such as the consolidation center and flexible micro facility structures such as the dark store and micro-fulfillment center have gained importance. Consolidation centers can find solutions to problems such as urban traffic congestion and high costs of the low number of shipments, increasing the scale in the final distribution leg. On the other hand, micro-fulfillment centers as small storage areas close to customers in urban areas provide good management of online trade volume and rapid distribution to end consumers by using artificial intelligence analytics and automation systems. In addition, the click and collect model can be integrated with these depots to make the process more operationally efficient.
- Suggestions such as crowdsourcing technology, night deliveries, and increasing usage of clean vehicles can shed light on the future of outbound logistics.
- While the old generation supply chain business models were product flow focused, the current perspective has turned into a value chain focus. Today, service and product must move together along the entire chain.
- Almost all sectors were caught unprepared for emergency and crisis management and tended to save the day. Therefore, more efficient and flexible supply chains need to be redesigned according to capacity, reliability, flexibility, collaboration, speed and visibility.
- New generation supply chains will adopt a result-oriented structure that produces solutions with digitalization and artificial intelligence. In addition, multi-channel marketing, cloud and hub sales points rather than physical stores, integration of different formats and categories, efficiency, and system development will come to the fore.
- After the pandemic, it is expected that there will be a return from complex supply chains to a leaner and shorter supply chain structure with supporting new business models.
- It is estimated that the zero stock working policies adopted in strategies such as the just-in-time (JIT) strategy will be put in the background, and alternatives will always be prioritized in storage for the risk of being out of stock.

- For the food supply chain to be sustainable, the issue of vertical fields where vegetables and fruits will be grown has come to the fore, and various countries have started to prepare some regulations regarding this.
- In the future, sharing of vehicles, loads, production machines, and workers within the scope of the sharing economy and the existence of win-win strategies will gain even more importance. In addition, many new business models will arise for subscription and rental systems for the consumption of products and services rather than purchasing.
- Design and differentiation in the supply chain are not one of the areas invested by companies. In this area, plans and strategies should be developed for more flexible and agile chains.

In the light of the findings reached within the scope of the study, the three most essential and promising concepts for constructing a more resilient supply chain network were determined as technology-intensive business models, collaborative network design, and corporate sustainability.

Technology-Intensive Business Models

The prevalence of information and communication technologies means that digitalization, connectivity, and intelligence features of technology can create quite vast opportunities in supply chain processes. The digital revolution that started with Industry 4.0 includes many modern automation systems, data exchanges, and production technologies. In this context, many leading technologies such as internet of things, cloud computing, big data, artificial intelligence, virtual reality, augmented reality, block chain technology provide significant contributions to business processes.

For example, within the scope of urban logistics, economic, social, and environmentally sustainable solutions are supported by carrying out technology-intensive processes in many different areas, such as instantaneously directing city traffic, reducing accidents, keeping air pollution under control, and saving energy. Many advantages such as creating flexible distribution solutions with dynamic routing, preventing unnecessary waiting with intelligent traffic lights in the city, obtaining real-time information about the traffic situation, and storing operational data regarding delivery have emerged with the support of these technological developments (Bektas et al., 2017).

At the point of integrating modern technologies into the supply chain processes, it is evident that a large fixed investment is required in R&D (Lee et al., 2020). However, it is known that business models built on these technologies show promise in terms of being more efficient and more resistant to unexpected disruptions compared to traditional systems (Shcherbakov and Silkina, 2021).

Collaborative Network Design

Today, the competition of supply chains has gained importance rather than the competition of companies. For a competitive supply chain design, the members' information sharing, communication, and harmony are fundamental. At this point, the concept of collaboration emerges when at least two actors share their efforts to achieve a common goal and is expressed with approaches that rise over the concepts of trust, sharing, and synergy (Paddeu et al., 2018; Pınarbaşı, 2020). The collaboration approach, which focuses on the co-creation of processes such as joint planning, joint designing, coordination, and process integration, includes a motivation beyond the mere idea of realizing the individual goals of the companies (Çotur and Öztürkoğlu, 2016).

In collaborative network environment, companies can design this approach with their suppliers, customers, and even with their competitors (Doganay and Ergun, 2017). For example, in the outbound logistics, the use of information, infrastructure, vehicles, route, and human resources, which are the essential logistics resources, by the competing logistics service providers through acting together can be seen as a type of this. Harmonization and sharing of data to create a mutually accessible plan (data sharing), operating over common facilities (infrastructure sharing), distributing over common vehicles (vehicle sharing), load pooling, and labor sharing can be exemplified as collaborative practices (Gonzalez-Feliu et al., 2011). In this way, achieving successes such as increasing operational efficiency and urban access and reducing transportation costs and environmental externalities while providing superior service to customers can be possible (Alarçin and Kırçova, 2014).

In particular, it is seen that the idea of "co-creation and development of new proposals for unique solutions" is gradually being implemented based on increasing collaboration between the main actors of the supply chain. Collaborative network design can be seen as a promising concept in increasing overall system productivity without compromising competitive advantages by synchronizing members' activities in the supply chain (Cleophas et al., 2019). Thus, providing the alignment of proactive and reactive risk management approaches among the different stakeholders can be achieved (Dorgham et al., 2020).

Corporate Sustainability

Sustainability, in general, refers to the capacity to sustain a situation or process for an indefinite period. In a world where it is difficult to meet the increasing consumption needs, the concept of "sustainability" is seen as an even more significant concept regarding the continuity of production and consumption balance. The concept of corporate sustainability is integrating the essential dynamics of sustainability into business priorities and activities by pursuing social objectives such as environmental protection, social equality, justice and economic development, and the corporate growth and profitability of businesses (Çalışkan, 2012). Along with this approach, the idea of being permanent brought by sustainability has brought forward that companies design their assets to be long-lasting and exhibit a constantly dynamic structure with strategies for this.

Today, rising demands and expectations on the customer's side have now exceeded the point of product and service features offered, and the image of the company has begun to be evaluated in a context shaped by the activities carried out. If the company's competition is only ensured by factors such as economically competitive price, providing speed, following the technology, the customer will choose the lower cost company among the companies that create the same opportunities. In contrast, a company that integrates sustainability into company activities can be perceived differently in many respects, such as trust, reputation, and quality. In this context, companies are increasingly positioning themselves as creating more value via differentiating on economic, social, and environmental dimensions (Özbekler and Akgül, 2020).

The adoption of corporate sustainability by supply chain members, both individually and within an integrated network structure, may offer the opportunity to recover faster in case of breaks in the chain (Özbekler and Öztürkoğlu, 2020). In particular, the trust in the company from the customer's point of view can facilitate the steps to be taken during and after the crisis, and the supply chain coordination can be reconstructed efficiently. In this context, priority should be given to integrating the corporate sustainability approach into the activities of the entire supply chain life cycle, from supply to the last mile distribution, and in the way chain members do business (Arslan, 2020).

FUTURE RESEARCH DIRECTIONS

This study addresses supply chain disruptions in the Covid-19 era from two perspectives: providing insight into areas of disruptions and enhancing supply chain resilience. Especially, this study focuses on disruptions in transportation, production and services, supply-demand sides, outbound logistics, crisis management. Recent studies of supply chain management show that the Covid-19 pandemic has had significant effects in many specific areas such as relationship management, financial management, and production management. In this study, the most critical limitation can be seen as impacts in only selected areas are explained in general terms. Therefore, the main recommendation for future research is to conduct studies in which the effects on disruptions in specific areas of the supply chain are examined in a detailed view.

The Covid-19 outbreak has revealed different levels of disruption in networked supply chains on a local, national, international, and global scale. Accordingly, depending on the magnitude of the impact felt during the crisis, the level of response of the supply chains and the agility of the recovery processes varied. In this respect, a second suggestion for future studies is to prioritize studies that evaluate the impact of disruptions in the supply chain within the scope of the scale in which they are experienced and offer solutions.

With the rapidly developing technology age, the future of supply chains will be associated with how integrated information technologies are into systems. In this sense, the increase in studies on innovative business models that provide developments in concepts such as real-time tracking, visibility, and traceability and the technology-oriented development of the resilience of supply chains against unexpected crises should be examined.

Lastly, technology-intensive businesses models, collaborative network design, and corporate sustainability are highlighted as the most promising concepts for a more resilient supply chain structure. In future studies, it is recommended that these solutions, which are reached by current trends in the literature and practical applications, should be evaluated in detail in terms of compliance with the expectations of supply chain members and the steps to be taken in terms of their implementation.

CONCLUSION

Along with the Covid-19 pandemic, many sectors, mainly tourism, travel, transportation, logistics, accommodation, food, retail, and health sectors, have experienced a critical risk globally. This pandemic, which is called the black swan and creates an unpredictable breaking effect for supply chains, reveals the need for organizations to take the most accurate and sustainable decisions quickly and transform their supply chain structures for the future.

In cases such as sharp changes in the market, pandemics, and natural disasters, it has been understood that traditional supply chains cannot meet the needs of the industry, and the need for resilient business models and sustainable supply chains has emerged. In this respect, the study aims to improve the resilience of supply chains with contemporary solutions by using the supply chain, marketing, and logistics management literature and examples from real-life cases.

In order to highlight the impact of Covid-19 on supply chain processes, this study focuses on disruptions in transportation, the slowdown in production and services, supply-demand imbalances, operational inefficiency in outbound logistics, and deficiencies in dealing with the crisis. The solutions proposed in the study are explained by presenting short, medium, and long-term predictions for the inbound logistics, production, and outbound logistics processes through the elements of supply chain resilience in order to increase the responsiveness of supply chains to possible disruptions. Also, the promising concepts proposed as a result of the study are mainly gathered under the headings of technology-intensive business models, collaborative network design, and corporate sustainability.

REFERENCES

Adenso-Diaz, B., Mena, C., García-Carbajal, S., & Liechty, M. (2012). The impact of supply network characteristics on reliability. *Supply Chain Management*, *17*(3), 263–276. doi:10.1108/13598541211227108

Alarçin, M., & Kırçova, İ. (2020). A Conceptual Study On car-sharing Services Based On Sharing Economy. *Business & Management Studies: An International Journal*, *8*(5), 4521–4545.

Ali, A., Mahfouz, A., & Arisha, A. (2017). Analysing supply chain resilience: Integrating the constructs in a concept mapping framework via a systematic literature review. *Supply Chain Management*, *22*(1), 16–39. doi:10.1108/SCM-06-2016-0197

Arslan, M. (2020). Corporate social sustainability in supply chain management: A literature review. *Journal of Global Responsibility*, *11*(3), 233–255. doi:10.1108/JGR-11-2019-0108

Bektaş, T., Crainic, T. G., & Van Woensel, T. (2017). From Managing Urban Freight to Smart City Logistics Networks. In Network Design and Optimization for Smart Cities (143-188). Academic Press.

Brindley, C. (Ed.). (2004). Supply Chain Risks. Ashgate Publishing.

BSI. (2014). *Supply Chain Impact of 2014 Ebola Outbreak*. Retrieved April 20, 2021, from https://www.bsigroup.com/globalassets/localfiles/aaa/Whitepaper%20Ebola_10.14_7.pdf

Çalışkan, A. Ö. (2012). *İşletmelerde Sürdürülebilirlik ve Muhasebe Mesleği İlişkisi. In Mali Çözüm Dergisi*. İSMMMO.

Calnan, M., Gadsby, E. W., Kondé, M. K., Diallo, A., & Rossman, J. S. (2018). The response to and impact of the Ebola epidemic: Towards an agenda for interdisciplinary research. *International Journal of Health Policy and Management*, *7*(5), 402–411. doi:10.15171/ijhpm.2017.104 PMID:29764104

Chang, W., Ellinger, A. E., & Blackhurst, J. (2015). A contextual approach to supply chain risk mitigation. *International Journal of Logistics Management*, 26(3), 642–656. doi:10.1108/IJLM-02-2014-0026

Chiaramonti, D., & Maniatis, K. (2020). Security of supply, strategic storage and Covid19: Which lessons learnt for renewable and recycled carbon fuels, and their future role in decarbonizing transport? *Applied Energy*, 271, 115216. doi:10.1016/j.apenergy.2020.115216

Chou, J., Kuo, N. F., & Peng, S. L. (2004). Potential impacts of the SARS outbreak on Taiwan's economy. *Asian Economic Papers*, 3(1), 84–99. doi:10.1162/1535351041747969

Chowdhury, P., Paul, S. K., Kaisar, S., & Moktadir, M. A. (2021). COVID-19 pandemic related supply chain studies: A systematic review. *Transportation Research Part E, Logistics and Transportation Review*, 148, 102271. doi:10.1016/j.tre.2021.102271 PMID:33613082

Christopher, M., & Peck, H. (2004). Building the Resilient Supply Chain. *International Journal of Logistics Management*, 15(2), 1–14. doi:10.1108/09574090410700275

Cleophas, C., Cottrill, C., Ehmke, J. F., & Tierney, K. (2019). Collaborative urban transportation: Recent advances in theory and practice. *European Journal of Operational Research*, 273(3), 801–816. doi:10.1016/j.ejor.2018.04.037

Çotur, Ö. K., & Öztürkoğlu, Y. (2016). Partnerships in supply chain management. In *Handbook of Research on Global Supply Chain Management* (pp. 161–185). IGI Global. doi:10.4018/978-1-4666-9639-6.ch010

Darchambeau, M. (2020). *Covid-19 and The Last Mile*. Retrieved April 20, 2021, from https://postandparcel.info/120509/podcasts/covid-19-and-the-outbound logistics/

Doganay, A., & Ergun, S. (2017). The effect of supply chain collaboration on supply chain performance. *Journal of Management Marketing and Logistics*, 4(1), 30–39. doi:10.17261/Pressacademia.2017.377

Dohale, V., Ambilkar, P., Gunasekaran, A., & Verma, P. (2021). Supply chain risk mitigation strategies during COVID-19: exploratory cases of "make-to-order" handloom saree apparel industries. *International Journal of Physical Distribution & Logistics Management*.

Dorgham, K., Nouaouri, I., Nicolas, J. C., & Goncalves, G. (2020). A Collaborative Supply Chain Network Design within a Territory Hospital Group. In *13ème Conference Internationale De Modelisation*. AGADIR.

Dun & Bradstreet. (2020). *Blindsided on the Supply Side*. Retrieved March 20, 2021, from https://foreignpolicy.com/2020/03/04/blindsided-on-the-supply-side/

Fan, Y., & Stevenson, M. (2018). A review of supply chain risk management: Definition, theory, and research agenda. *International Journal of Physical Distribution & Logistics Management, 48*(3), 205–230. doi:10.1108/IJPDLM-01-2017-0043

FAO. (2020). *COVID-19 pandemic – impact on food and agriculture*. Retrieved March 25, 2021, from https://www.fao.org/2019-ncov/q-and-a/impact-on-food-and-agriculture/en/

Farahani, R. Z., Lotfi, M. M., & Rezapour, S. (2020). Mass casualty management in disaster scene: A systematic review of OR&MS research in humanitarian operations. *European Journal of Operational Research, 287*(3), 787–819. doi:10.1016/j.ejor.2020.03.005

Fiksel, J., Polyviou, M., Croxton, K. L., & Pettit, K. J. (2015). From risk to resilience: Learning to deal with disruption. *MIT Sloan Management Review, 56*, 79–86.

Fortune. (2020). *94% of the Fortune 1000 are seeing coronavirus supply chain disruptions: Report*. Retrieved April 10, 2021, from https://fortune.com/2020/02/21/fortune-1000-coronavirus-china-supply-chain-impact/

Gonzalez-Feliu, J., & Morana, J. (2011). Collaborative transportation sharing: from theory to practice via a case study from France. In *Technologies for Supporting Reasoning Communities and Collaborative Decision Making: Cooperative Approaches* (pp. 252–271). IGI Global. doi:10.4018/978-1-60960-091-4.ch014

Heckmann, I., Comes, T., & Nickel, S. (2015). A critical review on supply chain risk – definition, measure and modeling. *Omega, 52*, 119–132. doi:10.1016/j.omega.2014.10.004

Hobbs, J. E. (2020). Food supply chains during the COVID-19 pandemic. *Canadian Journal of Agricultural Economics/Revue canadienne d'agroeconomie, 68*(2), 171-176.

IRU. (2021). *COVID-19 Impact on the Road Transport Industry*. Retrieved July 25, 2021, from https://www.iru.org/resources/iru-library/covid-19-impacts-road-transport-industry-executive-summary-update-june-2021

Ivanov, D. (2020). Predicting the impacts of epidemic outbreaks on global supply chains: A simulation-based analysis on the coronavirus outbreak (COVID-19/SARS-CoV-2) case. *Transportation Research Part E, Logistics and Transportation Review, 136*, 101922. doi:10.1016/j.tre.2020.101922 PMID:32288597

Ivanov, D., & Dolgui, A. (2021). OR-methods for coping with the ripple effect in supply chains during COVID-19 pandemic: Managerial insights and research implications. *International Journal of Production Economics*, *232*, 107921. doi:10.1016/j.ijpe.2020.107921 PMID:32952301

Ivanov, D., Sokolov, B., & Dolgui, A. (2014). The Ripple effect in supply chains: Trade-off 'efficiency-flexibility-resilience' in disruption management. *International Journal of Production Research*, *52*(7), 2154–2172. doi:10.1080/00207543.2013.858836

Juttner, U., Peck, H. L., & Christopher, M. G. (2003). Supply chain risk management: Outlining an agenda for future research. *International Journal of Logistics Research and Applications*, *6*(4), 197–210. doi:10.1080/13675560310001627016

Lee, J., Krishnan, V., & Shin, H. (2020). Business models for technology-intensive supply chains. *Management Science*, *66*(5), 2120–2139. doi:10.1287/mnsc.2019.3306

MMH. (2020). *Other Voices: Pop-up distribution centers help overcome outbound logistics delivery obstacles*. Retrieved May 25, 2021, from https://www.mmh.com/article/other_voices_pop_up_distribution_centers_help_overcome_last_mile_delivery_o

NAM. (2020). *Manufacturers' Survey Reveals Current Industry Impact of COVID-19*. Retrieved May 20, 2021, from https://www.nam.org/manufacturers-survey-reveals-current-industry-impact-of-covid-19-7411/?stream=series-press-releases

Özbekler, T. M., & Akgül, A. K. (2020). An Ex-Ante Assessment of City Distribution Alternatives Based on Multi Actor Multi Criteria Framework. *Business & Management Studies: An International Journal*, *8*(5), 4241–4272. doi:10.15295/bmij.v8i5.1650

Özbekler, T. M., & Öztürkoğlu, Y. (2020). Analysing the importance of sustainability-oriented service quality in competition environment. *Business Strategy and the Environment*, *29*(3), 1504–1516. doi:10.1002/bse.2449

Paddeu, D., Parkhurst, G., Fancello, G., Fadda, P., & Ricci, M. (2018). Multi-stakeholder collaboration in urban freight consolidation schemes: Drivers and barriers to implementation. *Transport*, *33*(4), 913–929. doi:10.3846/transport.2018.6593

Pınarbaşı, F. (2020). Sharing Economy and Applications: Business and Marketing Perspective. In Networked Business Models in the Circular Economy (pp. 82-102). IGI Global.

PMI. (2020). *Turkey: PMI falls to 48.1 due to COVID-19 outbreak.* Retrieved May 20, 2021, from https://www.aa.com.tr/en/economy/turkey-pmi-falls-to-481-due-to-covid-19-outbreak/1787549

Polyviou, M., Croxton, K. L., & Knemeyer, A. M. (2019). Resilience of medium-sized firms to supply chain disruptions: The role of internal social capital. *International Journal of Operations & Production Management, 40*(1), 68–91. doi:10.1108/IJOPM-09-2017-0530

Rafiei, M., Mohammadi, M., & Torabi, S. (2013). Reliable multi period multi product supply chain design with facility disruption. *Decision Science Letters, 2*(2), 81–94. doi:10.5267/j.dsl.2013.02.002

Ribeiro, J. P., & Barbosa-Povoa, A. (2018). Supply Chain Resilience: Definitions and quantitative modelling approaches–A literature review. *Computers & Industrial Engineering, 115*, 109–122. doi:10.1016/j.cie.2017.11.006

Rice, J. B., & Caniato, F. (2003). Building a secure and resilient supply network. *Supply Chain Management Review, 7*(5), 22–30.

Sá, M. M. D., Miguel, P. L. D. S., Brito, R. P. D., & Pereira, S. C. F. (2019). Supply chain resilience: The whole is not the sum of the parts. *International Journal of Operations & Production Management, 40*(1), 92–115. doi:10.1108/IJOPM-09-2017-0510

Sawik, T. (2013). Integrated selection of suppliers and scheduling of customer orders in the presence of supply chain disruption risks. *International Journal of Production Research, 51*(23-24), 7006–7022. doi:10.1080/00207543.2013.852702

Schmitt, A. J., & Singh, M. (2012). A quantitative analysis of disruption risk in a multi-echelon supply chain. *International Journal of Production Economics, 139*(1), 23–32. doi:10.1016/j.ijpe.2012.01.004

Scholten, K., & Schilder, S. (2015). The role of collaboration in supply chain resilience. *Supply Chain Management, 20*(4), 471–484. doi:10.1108/SCM-11-2014-0386

Scholten, K., Scott, P. S., & Fynes, B. (2014). Mitigation processes-antecedents for building supply chain resilience. *Supply Chain Management, 19*(2), 211–228. doi:10.1108/SCM-06-2013-0191

Scholten, K., Stevenson, M., & van Donk, D. P. (2019). Dealing with the unpredictable: Supply chain resilience. *International Journal of Operations & Production Management, 40*(1), 1–10. doi:10.1108/IJOPM-01-2020-789

Shcherbakov, V., & Silkina, G. (2021). Supply Chain Management Open Innovation: Virtual Integration in the Network Logistics System. *Journal of Open Innovation*, *7*(1), 54. doi:10.3390/joitmc7010054

Shokrani, A., Loukaides, E. G., Elias, E., & Lunt, A. J. (2020). Exploration of alternative supply chains and distributed manufacturing in response to COVID-19; a case study of medical face shields. *Materials & Design*, *192*, 108749. doi:10.1016/j.matdes.2020.108749 PMID:32341616

Stone, J., & Rahimifard, S. (2018). Resilience in agri-food supply chains: A critical analysis of the literature and synthesis of the novel framework. *Supply Chain Management*, *23*(3), 207–238. doi:10.1108/SCM-06-2017-0201

Swierczek, A. (2020). Investigating the role of demand planning as a higher-order construct in mitigating disruptions in the European supply chains. *International Journal of Logistics Management*, *31*(3), 665–696. doi:10.1108/IJLM-08-2019-0218

Tardivo, A., Carrillo Zanuy, A., & Sánchez Martín, C. (2021). COVID-19 Impact on Transport: A Paper from the Railways' Systems Research Perspective. *Transportation Research Record: Journal of the Transportation Research Board*, *2675*(1), 12. doi:10.1177/0361198121990674

Taymaz, E. (2020). *Covid-19 tedbirlerinin Türkiye ekonomisine etkisi ve çözüm önerileri*. Retrieved May 20, 2021, from https://sarkac.org/2020/04/covid19-tedbirlerinin-turkiye-ekonomisine-etkisi-cozum-onerileri/

Tukamuhabwa, B. R., Stevenson, M., Busby, J., & Zorzini, M. (2015). Supply chain resilience: Definition, review and theoretical foundations for further study. *International Journal of Production Research*, *53*(18), 5592–5623. doi:10.1080/00207543.2015.1037934

Turkey, K. M. P. G. (2020). *Perakende COVID-19 Sınavında*. Retrieved May 25, 2021, from https://home.kpmg/tr/tr/home/medya/press-releases/2020/03/perakende-covid-19-sinavinda.html

Um, J., & Han, N. (2020). Understanding the relationships between global supply chain risk and supply chain resilience: The role of mitigating strategies. *Supply Chain Management*, *26*(2), 240–255. doi:10.1108/SCM-06-2020-0248

United Nations. (2021). *Trade trends under the COVID-19 pandemic*. Retrieved June 15, 2021, from https://unctad.org/webflyer/key-statistics-and-trends-international-trade-2020

Uta Lojistik Magazine. (2020). *Lojistik Sektörünün Koronavirüs Envanteri*. Retrieved April 15, 2021, from https://lojistikhatti.com/images/pdf/UTA_LOJISTIK_DERGISI_NISAN_2020_SAYISI.pdf

UTİKAD. (2020). *COVID-19 Dolayısıyla Taşımacılık Faaliyetlerinde Alınan Önlemler*. Retrieved June 15, 2021, from https://www.utikad.org.tr/Covid-19

Vahdani, B., Zandieh, M., & Roshanaei, V. (2011). A hybrid multi-stage predictive model for supply chain network collapse recovery analysis: A practical framework for effective supply chain network continuity management. *International Journal of Production Research, 49*(7), 2035–2060. doi:10.1080/00207540903289748

Van der Vegt, G., Essens, P., Wahlstrom, M., & George, G. (2015). Managing risk and resilience: From the editors. *Academy of Management Journal, 58*(4), 971–980. doi:10.5465/amj.2015.4004

Vanpoucke, E., & Ellis, S. C. (2020). Building supply-side resilience – a behavioural view. *International Journal of Operations & Production Management, 40*(1), 11–33. doi:10.1108/IJOPM-09-2017-0562

Wells, J. (2020). *Amazon's Woodland Hills supermarket is now a dark store*. Retrieved June 15, 2021, from https://www.grocerydive.com/news/amazons-woodland-hills-supermarket-is-now-a-dark-store/575953/

Wieland, A., & Wallenburg, C. M. (2013). The influence of relational competencies on supply chain resilience: A relational view. *International Journal of Physical Distribution & Logistics Management, 43*(4), 300–320. doi:10.1108/IJPDLM-08-2012-0243

Xu, Z., Elomri, A., Kerbache, L., & El Omri, A. (2020). Impacts of COVID-19 on global supply chains: Facts and perspectives. *IEEE Engineering Management Review, 48*(3), 153–166. doi:10.1109/EMR.2020.3018420

Zhu, Q., Krikke, H., & Caniels, M. (2016). Collaborate or not? A system dynamics study on disruption recovery. *Industrial Management & Data Systems, 116*(2), 271–290. doi:10.1108/IMDS-05-2015-0209

KEY TERMS AND DEFINITIONS

Collaboration: The situation where actors with common interests work together to achieve goals.

Corporate Sustainability: An approach aiming to create long-term value through the activities of companies with environmental and social sensitivity as well as economic expectations.

Digital-Intensive Business Model: A model that leverages digital technologies to create value in a way of doing business.

Operational Efficiency: Measurement of resource allocation and aiming more output with less input.

Resilient Supply Chain: The capacity of the supply chain to resist or even quickly recover through disruptions.

Supply Chain Disruption: A disturbance that interrupts activities and processes in the supply chain network.

Supply Chain Risk Management Strategies: Strategies to minimize the impact of risks on the supply chain and overcome bottlenecks.

Chapter 5
Commercial Product Returns:
Emerging Trends via Network Analysis

Metehan Feridun Sorkun
Izmir University of Economics, Turkey

EXECUTIVE SUMMARY

The increasing use of online shopping has escalated product returns and consequently the importance of their management. In parallel, the increasing scholarly interest on the subject is reflected in the number of publications. In such fast-growing research fields, mapping the whole research activity is useful in highlighting research areas that could provide a better knowledge accumulation in the field. With this aim, this chapter conducts co-citation and co-word analysis to identify future research directions. According to results, there is a need for future research to investigate 1) the consumer reaction when the service level received conflicts with the retailer environment (un)friendly operations, 2) the impacts of retailer return policies on their reverse logistics management, 3) the implementation difficulties of handling omni-channel returns in different organizational structures, and 4) the effectiveness of technological tools and applications used to avoid returns. This chapter also discusses the implications of COVID-19 on the commercial product returns research.

INTRODUCTION

Commercial product returns, defined as "products returned by customers for any reason within up to 90 days of sale" (Blackburn et al., 2004, p. 6), have become the key focus of practitioners and scholars with the rise of Internet. The increasing demand for online shopping is escalating product returns to a level much greater than those of brick-and-mortar store sales (Rao et al., 2018). According to recent market

DOI: 10.4018/978-1-7998-9140-6.ch005

research, 36% of the surveyed online shoppers returned an item at least once within the last three-month-period (UPS, 2019). Besides the increasing rate of returns, the variation in the reasons for product returns makes its management quite complex for retailers. The reasons for product returns can broadly be categorized as true failure returns and false failure returns (Ferguson et al., 2006). True failure returns consist of those that occur due to the verifiable fault of retailers, such as defective/broken items and logistics failures (e.g. late delivery and improper packaging). In addition to these, retailers have to handle false failure returns which are the items returned by consumers although they have neither functional nor cosmetic problems (Ferguson et al., 2006). Consumers' impulsive purchasing behaviour, value and fit uncertainties especially in online purchases, and remorse because of simply changing their mind or finding a better price are the main reasons for false failure returns. Opportunistic returns (Akturk et al., 2021) are also another type of false failure returns, in which consumers may exploit liberal return policies of retailers for their benefits, for example, in order to reduce value and fit uncertainties in online purchases, they may order multiple alternative items with the intention of returning all but one (Asdecker et al., 2017).

Retailers should take into account many factors in managing commercial product returns. On one hand, processing returns can be very costly, considering the costs of sorting, testing, holding, transportation, disposal, and secondary market (Difrancesco et al., 2018; Shang et al., 2017). Other negative financial aspects for retailers are refunds to consumers, restocking, and product value depreciation after returns. On the other hand, attempting strictly to avoid product returns or charging consumers for these costs may also be damaging for retailers in overall. These measures could negatively affect sales (Wood, 2001), repurchasing behaviour (Petersen & Kumar, 2010), and brand loyalty (Griffis et al., 2012). Moreover, the resulting negative word-of-mouth may discourage potential consumers (Petersen & Kumar, 2009). In contrast, the hassle-free returns could increase customer satisfaction (Vakulenko et al., 2019) and provide useful feedback for improving retailers' processes (Röllecke et al., 2018). Table 1 below summarizes the potential negative outcomes associated with product returns management by separately listing the costs and negative impacts of accepting and avoiding returns respectively:

Table 1. The potential negative outcomes associated with product returns management

The costs of accepting returns	The negative impacts of avoiding returns
Collecting returns	The decrease in sales
Inspecting/testing returns	The decrease in repurchasing behaviour
Sorting returns	No brand loyal consumers
Transporting returns	Negative word-of-mouth
Remanufacturing / refurbishing returns	The decrease in customer satisfaction
Restocking	The lack of feedback for improving processes
Product value depreciation	

Paradigm shifts have occurred in the research field of commercial product returns over the years. Returns used to be seen as "a necessary evil" (Petersen & Kumar 2009), "a necessary cost of doing business" (Rao et al., 2014), and it was considered that "no return is the best return" (Stock, 2001), but these have become a key focus, especially after the dramatic growth of online sales. The exploitation of returns as a strategic tool and a means of supporting revenues (Röllecke et al., 2018) are new paradigms for which different business functions and supply chain members (Difrancesco et al., 2018; Mollenkopf et al., 2011) should work together collaboratively.

Further paradigm shifts are expected, given the continuing rapid emergence of new concepts and technological advancements in e-commerce (Robertson et al., 2020). The extreme external shocks at global scale, for example Covid-19, are also triggering these paradigm shifts. Despite the dramatic growth of publications on commercial product returns, in parallel to developments, there is a need for a better knowledge accumulation in order to match the rapidly changing dynamics of online retailing. In addition, the involvement of multiple factors into commercial product returns management requires an integrative perspective.

Shedding a light on the whole research activity, by revealing emerging trends and the intellectual structure in the field, could indicate future research directions that will improve knowledge accumulation in the field. Specifically, knowledge accumulation could be accelerated by guidance on how emerging themes can be catalysed with currently prominent themes, and how different research clusters can be bridged. The author believes that this contribution would be considerable, given the relative immaturity of the literature of commercial product returns (Röllecke et al., 2018) despite its fast growth. Furthermore, to the best knowledge of the author, there is very limited research particularly examining the effects of Covid-19 on retailers' product returns management processes. The only conclusion possible to draw from the state-of-the-art research is that consumers' steering towards online channels for shopping and lockdowns during Covid-19 have increased the rate (Končar et al., 2020; Masudin et al., 2021) and cost (Suguna et al., 2021) of product returns respectively, hence the importance of product return management for retailers. As another contribution, this chapter outlines the potential future research implications of Covid-19 on the commercial product returns research.

BACKGROUND

Factors Affecting the Rate of Commercial Product Returns

The literature reveals a long list of factors that affect the rate of commercial product returns, most of which can be grouped as factors related to product, retailer, consumer, and website design. Each of these factors may play a role in product returns at different time stage, which are pre-purchase, at purchase, order fulfilment, and post-delivery.

Product Related Factors at Pre-Purchase Time Stage

Previous studies have revealed many product related factors that affect the rate of returns. As these factors are related to the characteristics and features of products, their return likelihood can be projected before consumers purchase them, i.e. at pre-purchase time stage. Returns are more likely with products that have sensory (Wood, 2001), non-digital (Gallino & Moreno, 2018) and unobservable features (Anderson et al., 2009). Popular products inherently cause more returns because of their high sales numbers (Rao et al., 2014). Bulky and low price items are less likely returned due to inconvenience (Rao et al., 2014; Sahoo et al., 2018). However, according to another viewpoint, high-price items are less likely to be returned, because of the more informed decisions made while purchasing these (Shang et al., 2019). Similarly, products to which consumers are familiar (i.e. product maturity) or for which they have different alternatives for comparison (i.e. product variety) reduce returns owing to a more informed decision making (Shang et al., 2019). Rate of returns are also influenced by the product's competitiveness (Lee, 2015; Shang et al., 2017) and salvage value (Shang et al., 2017). When product is competitive, retailers may accept a higher rate of returns to maintain their competitiveness. Likewise, retailers may permit the returns of high salvage value items because of their positive effects on profit. As seen, all listed factors above affect the rate of returns at the pre-purchase stage due to product characteristics.

Retailer Related Factors at Pre-Purchase, Order Fulfilment and Post-Delivery Time Stages

Retailers' decisions at pre-purchase time stage and their performance during order-fulfilment process influence the rate of product returns. Product defections cause returns (Ahsan & Rahman, 2016), which may be due to retailers' lack of control over production processes, e.g. due to the decision to move production offshore (Mollenkopf et al., 2011). To increase sales, retailers may receive pre-orders, but according to Shi et al. (2018), this increases returns because of the consumer difficulty in product valuation. In addition, the retailer's return policy influences the return rate. Whereas returns are increased by money-back guarantee (Walsh & Möhring, 2017) and return convenience (Janakiraman & Ortonez, 2012), they are decreased by time and exchange leniency (Janakiraman et al., 2016; Minnema et al., 2018). Furthermore, the retailer's product shipping fee policy and discounts could have contradictory effects. While free shipping and discounts could reduce the likelihood of returns by positively affecting consumer perceptions (Minnema et al., 2018; Shang et al., 2019), they might equally escalate them by encouraging consumers to purchase more than their needs (Petersen & Kumar, 2009; Sahoo et al., 2018). Product returns also occur due to the retailers' poor logistics performance (de Araújo et al., 2018) during the order fulfilment process, such as missing purchased items, providing wrong & late delivery (Rao et al., 2014), or improper packaging (Mollenkopf et al., 2011). Finally, some retailer related issues cause returns also after product delivery. The research shows that consumers are more likely to return products due to the expectation-perception gap after physical delivery when products are not provided by reputable and specialized retailers (Walsh et al., 2016). It is also revealed that the retailer's gestures, such as gifts (Asdecker et al., 2017; Rao et al., 2014), could decrease the propensity of returns by positively influencing perceptions.

Consumer Related Factors at Pre-Purchase, Purchase and Post-Delivery Time Stages

Consumer related factors play a role in the rate of product returns. After consumers physically receive products (i.e. at post-delivery time stage), they may feel regret and decide to return, for example, because they simply change their minds or find a better product (Powers & Jack, 2015). These tendencies may vary with respect to gender (Walsh et al., 2016) and the country (Yu & Kim, 2019). Another interesting finding is that even if consumers dislike a single item in multiple item purchases, they tend to return all (Sahoo et al., 2018). Consumer related returns may also occur at the time of purchase. They may simply make mistakes in ordering (X. Li et al., 2019) or over-purchase due to their inexperience in online shopping (Shang et al., 2017). Additionally, some consumers may already have return tendency at the pre-purchase stage, e.g. selfish consumers (X. Li et al., 2019). Their opportunistic, fraudulent and strategic behaviours increase the rate of returns. It is becoming more common for consumers to order multiple alternative items with the intention of returning all but one (Asdecker et al., 2017). Moreover, consumers may make strategic returns, for example, in order to qualify for free shipping by exceeding the minimum order amount, they may add items to their shopping carts with the sole intention of returning them later (Lepthien & Clement, 2019). Furthermore, it is observed that consumers may abuse return policies by engaging in fraudulent behaviour, e.g. "retail borrowing" (Piron & Young, 2000), in which a product is used for a single occasion or short period before being returned.

Website Related Factors at Purchase Time Stage

Although it could be argued that website design related factors are under retailer control, it is better to analyse them separately, because, some retailers may not able to control them due to their presence in e-marketplaces. Website design related factors determine the rate of returns at the time of purchase by mainly influencing consumer decision quality, which is highly critical due to high value and fit uncertainties in online purchases. Users' product reviews on a website enable shoppers to make better informed decisions (Sahoo et al., 2018; Walsh & Möhring, 2017), decreasing returns, unless these reviews create misleading expectations (Li et al., 2021). Similarly, the technologies incorporated into websites, such as virtual fitting-room (Gallino & Moreno, 2018) and zoom technology (De et al., 2013) could decrease returns by increasing the decision quality. In contrast, stock information available on websites (Gupta & Gentry, 2019; Rao et al., 2014) might lower decision quality by encouraging instantaneous decisions. Similarly, diminished decision quality, thus increases returns, may result from webstore design incompatible with small screen devices (Seeger et al., 2019) and lack of product information (Minnema et al., 2018).

Table 2 below summarizes the list of items affecting the rate of commercial product returns with respect to related factors and time stages.

Table 2. Factors affecting commercial product returns rates with respect to time stages

		Pre-purchase	At purchase	Order fulfilment	Post-delivery
Product related factors	- Salvage / time value	X			
	- Size	X			
	- Price	X			
	- Type (e.g. hard good)	X			
	- Maturity	X			
	- Variety	X			
	- Popularity	X			
	- Competitiveness	X			
Retailer related factors	- Product quality	X			
	- Outsourcing production	X			
	- Receiving pre-orders	X			
	- Money-back guarantee	X			
	- Product exchange leniency	X			
	- Return convenience	X			
	- Allowable return time period	X			
	- Discounts	X			
	- Shipping fee	X			
	- Delivery accuracy			X	
	- Delivery time			X	
	- Packaging			X	
	- Retailer reputation				X
	- Retailer type				X
	- Retailer gestures				X
Consumer related factors	- Remorse				X
	- Gender				X
	- Country				X
	- Multiple item purchase				X
	- Consumer order accuracy		X		
	- Shopping frequency		X		
	- Shopping experience		X		
	- Consumer type	X			
	- Opportunistic behaviour	X			
	- Fraudulent behaviour	X			
	- Strategic returns	X			

Continued on following page

Table 2. Continued

		Pre-purchase	At purchase	Order fulfilment	Post-delivery
Website design related factors	- Value uncertainty		X		
	- Fit uncertainty		X		
	- Device compatibility		X		
	- Product info availability		X		
	- Stock information		X		
	- Consumer ratings		X		
	- Online product reviews		X		
	- Technological apps		X		

Different Channels Available for Commercial Product Returns

Consumers currently have many return channel options, which are the physical store, predetermined drop point, parcel carrier, parcel lockers, and by post (Bernon et al., 2016; Iannaccone et al., 2021). Not long ago, consumers had to return items only to the physical store from which they had originally made the purchase. Likewise, when consumers used to make an online purchase, they might not be able to make an in-store return. Differently, retailers nowadays tend to integrate both their online and offline channels to make the return process more convenient for consumers, e.g. "buy-online-and-return-in-store" (Huang and Jin, 2020; Jin et al., 2020; Mandal et al., 2021). That is, consumers are able to return items to any physical store of retailers regardless of their initial purchase point. Even, for the convenience of consumers, retailers may be working with courier companies that collect returns from consumer homes or consumers may drop off the returned items to the branches of these courier companies. There are also options removing the need for contact between consumer and courier. For instance, retailers may include third parties, such as grocery shops closer to the neighborhood of consumers, into their reverse logistics networks. Parcel lockers are used for the same purpose, which also allows unattended return pickup (Iannaccone et al., 2021).

METHODOLOGY

Bibliometrics is a scientific approach used to examine the published literature via quantitative and statistical methods (Pritchard, 1969). Bibliometric studies require publication metadata, including title, keywords, author names, institutions, citations, publication year, and source. In this study, these metadata were collected from the two main academic databases, Scopus and Web of Science (WoS). In the data collection, only published and early access articles were considered, given that their findings are generally subject to a more rigorous peer-review process.

For the data collection, a preliminary analysis was conducted to identify the Boolean search strings. After a comprehensive evaluation of approximately 100 papers, the following eight search strings were determined to identify articles: *"consumer return"*, *"product return"*, *"return management"*, *"return policy"*, *"money-back guarantee"*, *"return period"*, *"return behaviour"* and *"online return"*. The articles including one of these eight search strings in their titles, abstracts, or keywords were initially listed in WoS and Scopus with no publication year restriction. In the next step, the search list on WoS was refined to the three categories relevant to the commercial product returns research, which are "operations research and management science", "management", and "business". After this refinement, the number of remaining articles identified on WoS was 369. Similarly, the search on Scopus allowed refining articles using the "keyword limitation" option. After excluding the keywords obviously irrelevant to commercial product returns, the number of remaining articles identified on Scopus was 362.

The abstracts of the remaining articles were examined to confirm their relevance, and if necessary, their introduction and conclusion sections. The main inclusion criterion was whether the commercial product returns were in B2C context; articles that examined returns in B2B context were excluded, unless consumer behaviour and profiles were involved in the analyses. Many other articles were excluded for a number of distinct reasons. In some, the term "return" referred to other research areas, such as in finance, tourism, healthcare, and disaster management. Also excluded were articles on postconsumer returns (e.g. end-of-use and end-of-life returns), renting models, and service cancellation and articles solely on closed-loop supply chain, circular economy, and reverse logistics activities, such as remanufacturing and recycling, since their focus was not on commercial product returns. After these exclusions, the remaining number of articles in WoS and Scopus were 230 and 211 respectively (in total 441). After removing the duplicate records (112) across databases, 329 articles remained in the final collection.

A number of analyses were conducted after the data collection. First, the descriptive analysis revealed the most influential articles and country productivity & collaboration. Next, citation network analyses highlighted the intellectual and conceptual structures of the field. To this end, co-citation and co-word analyses were performed to display the research clusters, and the thematic map of the field over time respectively. In these analyses, this study mainly used an open source tool (R-package), *"bibliometrics"* (Aria & Cuccurullo, 2017), which allows the use of metadata available in both WoS and Scopus.

DESCRIPTIVE ANALYSIS OF COMMERCIAL PRODUCT RETURNS RESEARCH

The timespan of 329 articles in the collection covers the period from 1995 to the first half of 2020. The number of articles per year during this time has grown very fast with an annual rate over 15%. As Figure 1 highlights, the literature is relatively young, with more than half of articles (53.6%) published within the last 5 years. Although the number of published articles in 2020 shows a slight decrease in Figure 1, it should be noted that this number (34) only represents the first six months of 2020.

Figure 1. The number of articles per year in the field of commercial product returns

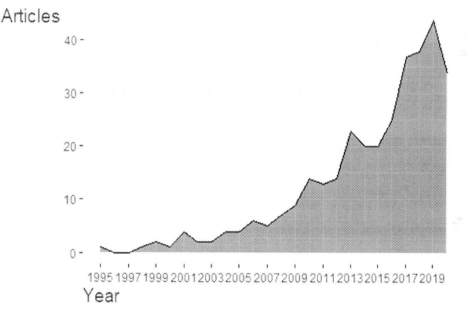

The total number of contributing authors in the collection is 680. The articles are mainly multi-authored (2.78 authors per article on average), with a small percentage of single-authored articles (9.7%). In terms of author affiliation, the countries with the most significant contributions to the field are the USA (79 articles) and China (44 articles). Here, the interesting finding is that USA affiliated authors prefer collaborating with each other; 75 of 79 articles contributed by USA-affiliated authors are single country articles.

A well-established measure of the scientific impact is citation frequency. In the reviewed collection, each article has an average of 25.53 citations, and receives around 3.2 citations per year. The influence of USA affiliated authors is high, with respect to not only number of publications, as abovementioned, but also of citations, 3948, followed by China-affiliated authors, with 951 citations. A citation analysis also reveals influential articles according to their total citations per year, as shown in Table 3.

Table 3. Top 10 articles according to total citations per year

	Article (Year)	Journal	Total Citations	Total Citations per Year
1	Guo et al. (2020)	European Journal of Operational Research	20	20.000
2	Guide et al. (2006)	Management Science	253	16.867
3	Ofek et al. (2011)	Marketing Science	164	16.400
4	Gao & Su (2017)	Manufacturing & Service Operations Management	63	15.750
5	Blackburn et al. (2004)	California Management Review	246	14.471
6	Hong & Pavlou (2014)	Information Systems Research	100	14.286
7	Su (2009)	Manufacturing & Service Operations Management	170	14.167
8	G. Li et al. (2019)	International Journal of Production Economics	27	13.500
9	Petersen & Kumar (2009)	Journal of Marketing	155	12.917
10	Özkır & Başlıgil (2013)	Journal of Cleaner Production	103	12.875

THE RESULTS OF THE CITATION NETWORK ANALYSIS

Intellectual Structure of the Field: Co-Citation Analysis

Co-citation analysis, which establishes similarity between articles to the degree that they appear together in the reference lists of other publications, was carried out to identify clusters in the field of commercial product returns. The clustering algorithm "Louvain" was used, which aims to maximize the modularity degree of network for identifying well-separated clusters (Blondel et al., 2008). By plotting the top 50 articles according to the degree centrality scores, Figure 2 shows the results of the co-citation analysis performed over 11887 references.

Figure 2. Co-citation analysis

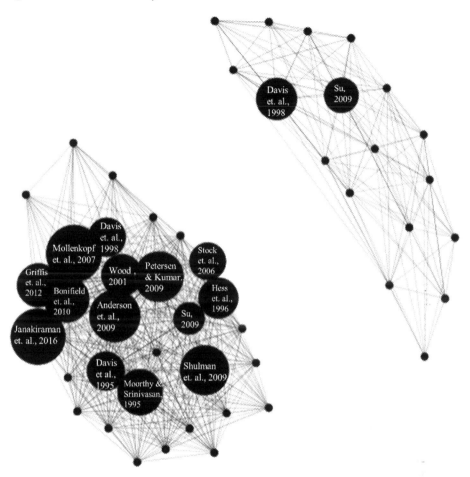

The cluster analysis clearly shows two distinct facets of commercial product returns. The articles in the first cluster (the larger one on the left in Figure 2) mainly focuses on the strategic role of returns, hence their effects on future demand (e.g. Anderson et al., 2009; Griffis et al., 2012; Janakiraman et al., 2016; Petersen & Kumar, 2009), loyalty (Mollenkopf et al., 2007) and competitiveness (e.g. Stock et al., 2006). The articles in the second cluster are distinguished by their attempt to reveal a suitable operational design while handling returns, encompassing necessary organizational structures, activities, and capabilities. For instance, they indicate the appropriate type of reverse supply chain (efficient versus responsive) with respect to the returned product's marginal value of time (Blackburn et al., 2004; Guide et al., 2006), and emphasize the capabilities needed for good return management, e.g. information technology capabilities (Daugherty et al., 2005). There are also studies that bridge these two clusters, appearing in both, e.g. Davis et al. (1998) and Su (2009), as seen in Figure 2. These studies consider both facets of returns via their analytical models, and accordingly, include wide range of variables into their models, such as price level, cross-selling, sales rebate, salvage value, hassle cost, processing cost, return policies, and supply chain coordination.

Conceptual Structure of the Field: Thematic Analysis

Article keywords are important metadata because they illustrate the key themes on which the research is built. The authors of articles, as the executors of research, should be the most competent to identify the keywords depicting their research. Currently, academic databases also automatically generate keywords for articles via various algorithms applied on their titles and abstracts. Although useful in categorizing a mass of articles, these algorithms cannot determine the keywords of one particular article as successfully as its authors, therefore this chapter used the author keywords for the thematic analysis. Please note that the keywords that indicate the name of whole field, such as "product returns" and "returns" were not considered in the analysis.

An examination on the frequency of keywords over the last five years indicates four main trends. First, as expected, in this digital age, certain keywords appear more frequently, such as "e-commerce", "online retailing", and "online shopping" (in total 31 articles). Also, the distinct features of online shopping, such as temporal and spatial separation (Sorkun, 2019), seem to have increased the scholarly interest on "return policy" (36 articles). Secondly, the need to sell products via both physical and online channels has shifted the focus to terms such as "supply chain" (25 articles), "pricing" (23 articles), "game theory" (16 articles), and "omni-channel" (12 articles) regarding the goal alignment and operational coordination among distinct entities in the whole distribution network. Thirdly, a focus on the operational design of the more efficient and effective handling of returns should account for the high frequency of the keywords "reverse logistics" and "reverse supply chain" (in total 18 papers). Finally, the recent emphasis on sustainability seems to influence scholarly work in the field, given the frequency of keywords including the terms "closed-loop" (19 articles) and "green" (4 articles in the last two years).

In order to reveal the thematic evolution of the field, the articles in the collection were divided according to their publication years to distribute the studies as evenly as possible across groups. This yielded three groups with the following time zones: 1995-2013 (112 articles), 2014-2017 (101 articles), and 2018-2020 (116 articles). The co-word analysis on author keywords was performed to classify themes with respect to their centrality and density scores. Centrality shows the strength of a theme's connection with other themes in the field, implying its importance in the

Commercial Product Returns

evolution of the whole field. Density indicates the level of development for each theme. As themes emerge from a cluster analysis on keywords, the interconnection between keywords within each cluster (i.e. density score) shows how well themes are developed.

As illustrated in Figures 3, 4 and 5 below, the four quadrants can be depicted according to centrality and density scores. The position of each theme provides useful information, such as how well a theme is conceptually developed, how important it is for the field's evolution, and whether it is emerging or transversal theme for the field. Applying this thematic analysis on different time zones makes possible to observe changes in a particular theme's positions over time. Accordingly, Figure 3, Figure 4, and Figure 5 show the thematic evolution of the commercial product returns research. Please note that the volume of nodes (i.e. themes) in these figures varies according to the number of articles identified relevant to themes.

Figure 3. Themes between the years of 1995 and 2013

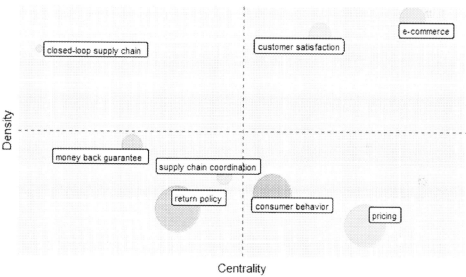

Figure 4. Themes between the years of 2014 and 2017

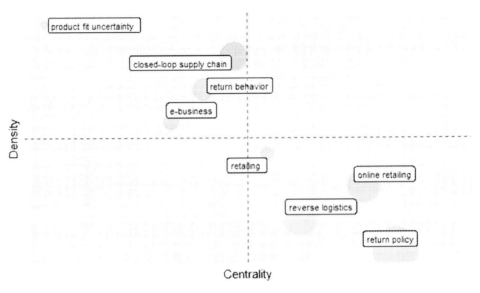

Figure 5. Themes between the years of 2018 and 2020

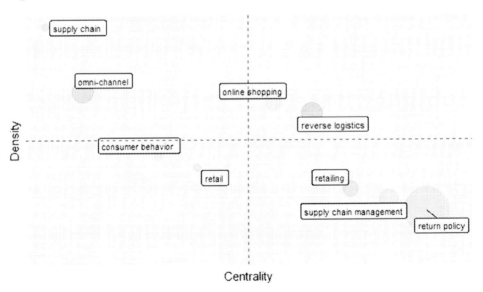

A number of various themes have emerged from the analysis. The themes – "e-commerce", "e-business", and "online retailing" – imply that online transactions have increased the importance and rate of product returns, which might be mainly due to "product fit uncertainty" because consumers cannot try on products at the time of purchase. Associated with this, the themes - "reverse logistics management" and "closed-loop supply chain" – indicate that the management of reverse product flows have become as critical as the management of the forward flows in supply chains because there are many activities needed to process the consumer return claims, including the returned products' transportation, gatekeeping, repairing, reselling, etc., which should be synchronized with the forward product flows in supply chains. Moreover, as return management has an impact on "customer satisfaction", retailers are aiming to enhance the consumer experience in return management processes as well. Many of them have adopted the "omni-channel" management strategy to make the return processes more convenient for consumers by fully integrating their physical and digital channels, however, this requires a good "supply chain coordination and management". Besides, it is also necessary to keep costs under control while aiming to increase "customer satisfaction". Here, the "return policy" of retailers plays a crucial role, because it determines the principles guiding retailers' decisions on product returns, e.g., which items consumers can return, what the maximum allowable time is for return claims, or whether consumers are fully refunded after a product return, i.e. "money-back guarantee". For the development of a good return policy, retailers ought to understand the "consumer behaviour" well, including their "return behaviour", which could also allow retailers to influence the number of returns for their benefits via a proper "pricing" strategy.

An examination on themes along three time zones provides a number of remarkable findings. First, "e-commerce" and "customer satisfaction" are motor themes in the first time zone (from 1995 to 2013), i.e. they have high scores for both density and centrality. However, these themes lost their particularity for the field in the later time zones. In contrast, the centrality of the "closed-loop supply chain" and the density of "reverse logistics" have increased over time, and in the last few years, the latter, together with "online shopping", has become the current motor theme in the field. Two other notable changes in the field are evident over the period. One is that "return policy" is becoming more prominent (centrality) for the field over the time; nevertheless, it seems that there remains scope for the development of its conceptualization. The other remarkable finding is the appearance of theme "omni-channel" towards the end of the decade (2018-2020). Despite its currently limited impact on the evolution of the field, its well-established conceptual development could make significant impact in future.

FUTURE RESEARCH DIRECTIONS

A high growth rate in the number of articles on commercial product returns indicates that the scholarly activity in the field will intensify in the following years. The author believes that the review studies in such fast-growing research fields are useful in coordinating future work, by raising awareness on research avenues to accelerate knowledge creation and accumulation. Mapping the research activity across the whole field provides a holistic view, increasing scholars' ability to incorporate the perspectives of other research streams into their work. In alignment with these, this chapter identifies future research directions based on the results of the thematic and co-citation analyses. Understanding prominent and emerging themes (Figures 3, 4, and 5), and their possible linkages has the potential to accelerate the knowledge accumulation in the field. To further this end, this chapter also considers these linkages' potential on bridging two distinct clusters in the field (Figure 2).

The Effects of Reverse Logistics Activities on Return Behaviour in Online Shopping

As seen in Figure 5, some remarkable recent themes in the field are "reverse logistics", "online shopping / retailing", and "consumer / return behaviour". As these themes are examined in association with the co-citation analysis, it is observed that papers related to themes "online shopping / retailing" and "consumer / return behaviour" usually focus on the strategic role of returns, thus they are the part of the first cluster (on the left in Figure 2). In contrast, the theme "reverse logistics" is more associated with papers in the second cluster, which aims to reveal the organizational structures most effective in enabling the management of returns. Thus, by bringing the abovementioned themes together, future studies could make solid contribution to the evolution of the field.

Online returns occur not only due to product and logistics failures, but also due to the negative disconfirmation of expectations (Seeger et al., 2019) and dissonance (Powers & Jack, 2015). This implies the involvement of psychological elements in online shopping behaviour, including return behaviour. Therefore, it would be interesting to explore the effects of the retailers' reverse logistics operations on the perceptions of consumers, who are increasingly emphasizing the concepts of sustainability and circularity. An area for exploration is the discrepancy between expected and perceived product performance (i.e. consumer return behaviour), and how this discrepancy is affected by the environmentally-friendliness of the retailers' reverse logistics operations. Also, it is known that the majority of consumers currently consider retailers' return policy before their purchasing decisions (Su, 2009). It would therefore be valuable if future research examines how consumer purchasing decisions are affected by the degree to which the retailer stresses sustainable reverse logistics activities in return policy terms.

Uncertainty in the timing and quantities of returns (Jayaraman & Luo, 2007), combined with the pressure on retailers to process return claims faster for customer satisfaction inevitably leads to partial-truck load shipments. In view of the negative environmental effects of such practices (Schleiden & Neiberger, 2020), future research is needed to reveal whether, and if so, how long, consumers could be persuaded to wait for the processing of their return claims to promote greener reverse logistics operations. Likewise, given that a good product returns management positively affects consumer repurchasing behaviour (Petersen & Kumar 2010; Piroth et al., 2020) and loyalty (Griffis et al., 2012), future research could investigate whether the retailer's environmental-friendly reverse logistics operations stimulates (i.e. positively moderates) this repurchasing behaviour. In addition, many retailers are now offering services, such as wardrobing (Shang et al., 2017), in order to increase sales by eliminating value and fit uncertainties in online shopping. This enables consumers to order many items and keep only those selected. Although such services may bring customer satisfaction, they might have negative environmental consequences (e.g. due to extra transportation). Hence, future studies could examine how these services could affect general consumer perception towards the retailer's brand image from a sustainability aspect.

Alignment between Return Policy Factors and Reverse Logistics Activities and Design

The thematic evolution of the field (see Figures 3, 4, and 5) indicates an increasing prominence (i.e. centrality) of the theme "return policy", but its density score is still low, implying a wide range of keywords used in the respective papers. Steering future work on return policy towards particular areas would help providing a good knowledge accumulation in the field. In this regard, "reverse logistics" appears to be a suitable option because it has high prominence and is well-conceptualized. In addition, as stated in the previous section, the intellectual structure of the field demonstrates that papers associated with the theme "reverse logistics" are usually part of the second cluster (on the right in Figure 2). Therefore, the two distinct research clusters could be bridged by studies combining reverse logistics issues with return policy factors reflecting the return strategy of retailers (i.e. the first cluster).

Exploring the effects of return policy on reverse logistics activities could be a good future research direction. Janakiraman et al. (2016) list five factors that determine the leniency of return policies: time, money, effort, scope, and exchange leniency, any of which could influence the importance of the particular reverse logistics activity. For example, an extended return period could increase wear on returned items, making recycling and refurbishing more critical, whereas, in the case of a shorter period, reselling on the second-hand market could become the most critical reverse logistics activity, due to the expected minor value deprecation in returned items.

Identifying highly critical reverse logistics activities with respect to one return policy factor in isolation is relatively straightforward, but future studies should also aim to predict the joint effects of multiple factors, requiring much more complex analyses. For example, would it be possible for retailers to offer both time leniency and money-back guarantee (i.e. exchange leniency)? If so, how should the retailer's reverse logistics activities support this return policy while avoiding a significant financial burden due to consumer opportunistic behaviours? In the opposite direction, future research could also portray the ideal return policy (i.e. the optimal leniency of return policy factors) for the a retailer's given capabilities and resources in each reverse logistics activity, e.g. gatekeeping, collection, sorting, reselling, repairing, remanufacturing, and recycling.

Another possible avenue for future research is uncovering the most appropriate reverse logistics network design with respect to return policy factors. As revealed by previous research, reverse logistics network design should take into account company motivations (Sorkun & Onay, 2018) and product characteristics (Blackburn et al., 2004). In parallel, it is recommended that future research explore how return policy factors should influence the designs of reverse logistics networks. For example, to what degree should the effort leniency offered by retailers lead to an increase in the number of easily accessible return collection points? Alternatively, since the extended return period for returns (i.e. time leniency) decreases the likelihood of direct reselling due to wear, could time leniency lead to an increase in the number and size of the remanufacturing / repairing facilities in reverse logistics networks?

Return policy factors could also play a role in make-or-buy decisions. One commonly stated risk of outsourcing is the loss of control on activities. However, for retailers, lenient return policies decrease the relative importance of gatekeeping, because claims for product returns are usually accepted to ensure customer satisfaction. Therefore, would it be possible to argue that retailers adopting a lenient return policy are more likely to outsource their reverse logistics operations, such as collection? As an alternative perspective, considering that lenient return policies encourage consumer returns, it would also be interesting to investigate whether a high rate of return (i.e. sufficiently large scale) would induce retailers to establish their own reverse logistics network to conduct the respective operations themselves.

Omni-Channel Returns

Omni-channel, a current popular channel strategy and an emerging theme in the commercial product returns research, refers to the integration of a retailer's all physical and online channels, i.e. all touchpoints including physical stores, web stores, mobile applications, social media and etc. (Verhoef et al., 2015). The aim is to provide consumers with a "seamless shopping experience", enabling to use multiple touchpoints simultaneously within the same sales transaction (Piotrowicz & Cuthbertson, 2014) and providing the same level of service in each touchpoint, including the product returns (de Borba et al., 2020).

The thematic evolution of the field reveals that "omni-channel" is well conceptualized (i.e. high density score) but has a low centrality score, probably due to being a novel term. We suggest that future research on omni-channel returns is critical in providing a good knowledge accumulation in the field, because of its potential to bridge the two research clusters (Figure 2) due to its emphasis on both strategic and operational aspects of commercial product returns.

While omni-channel strategy boosts customer satisfaction (Sorkun et al., 2020), cross-channel returns may complicate retailers' operations. As reported by previous research, for convenience, consumers purchasing online prefer in-store returns to mailing (Jones & Livingstone, 2018). The implications can be investigated in future research, which can indicate under which circumstances retailers should encourage these cross-channel returns. More specifically, in case of "buy-online and return in-store", some potential advantages for the retailer can be listed as the possible additional purchases made while returning products, return shipping fee savings, and the opportunity for face-to-face discussion with consumers to understand the causes of return. In contrast, potential disadvantages are stock imbalances, longer return processing times, and extra product handling (Bernon et al., 2016). Future research might attempt a detailed discussion of the circumstances under which these advantages outweigh the disadvantages of "buy-online and return in-store", and in the absence of these circumstances, should focus on the ways of making returns by mail as convenient as in-store returns.

In addition to cross-channel returns, omni-channel returns encompass another type of return, i.e., across different physical store locations. Thus, consumers are able to return products to any store location, regardless of where the product was purchased. However, the stores of a particular brand may be franchisees with different owners, leading to lack of goal alignment, and hindering a policy of allowing returns across different physical store locations under omni-channel strategy. Future research could delve into these cases and propose solution alternatives.

Technology Use for Mitigating Online Returns Due to Uncertainty

A remaining barrier to the further growth of online retailing is the issue of value and fit uncertainties due to consumers' inability to touch, feel, and try on products before purchase (Saarijärvi et al., 2017). These uncertainties cause retailers a higher rate of returns and dissatisfied customers. Interestingly, few studies have examined the use of technology to reduce uncertainty in online shopping, and thus, avoiding returns. The theme "product fit uncertainty" appears in Figure 4 only between the years of 2014 and 2017 with high density and low centrality scores. This is due to the narrow range of technologies studied, mainly limited to visual media, zoom technology and virtual fitting rooms (Bell et al., 2014; De et al., 2013; Hong & Pavlou, 2014). Future research could also explore the effectiveness of other novel applications and practices in decreasing uncertainties, i.e. product returns, such as one-to-one videoconference calls with experts / influencers, and online shopping parties where consumers are able to interact with each other (PSFK Research, 2020).

Another future research direction could be the ways of overcoming practical obstacles to the exploitation of the technology-powered applications in reducing consumer uncertainty. For instance, virtual fitting rooms enable consumers to virtually try on clothing products before online purchase. Although recent research (Gallino & Moreno 2018; Yang & Xiong 2019) show that virtual fitting rooms decrease the rate and fulfilment costs of returns, it is not clear why such applications are not more widely-used. Hence, a rigorous examination is needed to uncover the causes of this situation, and future studies should aim to shed light on the degree to which consumers find these applications useful and easy-to-use. Alternatively, future studies might reveal how retailers can improve and simplify them, and for this, which capabilities and resources retailers should have.

To tackle uncertainties in online shopping, there is considerable progress of exploiting cutting-edge technologies in the market. Especially noteworthy is the use of artificial intelligence. For example, using click statistics, retailers are able to instantly recognize consumers who experience uncertainty while examining a particular item (SmarterCX Team, 2020); in these circumstances, retailers' chatbots are able to provide an instant guidance and help. As another example, the start-up company Octane AI has developed a tool called "shoppable quizzes", giving consumers the opportunity to ask questions to chatbots, and get guidance as in physical stores (Swant, 2020). The company argues that such interaction decreases uncertainties by giving a clearer understanding of consumers' exact requirements. Although all these technological tools have the potential to effectively reduce returns, their performances have not yet been validated. Hence, future studies are needed to investigate the magnitude of positive effect on returns provided by these technological tools.

3D printing technology is promising to radically change the dynamics of online retailing, encompassing the online returns management. Some retailers are already introducing business models that make use of 3D printers (Baranov, 2019). In these models, retailers produce products designed by consumers themselves using

3D printers. Although consumer involvement is expected to reduce value and fit uncertainties, the task of 3D printing itself is carried out by retailers, not by consumers. In future, the wide availability of home 3D printers could radically impact online retailing by eliminating uncertainties and the need to physically return products. Future studies could explore the very interesting area of possible scenarios and potential impacts on product returns when 3D printers are in widespread use in homes.

FUTURE RESEARCH IMPLICATIONS OF COVID-19

Restrictions, lockdowns, and the fear of Covid-19 transmission steer consumers towards online shopping further. As discussed earlier, due to spatial and temporal separation, online shopping has an effect of increasing returns (Končar et al., 2020; Masudin et al., 2021) which retailers have to handle. Moreover, the Covid-19 pandemic has influenced the return behaviour of consumers who prefer now contactless collection alternatives, such as making returns by mail, to returning them in stores (Cycleon, 2021; Ryan, 2020), because consumers have not felt comfortable with the situation of having time in stores with many other people (Ward, 2020). During the pandemic, many retailers have indeed made their return policies more lenient, for example, by extending the return time windows (Barkho, 2020). They also take measures against the risk of virus transmission in return processes. Accordingly, while the return of some items (e.g. cosmetics and beauty products) may not be accepted (Barkho, 2020), all returned items are put in quarantine for some time and sanitized before any further process (Barkho, 2020; Ryan, 2020).

Based on the above depicted new situation in commercial product returns, it is possible to discuss the implications of Covid-19 on future research directions identified in this chapter. The first research direction emphasizes the recent importance, given by consumers, to environmental and sustainability issues during the reverse logistics activities of retailers, e.g. the transportation of returned items. However, after Covid-19, consumers have health concerns and do not prefer making returns to stores (Cycleon, 2021; Ryan, 2020), which increases the number of shipments that need to be made for handling product returns. Future research could compare the relative importance of health issues with environmental concerns in the eyes of consumers. The second research direction identified by this chapter draws attention to the need for aligning the retailers' return policies and reverse logistics networks. The Covid-19 pandemic shows that retailers are still attempting to liberalize their return policies due to competition, even though they have more operational challenges, such as keeping the returned items in quarantine for a while, sanitizing the packages, and providing the contactless collection service (Barkho, 2020; Downes, 2021; Ryan, 2020). Future research could investigate what kind of changes retailers need to make in their reverse logistics networks and activities to overcome these additional difficulties. The topic of omni-channel returns is another future research direction revealed by this study. As a part of the omni-channel strategy, retailers encourage "buy-online-and-return-in-store", which enables them to make extra sales in stores and save shipping and transportation costs (Webster, 2020). Nevertheless, due to the risk of virus transmission in stores, consumers are willing to make their returns by mail. Future studies could research the financial impact of Covid-19 on retailers in this regard and explore strategies able to bring consumers back to stores for returns. Finally, recent research (Kunovjanek and Wankmüller, 2020; Manero et al., 2020) has proposed that 3D printing technology can decrease the risk of supply chain disruptions against external global shocks, e.g. due to Covid-19, by bringing production and consumption points closer to each other. To this end, future research is suggested to study how 3D printing technology can be exploited in product return processes.

CONCLUSION

The very rapid growth in research on commercial product returns in recent years is expected to continue, given consumers' increasing preference for online shopping, which will lead to the emergence of many intriguing research questions. However, a possible problem in such fast-growing research fields is an insufficient rate of knowledge accumulation due to a lack of coordination across different research streams. In this regard, review studies are valuable in revealing current scientific activity, knowledge domains, and emerging research themes. They also enable scholars to recognize research gaps, and potential collaborators with whom they can address these.

This chapter carries out various analyses to examine the field of commercial product returns. The descriptive analysis in the first stage shows very fast growth in the number of articles published on commercial product returns, with a significant contribution from USA affiliated authors, in terms of both publication and citation frequency. However, the examination on multi-authored articles indicates a general lack of collaboration between USA affiliated authors and authors in other countries; reinforcing a cross-border collaboration could therefore accelerate the creation of knowledge in the field. In the second stage, this chapter illustrates the intellectual structure of the field, revealing two main research clusters focusing respectively on the strategic role of returns, and appropriate operational design enabling the efficient and effective handling of returns. In a field characterized by such a network structure, future studies should aim to deliver a holistic approach and bridge these two clusters. In the third stage, this chapter's thematic analysis highlights prominent and emerging research themes in the field over the time. The results show a number of emerging themes, e.g. omni-channel, and also current prominent themes in the field, e.g. reverse logistics and return policy.

This chapter finally suggests four major avenues for future research based on the abovementioned analyses and discusses the implications of Covid-19 on future research. The first emphasis is made on consumers' current high level of environmental consciousness, and accordingly, it is recommended that future research investigates the consumers' reaction when the service level received conflicts with the retailers' environment (un)friendly reverse logistics operations in product returns. Second, there is a need for more comprehensive future research to provide a detailed examination of the impacts of retailers' return policies on their reverse logistics activities and network designs. Third, it is important to encourage studies that will investigate omni-channel returns and their implementation difficulties in different organizational structures, because they will be able to increase the scope of the field of product returns management, embracing both strategic and operational issues. Finally, underlining the continuing role of uncertainty as a main driver of returns, and a barrier to the further growth of online retailing, there is a need to magnify the effectiveness of recent practices, technological tools and applications in mitigating these uncertainties, and concordantly also to reveal practical obstacles preventing the application and tools' full exploitation. Additionally, it is emphasized that some existing technologies, such as artificial intelligence and 3D printing, are likely to change the dynamics of retailing and product returns management in the near future. Hence, investigations on the potential implications of these technologies are called for.

ACKNOWLEDGMENT

This research received no specific grant from any funding agency in the public, commercial, or not-for-profit sectors.

REFERENCES

Akturk, M. S., Ketzenberg, M., & Yıldız, B. (2021). Managing consumer returns with technology-enabled countermeasures. *Omega*, *102*, 102337. doi:10.1016/j.omega.2020.102337

Anderson, E. T., Hansen, K., & Simester, D. (2009). The option value of returns: Theory and empirical evidence. *Marketing Science*, *28*(3), 405–423. doi:10.1287/mksc.1080.0430

Aria, M., & Cuccurullo, C. (2017). Bibliometrix: An R-tool for comprehensive science mapping analysis. *Journal of Informetrics*, *11*(4), 959–975. doi:10.1016/j.joi.2017.08.007

Asdecker, B., Karl, D., & Sucky, E. (2017). Examining drivers of consumer returns in e-tailing with real shop data. In *Proceedings of the 50th Hawaii International Conference on System Sciences* (pp. 4192-4201). University of Hawaii. 10.24251/HICSS.2017.507

Baranov, D. (2019). *How 3D printers reshape retail business.* https://blog.dataart.com/how-3d-printers-reshape-retail-business

Barkho, G. (2020). *How the coronavirus changed retailers' returns policies.* https://www.modernretail.co/retailers/how-the-coronavirus-changed-retailers-returns-policies/

Bell, D. R., Gallino, S., & Moreno, A. (2014). How to win in an omnichannel world. *MIT Sloan Management Review*, *56*(1), 45–53.

Bernon, M., Cullen, J., & Gorst, J. (2016). Online retail returns management: Integration within an omni-channel distribution context. *International Journal of Physical Distribution & Logistics Management*, *46*(6/7), 584–605. doi:10.1108/IJPDLM-01-2015-0010

Blackburn, J. D., Guide, V. D. R. Jr, Souza, G. C., & Van Wassenhove, L. N. (2004). Reverse supply chains for commercial returns. *California Management Review*, *46*(2), 6–22. doi:10.2307/41166207

Blondel, V. D., Guillaume, J. L., Lambiotte, R., & Lefebvre, E. (2008). Fast unfolding of communities in large networks. *Journal of Statistical Mechanics*, *2008*(10), P10008. doi:10.1088/1742-5468/2008/10/P10008

Bonifield, C., Cole, C., & Schultz, R. L. (2010). Product returns on the internet: A case of mixed signals? *Journal of Business Research*, *63*(9-10), 1058–1065. doi:10.1016/j.jbusres.2008.12.009

Cycleon. (2021). *Consumer returns during and after COVID-19.* https://cycleon.com/wp-content/uploads/2021/06/how-consumer-return-whitepaper-.pdf

Daugherty, P. J., Richey, R. G., Genchev, S. E., & Chen, H. (2005). Reverse logistics: Superior performance through focused resource commitments to information technology. *Transportation Research Part E, Logistics and Transportation Review*, *41*(2), 77–92. doi:10.1016/j.tre.2004.04.002

Davis, S., Gerstner, E., & Hagerty, M. (1995). Money back guarantees in retailing: Matching products to consumer tastes. *Journal of Retailing, 71*(1), 7–22. doi:10.1016/0022-4359(95)90010-1

Davis, S., Hagerty, M., & Gerstner, E. (1998). Return policies and the optimal level of "hassle". *Journal of Economics and Business, 50*(5), 445–460. doi:10.1016/S0148-6195(98)00013-7

De, P., Hu, Y., & Rahman, M. S. (2013). *Product-oriented web technologies and product returns: An exploratory study.* https://cycleon.com/wp-content/uploads/2021/06/how-consumer-return-whitepaper-.pdfm doi:10.1287/isre.2013.0487

de Araújo, A. C., Matsuoka, E. M., Ung, J. E., Massote, A., & Sampaio, M. (2018). An exploratory study on the returns management process in an online retailer. *International Journal of Logistics Research and Applications, 21*(3), 345–362. doi:10.1080/13675567.2017.1370080

de Borba, J. L. G., de Magalhães, M. R., Filgueiras, R. S., & Bouzon, M. (2020). Barriers in omnichannel retailing returns: A conceptual framework. *International Journal of Retail & Distribution Management, 49*(1), 121–143. doi:10.1108/IJRDM-04-2020-0140

Difrancesco, R. M., Huchzermeier, A., & Schröder, D. (2018). Optimizing the return window for online fashion retailers with closed-loop refurbishment. *Omega, 78*, 205–221. doi:10.1016/j.omega.2017.07.001

Downes, H. (2021). *Coronavirus: Extended returns policies and your rights to a refund.* https://www.which.co.uk/news/2021/02/coronavirus-extended-returns-policies-and-your-rights-to-a-refund/

Ferguson, M., Guide, V. D. R. Jr, & Souza, G. C. (2006). Supply chain coordination for false failure returns. *Manufacturing & Service Operations Management, 8*(4), 376–393. doi:10.1287/msom.1060.0112

Gallino, S., & Moreno, A. (2018). The value of fit information in online retail: Evidence from a randomized field experiment. *Manufacturing & Service Operations Management, 20*(4), 767–787. doi:10.1287/msom.2017.0686

Gao, F., & Su, X. (2017). Online and offline information for omnichannel retailing. *Manufacturing & Service Operations Management, 19*(1), 84–98. doi:10.1287/msom.2016.0593

Griffis, S. E., Rao, S., Goldsby, T. J., & Niranjan, T. T. (2012). The customer consequences of returns in online retailing: An empirical analysis. *Journal of Operations Management, 30*(4), 282–294. doi:10.1016/j.jom.2012.02.002

Guide, V. D. R. Jr, Souza, G. C., Van Wassenhove, L. N., & Blackburn, J. D. (2006). Time value of commercial product returns. *Management Science, 52*(8), 1200–1214. doi:10.1287/mnsc.1060.0522

Guo, S., Choi, T. M., & Shen, B. (2020). Green product development under competition: A study of the fashion apparel industry. *European Journal of Operational Research, 280*(2), 523–538. doi:10.1016/j.ejor.2019.07.050

Gupta, S., & Gentry, J. W. (2019). 'Should I Buy, Hoard, or Hide?'-Consumers' responses to perceived scarcity. *International Review of Retail, Distribution and Consumer Research, 29*(2), 178–197. doi:10.1080/09593969.2018.1562955

Hess, J. D., Chu, W., & Gerstner, E. (1996). Controlling product returns in direct marketing. *Marketing Letters, 7*(4), 307–317. doi:10.1007/BF00435538

Hong, Y., & Pavlou, P. A. (2014). Product fit uncertainty in online markets: Nature, effects, and antecedents. *Information Systems Research, 25*(2), 328–344. doi:10.1287/isre.2014.0520

Huang, M., & Jin, D. (2020). Impact of buy-online-and-return-in-store service on omnichannel retailing: A supply chain competitive perspective. *Electronic Commerce Research and Applications, 41*, 100977. doi:10.1016/j.elerap.2020.100977

Iannaccone, G., Marcucci, E., & Gatta, V. (2021). What young e-consumers want? Forecasting parcel lockers choice in Rome. *Logistics, 5*(3), 57. doi:10.3390/logistics5030057

Janakiraman, N., & Ordóñez, L. (2012). Effect of effort and deadlines on consumer product returns. *Journal of Consumer Psychology, 22*(2), 260–271. doi:10.1016/j.jcps.2011.05.002

Janakiraman, N., Syrdal, H. A., & Freling, R. (2016). The effect of return policy leniency on consumer purchase and return decisions: A meta-analytic review. *Journal of Retailing, 92*(2), 226–235. doi:10.1016/j.jretai.2015.11.002

Jayaraman, V., & Luo, Y. (2007). Creating competitive advantages through new value creation: A reverse logistics perspective. *The Academy of Management Perspectives, 21*(2), 56–73. doi:10.5465/amp.2007.25356512

Jin, D., Caliskan-Demirag, O., Chen, F. Y., & Huang, M. (2020). Omnichannel retailers' return policy strategies in the presence of competition. *International Journal of Production Economics, 225*, 107595. doi:10.1016/j.ijpe.2019.107595

Jones, C., & Livingstone, N. (2018). The 'online high street' or the high street online? The implications for the urban retail hierarchy. *International Review of Retail, Distribution and Consumer Research, 28*(1), 47–63. doi:10.1080/09593969.2017.1393441

Končar, J., Grubor, A., Marić, R., Vučenović, S., & Vukmirović, G. (2020). Setbacks to IoT implementation in the function of FMCG supply chain sustainability during COVID-19 pandemic. *Sustainability, 12*(18), 7391. doi:10.3390u12187391

Kunovjanek, M., & Wankmüller, C. (2020). An analysis of the global additive manufacturing response to the Covid-19 pandemic. *Journal of Manufacturing Technology Management, 32*(9), 75–100. doi:10.1108/JMTM-07-2020-0263

Lepthien, A., & Clement, M. (2019). Shipping fee schedules and return behavior. *Marketing Letters, 30*(2), 151–165. doi:10.100711002-019-09486-8

Li, G., Li, L., Sethi, S. P., & Guan, X. (2019). Return strategy and pricing in a dual-channel supply chain. *International Journal of Production Economics, 215*, 153–164. doi:10.1016/j.ijpe.2017.06.031

Li, X., Ma, B., & Chu, H. (2021). The impact of online reviews on product returns. *Asia Pacific Journal of Marketing and Logistics, 33*(8), 1814–1828. Advance online publication. doi:10.1108/APJML-02-2020-0074

Li, X., Zhuang, Y., Fu, Y., & He, X. (2019). A trust-aware random walk model for return propensity estimation and consumer anomaly scoring in online shopping. *Science China. Information Sciences, 62*(5), 52101. doi:10.100711432-018-9511-1

Mandal, P., Basu, P., & Saha, K. (2021). Forays into omnichannel: An online retailer's strategies for managing product returns. *European Journal of Operational Research, 292*(2), 633–651. doi:10.1016/j.ejor.2020.10.042

Manero, A., Smith, P., Koontz, A., Dombrowski, M., Sparkman, J., Courbin, D., & Chi, A. (2020). Leveraging 3D printing capacity in times of crisis: Recommendations for Covid-19 distributed manufacturing for medical equipment rapid response. *International Journal of Environmental Research and Public Health, 17*(13), 4634. doi:10.3390/ijerph17134634 PMID:32605098

Masudin, I., Ramadhani, A., Restuputri, D. P., & Amallynda, I. (2021). The effect of traceability system and managerial initiative on Indonesian food cold chain performance: A Covid-19 Pandemic perspective. *Global Journal of Flexible Systems Management*. doi:10.1007/s40171-021-00281-x

Minnema, A., Bijmolt, T. H., Petersen, J. A., & Shulman, J. D. (2018). Managing product returns within the customer value framework. In R. W. Palmatier, V. Kumar, & C. M. Harmeling (Eds.), *Customer engagement marketing* (pp. 95–118). Palgrave Macmillan. doi:10.1007/978-3-319-61985-9_5

Mollenkopf, D. A., Frankel, R., & Russo, I. (2011). Creating value through returns management: Exploring the marketing–operations interface. *Journal of Operations Management*, *29*(5), 391–403. doi:10.1016/j.jom.2010.11.004

Mollenkopf, D. A., Rabinovich, E., Laseter, T. M., & Boyer, K. K. (2007). Managing internet product returns: A focus on effective service operations. *Decision Sciences*, *38*(2), 215–250. doi:10.1111/j.1540-5915.2007.00157.x

Moorthy, S., & Srinivasan, K. (1995). Signaling quality with a money-back guarantee: The role of transaction costs. *Marketing Science*, *14*(4), 442–466. doi:10.1287/mksc.14.4.442

Ofek, E., Katona, Z., & Sarvary, M. (2011). "Bricks and clicks": The impact of product returns on the strategies of multichannel retailers. *Marketing Science*, *30*(1), 42–60. doi:10.1287/mksc.1100.0588

Özkır, V., & Başlıgil, H. (2013). Multi-objective optimization of closed-loop supply chains in uncertain environment. *Journal of Cleaner Production*, *41*, 114–125. doi:10.1016/j.jclepro.2012.10.013

Petersen, J. A., & Kumar, V. (2009). Are product returns a necessary evil? Antecedents and consequences. *Journal of Marketing*, *73*(3), 35–51. doi:10.1509/jmkg.73.3.035

Petersen, J. A., & Kumar, V. (2010). Can product returns make you money? *MIT Sloan Management Review*, *51*(3), 85–89.

Piotrowicz, W., & Cuthbertson, R. (2014). Introduction to the special issue information technology in retail: Toward omnichannel retailing. *International Journal of Electronic Commerce*, *18*(4), 5–16. doi:10.2753/JEC1086-4415180400

Piron, F., & Young, M. (2000). Retail borrowing: Insights and implications on returning used merchandise. *International Journal of Retail & Distribution Management*, *28*(1), 27–36. doi:10.1108/09590550010306755

Piroth, P., Rüger-Muck, E., & Bruwer, J. (2020). Digitalisation in grocery retailing in Germany: An exploratory study. *International Review of Retail, Distribution and Consumer Research*, *30*(5), 479–497. doi:10.1080/09593969.2020.1738260

Powers, T. L., & Jack, E. P. (2015). Understanding the causes of retail product returns. *International Journal of Retail & Distribution Management*, *43*(12), 1182–1202. doi:10.1108/IJRDM-02-2014-0023

Pritchard, A. (1969). Statistical bibliography or bibliometrics. *The Journal of Documentation*, *25*(4), 348–349.

PSFK Research. (2020). *Building consumer confidence in retail's new virtual world*. https://www.psfk.com/2020/08/consumer-confidence-virtual-retail.html

Rao, S., Lee, K. B., Connelly, B., & Iyengar, D. (2018). Return time leniency in online retail: A signaling theory perspective on buying outcomes. *Decision Sciences*, *49*(2), 275–305. doi:10.1111/deci.12275

Rao, S., Rabinovich, E., & Raju, D. (2014). The role of physical distribution services as determinants of product returns in Internet retailing. *Journal of Operations Management*, *32*(6), 295–312. doi:10.1016/j.jom.2014.06.005

Robertson, T. S., Hamilton, R., & Jap, S. D. (2020). Many (un) happy Returns? The changing nature of retail product returns and future research directions. *Journal of Retailing*, *96*(2), 172–177. doi:10.1016/j.jretai.2020.04.001

Röllecke, F. J., Huchzermeier, A., & Schröder, D. (2018). Returning customers: The hidden strategic opportunity of returns management. *California Management Review*, *60*(2), 176–203. doi:10.1177/0008125617741125

Ryan, T. (2020). *Has COVID-19 exacerbated online return challenges?* https://www.retailwire.com/discussion/has-covid-19-exacerbated-online-return-challenges/

Saarijärvi, H., Sutinen, U. M., & Harris, L. C. (2017). Uncovering consumers' returning behaviour: A study of fashion e-commerce. *International Review of Retail, Distribution and Consumer Research*, *27*(3), 284–299. doi:10.1080/09593969.2017.1314863

Sahoo, N., Dellarocas, C., & Srinivasan, S. (2018). The impact of online product reviews on product returns. *Information Systems Research*, *29*(3), 723–738. doi:10.1287/isre.2017.0736

Schleiden, V., & Neiberger, C. (2020). Does sustainability matter? A structural equation model for cross-border online purchasing behaviour. *International Review of Retail, Distribution and Consumer Research, 30*(1), 46–67. doi:10.1080/09593969.2019.1635907

Seeger, M. K., Kemper, J., & Brettel, M. (2019). How information processing and mobile channel choice influence product returns: An empirical analysis. *Psychology and Marketing, 36*(3), 198–213. doi:10.1002/mar.21170

Shang, G., Ferguson, M. E., & Galbreth, M. R. (2019). Where should I focus my return reduction efforts? Empirical guidance for retailers. *Decision Sciences, 50*(4), 877–909. doi:10.1111/deci.12344

Shang, G., Pekgün, P., Ferguson, M., & Galbreth, M. (2017). How much do online consumers really value free product returns? Evidence from eBay. *Journal of Operations Management, 53*(1), 45–62. doi:10.1016/j.jom.2017.07.001

Shi, X., Dong, C., & Cheng, T. C. E. (2018). Does the buy-online-and-pick-up-in-store strategy with pre-orders benefit a retailer with the consideration of returns? *International Journal of Production Economics, 206*, 134–145. doi:10.1016/j.ijpe.2018.09.030

Shulman, J. D., Coughlan, A. T., & Savaskan, R. C. (2011). Managing consumer returns in a competitive environment. *Management Science, 57*(2), 347–362. doi:10.1287/mnsc.1100.1274

Smarter C. X. Team. (2020). *8 retail innovations reshaping your shopping experience.* https://smartercx.com/8-retail-innovations-reshaping-your-shopping-experience/

Sorkun, M. F. (2019). The impact of product variety on LSQ in e-marketplaces. *International Journal of Physical Distribution & Logistics Management, 49*(7), 749–766. doi:10.1108/IJPDLM-06-2018-0223

Sorkun, M. F., & Onay, M. (2018). The effects of companies' reverse logistics motivations on their reverse logistics networks. In H. Dinçer, Ü. Hacıoglu, & S. Yüksel (Eds.), *Strategic design and innovative thinking in business operations* (pp. 3–21). Springer. doi:10.1007/978-3-319-77622-4_1

Sorkun, M. F., Yumurtacı Hüseyinoğlu, I. Ö., & Börühan, G. (2020). Omni-channel capability and customer satisfaction: Mediating roles of flexibility and operational logistics service quality. *International Journal of Retail & Distribution Management, 48*(6), 629–648. doi:10.1108/IJRDM-07-2019-0235

Stock, J., Speh, T., & Shear, H. (2006). Managing product returns for competitive advantage. *MIT Sloan Management Review, 48*(1), 57–62.

Stock, J. R. (2001). Reverse logistics in the supply chain. *Revista Transport & Logistics*, 44-48.

Su, X. (2009). Consumer returns policies and supply chain performance. *Manufacturing & Service Operations Management, 11*(4), 595–612. doi:10.1287/msom.1080.0240

Suguna, M., Shah, B., Raj, S. K., & Suresh, M. (2021). *A study on the influential factors of the last mile delivery projects during Covid-19 era*. Operations Management Research., doi:10.100712063-021-00214-y

Swant, M. (2020). *From near death with chatbots to new life in e-commerce, Octane AI raises $4.25 million*. https://www.forbes.com/sites/martyswant/2020/08/21/from-celebrity-chatbots-to-new-life-in-e-commerce-octane-ai-raises-425-million/#540a3c474795

UPS. (2019). *UPS Pulse of the online shopper: A customer experience study*. https://solutions.ups.com/rs/935-KKE-240/images/UPS-Pulse-of-the-Online-Shopper-Report.pdf

Vakulenko, Y., Shams, P., Hellström, D., & Hjort, K. (2019). Online retail experience and customer satisfaction: The mediating role of last mile delivery. *International Review of Retail, Distribution and Consumer Research, 29*(3), 306–320. doi:10.1080/09593969.2019.1598466

Verhoef, P. C., Kannan, P. K., & Inman, J. J. (2015). From multi-channel retailing to omni-channel retailing: Introduction to the special issue on multi-channel retailing. *Journal of Retailing, 91*(2), 174–181. doi:10.1016/j.jretai.2015.02.005

Walsh, G., Albrecht, A. K., Kunz, W., & Hofacker, C. F. (2016). Relationship between online retailers' reputation and product returns. *British Journal of Management, 27*(1), 3–20. doi:10.1111/1467-8551.12120

Walsh, G., & Möhring, M. (2017). Effectiveness of product return-prevention instruments: Empirical evidence. *Electronic Markets, 27*(4), 341–350. doi:10.100712525-017-0259-0

Ward, D. (2020). *4 ways to reduce e-commerce returns during Covid-19*. https://www.threekit.com/blog/4-ways-to-reduce-ecomm-product-returns

Webster, T. (2020). *Covid-19: Policies and protocol for returns and exchanges*. https://downtownfrederick.org/wp-content/uploads/COVID-19-Policies-and-Protocol-for-Returns-and-Exchanges1.pdf

Wood, S. L. (2001). Remote purchase environments: The influence of return policy leniency on two-stage decision processes. *JMR, Journal of Marketing Research, 38*(2), 157–169. doi:10.1509/jmkr.38.2.157.18847

Yang, S., & Xiong, G. (2019). Try it on! Contingency effects of virtual fitting rooms. *Journal of Management Information Systems, 36*(3), 789–822. doi:10.1080/07421 222.2019.1628894

Yu, Y., & Kim, H. S. (2019). Online retailers' return policy and prefactual thinking: An exploratory study of USA and China e-commerce markets. *Journal of Fashion Marketing and Management, 23*(4), 504–518. doi:10.1108/JFMM-01-2019-0010

KEY TERMS AND DEFINITIONS

Commercial Product Returns: A type of return by consumers for any reason within a short time after their product purchase.

Omni-Channel: A distribution channel strategy that aims to fully integrate all distribution channels of retailers in the eyes of consumers, including both physical and digital channels.

Return Policy: The principles of retailers that guide their decisions on product returns, e.g., which items consumers can return or what the maximum allowable time is for return claims.

Reverse Logistics: A set of activities needed to process the consumer return claims, including the returned products' transportation, gatekeeping, repairing, reselling, etc.

Spatial Separation: A feature of online retailing implying that consumers cannot touch and feel products at the time of purchase because they are not within the same physical setting.

Strategic Returns: A type of returns by consumers with the aim of affording an advantage (e.g., free shipping, purchase discounts), not due to the logistics and product related problems.

Temporal Separation: A feature of online retailing implying that the purchase and delivery of products by consumers occur at different time points.

Chapter 6
Multicriteria Decision Support Model for Selection of Fiberglass Suppliers:
A Case Study in a Wind Industry Company

Celina Rodrigues
Polytechnic of Porto, Portugal

Ana Paula Lopes
https://orcid.org/0000-0003-1603-6959
Polytechnic of Porto, Portugal

EXECUTIVE SUMMARY

This chapter presents a real case of a decision problem in supplier selection of one of the main raw materials of a wind blades industry. The study considered all currently qualified suppliers according to considerably rigorous standards and specifications and one in qualification process. It is a complex choice, given the strategic importance of the product and the multiplicity of criteria to be considered, both quantitative and qualitative. The strong competitiveness requires a special attention which concerns the supplier selection; not only the price matters; in fact, a day of stoppage due to failure in a delivery, for example, corresponds to high losses that would have justified the purchase from a supplier with a higher price but with no delivery failures. In order to contribute to the problem resolution, the methodologies PROMETHEE and AHP were applied, whose results allow the authors to stablish a ranking of the considered suppliers. The results will support the company on the selection of fiberglass suppliers and in some cases clarify where they can find the main trade-offs.

DOI: 10.4018/978-1-7998-9140-6.ch006

INTRODUCTION

The literature is unanimous with regard to the growing importance of the purchasing process and the consequent selection of suppliers, as is the case of (de Boer, Labro, & Morlacchi, 2001) when they mention that with the increasing significance of the purchasing function, purchasing decisions become more important. As organisations become more dependent on suppliers the direct and indirect consequences of poor decisions making become more severe.

According to (Izadikhah, 2012) cited by (Azadfallah, 2017), the success of a supply chain is highly dependent on selection of good suppliers.

On (Katsikeas & Leonidou, 1996) perspective, international supplier selection is a complex decision-making problem. The complexity stems from a multitude of quantitative and qualitative factors influencing supplier choices as well as the intrinsic difficulty of making numerous trade- offs among these factors.

According to (Monczka et al., 1998), cited by (Chen, Lin, & Huang, 2006), the supplier selection problem has become one of the most important issues for establishing an effective supply chain system. The overall objective of supplier selection process is to reduce purchase risk, maximize overall value to the purchaser, and build the closeness and long- term relationships between buyers and suppliers. In fact, on the company herewith studied the invitation to one supplier to start the qualification process came from a long term relationship supplying similar material.

The impacts of this choice, according to (Dias, 2015) may spread from the specific purchasing area to other areas of the company, with a final impact on the profits obtained. According to (Çebi & Bayraktar, 2003) the supplier selection problem involves several criteria that conflict with each other. It is therefore important in decision making to consider as many criteria as possible, covering different perspectives, in order to make the choice sustained and informed.

With the COVID-19 pandemic, all of world's wind turbine and component factories are now open following the easing of restrictions across world. Sanitary measures are strengthened within sites to guarantee full compliance with government recommendations. Wind power installations in 2020 were down 30% compared to industry forecasts. It was also found that any continuous restriction on the movement of goods and people reduced activity and increased capital expenditures (CAPEX). Like many other manufacturing or service enterprises, supply chains in the wind sector will continue to be impacted in the months ahead. Some project milestones will be deferred, with impacts being felt throughout the whole value chain, whilst at the operational level; turbines, blades, component and material orders will be cancelled or unfulfilled (Eddie Rae, 2020). The biggest challenges for entities of any size is the dramatic reductions in revenue creation that have occurred and continue to occur. Unfortunately, in a business crisis, one of the first immediate solutions is to delay payments to creditors. You may be super-efficient in most aspects of your operations, have substantial reserves, long-term contracts, or access to deep corporate pockets or competitive financing, but sooner or later no cash generation equals no company.

The Wind Industry, as many others, with the globalization and the COVID-19 pandemic, faces high levels of competitiveness. To survive and get success, has now to play in a field much more sensitive and instable, everyday confronting other players fighting for the same.

In the company herewith studied, which is part of a multinational, the competitors are both inside and outside the group and located in many different geographies.

Despite the importance of the raw material price, which frequently have the main attention, each improvement, even small, in the supply chain, such as, lead times, transit times or supplier flexibility, has a positive impact in the company performance. For the most of decision makers it is easy to understand that a lack of material due a supply failure may have a huge impact in terms of stoppage costs, so, the roll of the supplier is much more than offer a good price.

One of the more 200 materials necessary in the production of wind blades is fiberglass. The fiberglass for this kind of product is very specific and subjected to tight quality criteria, and that is the main reason for not having many qualified suppliers all over the world. It turns out that this raw material is strategic as represents 20% of the Bill of Material (BOM) cost.

Figure 1. Bill of material cost distribution
(Source: own)

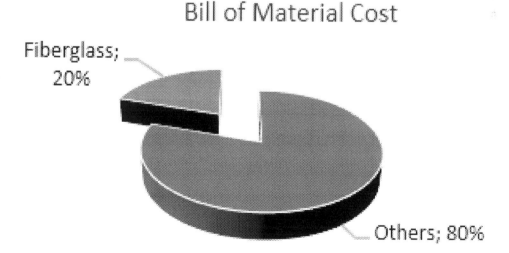

The company understands that despite the price and direct costs related with the purchasing, there are other factors that well managed, at the end of the day, will may represent different kind of savings. At a phases that the company is distributing the volume to five suppliers, the strategy is to select only two of them, the question is, which two have the best combination between the criteria which are considered more relevant. The company is clearly facing a challenge of a multicriteria decision in choosing the best suppliers, from one hand, suppliers with good price but located in the other side of the globe, and on the other, suppliers in the neighborhood but with higher prices. This combined with other criteria, such as lead time or quality makes this a traditional problem that can be supported by different Multicriteria Decision Analyses Methods.

For this case study, in order to support the decision-makers, two MCDA were applied, the PROMETHHE (Preference Ranking Organization Method for Enrichment Evaluation) and AHP (Analytic Hierarchy Process).

Both methods were often used in supporting Multicriteria Selection Analysis in many different areas including the supplier selection problematic.

MULTICRITERIA DECISION ANALYSIS

There are several methods with different approaches but with the same goal, to support multicriteria decision making problematic. To (Alves, 2018), the multicriteria decision analysis aim to be a support tool to analysts and decision makers in scenarios where is needed to identify priorities having multiple criteria and involving two or more alternatives.

Even according to the author, it is common to classify the methods in two groups, the ones developed by the American school, which aims to reduce the various criteria to a synthesis criterion, in most cases, through a weighted sum, from which the AHP, TODIM and MACBETH methods stand out, and those developed by the French school, based on prevalence relations as ELECTRE and PROMETHEE family methods.

In this case study, to support a traditional supplier selection, two methods will be applied, one from the American school AHP (Analytic Hierarchy Process) and other from the French one, the PROMETTHEE (Preference Ranking Organization Method for Enrichment Evaluation).

Both methods have been widely applied over time to support the problem of selecting suppliers, as they consider the decision-maker's perception in the model, which translates into results that are suitable with the strategic vision of each one.

METHODOLOGY

Criteria Definition

Studies over the years have addressed a variety of criteria that are important in seller selection. The major premise of these studies is that many organizations spend a considerable amount of time evaluating their supply chain partners by the fact the strategic importance of supplier selection (Bayazit, 2006).

The criteria in evaluation were the ones usually considered more relevant for the decision makers, according to their own perception of what should be considered for this kind of analysis. Same as been discussed with three decision makers from Finance, Production and Procurement departments.

Price: the unit measure of this criteria is kg, to make easier the calculations and comparison same has been treated by €/10 Kg. Refers to the cost that the company has to buy this material. It is obviously a quantitative criterion to be minimized.

Transport Cost: depending on the delivery conditions negotiated with the supplier (Incoterm), the transport can be at company responsibility or can be on supplier's side as well as the risk. As the price it will be represented by €/10Kg.

Duties: In the case that the supplier is based out of the UE, import duties may be applied by the TAX authorities depending on the country of origin. In certain cases, also antidumping rules are in the game.

Transit Time: as longer as the transit time is, and again depending on the delivery conditions, the company will have higher inventory costs and higher will be the risk of having delivery delays, is so a quantitative criterion to be minimized and will be presented in days.

Payment Terms: cash flow is highly dependent on the balance of payment/receiving conditions, as longer is the payment term as better, this will be a quantitative criterion to be maximized.

Lead Time: the lead time is the time occurred between the order placement and material reception. As lower the better, at it will give more flexibility to the supply chain in which concern the orders adjustments in terms of quantities and/or delivery dates.

Stock Days: material stopped at warehouse represent a cost, the inventory cost is an important KPI for the company and is reported in daily basis to the board. Beside the cost, the fiberglass is a voluminous material which occupies a considerable area, so the idea is to have the fiberglass stock as lower as possible.

Quality: this criterion is not about the material quality himself as this was already approved on the supplier qualification phasis. It´s mainly regarding the evaluation of supplier behavior in terms of accomplishment of deliveries, like time, quantity and right documentation. Not only the delay can be a reason for stoppage, wrong or incomplete shipping documents can be as well as can provoke retention at customs for days or weeks. It will be a qualitative criterion to be maximized.

Purchasing Complexity: purchasing decision maker considered that this criterion should be included in the study as they face some constraints with the purchasing process with some suppliers, losing more time to get confirmations and to have all the process clear. He preferred to keep it outside the quality criterion in order to be evaluated separately.

Flexibility: the production plan can have changes that have to be followed by adjustments to the materials orders, in order to anticipate or delays deliveries or even increase or decrease quantities. It is important to have suppliers which can be flexible on accepting as much as possible those changes without extra costs. It is so a criterion to be maximized.

Handling Complexity: this was a criterion raised by the production decision maker as he observed considerable deviations in terms of handling the fiberglass when it is coming from certain suppliers. From one side the transport system, truck or container, and from the other the way as the material is packed. The material goes through three handling processes: unloading from transport system; inbound picking and storage; picking for frontal feeding to cutting line.

Multicriteria Decision Methods

PROMETHEE: Preference Ranking Organization Method for Enrichment Evaluation

According to (J. P. Brans & De Smet, 2016) in order to build an appropriate multicriteria method some requisites could be considered:

Requisite 1: The amplitude of the deviations between the evaluations of the alternatives within each criterion should be taken into account:

$$d_j(a,b) = g_j(a) - g_j(b) \tag{1}$$

Requisite 2: As the evaluations $g_j(a)$ of each criterion are expressed in their own units, the scaling effects should be completely eliminated.

Requisite 3: In the case of pairwise comparisons, an appropriate multicriteria method should provide the following information:
- a is preferred to b;
- a and b are indifferent;
- a and b are incomparable

Requisite 4: Different multicriteria methods request different additional information and operate different calculation procedures so that the solutions they propose can be different. It is therefore important to develop methods being understandable by the decision-makers. "Black box" procedures should be avoided.

Requisite 5: An appropriate procedure should not include technical parameters having no significance for the decision-maker. Such parameters would again induce "Black box" effects.

Requisite 6: An appropriate method should provide information on the conflicting nature of the criteria.

Requisite 7: Most of the multicriteria methods are allocating weights of relative importance of the criteria. These weights reflect a major part of the "brain" of the decision-maker. It is not easy to fix them. Usually the decision-makers strongly hesitate. An appropriate method should offer sensitivity tools to test easily different sets of weight.

To the author the PROMETHEE methods and the associated GAIA visual interactive module are taking all these requisites into account.

PROMETHEE I (partial ranking) and PROMETHEE II (complete ranking) were developed by JP Brands and presented for the first time in 1982 at a conference organized by R. Nadeau and M. Landry at the Université Laval, Québec, Canada (L'Ingénierie de la Décision. Elaboration d'instruments d'Aide à la Décision) (Brans, Jean-Pierre, De Smet, 2017).

According to (Jalalvand, Teimoury, Makui, Aryanezhad, & Jolai, 2011), This methodology includes various types such as PROMETHEE I (partial ranking), PROMETHEE II (complete ranking) and PROMETHEE III (ranking based on intervals) applied in different conditions for different purposes.

The model considers some possible alternatives and evaluate them through pre-established criteria, prioritizing the most appropriate ones, enabling the management to gain an overview of the business and become able to make multifunctional decisions, with possible solution strategies to minimize losses in the system (Morais & Almeida, 2006).

In a most practical view, (Pinho & Lopes, 2020) explain that PROMETHEE method is based on the ordering of a finite set of actions, where a given weight is assigned to each criterion, taking into account its importance. Thus, preference is calculated by combining pairs of alternatives, considering the deviation between two alternatives in a single criterion.

The alternative pairwise comparison of PROMETHEE model requires that a preference function must be associated to each criterion.

The purpose of the preference function is to translate the difference observed between two actions on a given criterion, from the criterion scale to a normalized

0-1 degree of preference (Mareschal, 2018). The 0-1 preference degree presents the decision maker preference between the alternatives on each criteria; the higher the number, the greater the preference.

As stated, PROMETHEE is based on the pairwise comparison of the alternatives. According to (Mareschal, 2013) it means that the deviation between the evaluations of two actions on a particular criterion has first to be modelled. For small deviations, there will probably be either a weak preference or no preference at all for the best action as the decision-maker will consider this deviation as small or negligible. For larger deviations, larger preference levels are expected.

Means that, beside the weight assignment to the criteria, which is the information between criteria required to apply PROMETHEE method, the decision maker, the method goes deeper in the subconscious of the decision maker with the information within criteria which is modelled by the preference functions.

Figure 2. Type of preference functions (Brans e Smet, De, 2016)

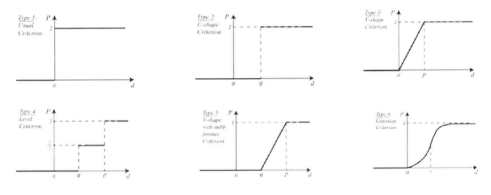

Depending on the chosen preference function, 0, 1 or 2 parameters have to be defined:

- q is a threshold or indifference;
- p is a threshold of strict preference;
- s is an intermediate value between q and p

The q indifference threshold is the largest deviation which is considered as negligible by the decision maker, while the p preference threshold is the smallest deviation which is considered as sufficient to generate a full preference (Brans, Jean-Pierre, De Smet, 2017).

To apply PROMETHEE method the first step is to compare each alternative with each other for all criteria.
So, given two alternatives *ai, aj*, we define the preference index as:

$$\pi(a_i, a_j) = \sum_{k=1}^{q} w_k P_k(a_i, a_j) \qquad (2)$$

where, w_k refers to the weight assigned to the criterion k and $P_k(a_i, a_j)$ refers to the value of the preference function according to the difference between the evaluation of the alternatives a_i and a_j on the criterion k, where

$$d_k(a_i, a_j) = g_k(a_i) - g_k(a_j) \qquad (3)$$

π(ai aj) to be calculated for all criteria and represents the intensity of preference of the decision maker of alternative *ai* over alternative *aj* when considering simultaneously all the criteria. It is a figure between "0" and "1" and

π(ai aj)=0 denotes a weak preference of "a1" over "a2" for all the criteria; and
π(ai aj)=1 denotes a strong preference of "a1" over "a2" for all the criteria (Anand & Kodali, 2008).

$$\sum_{k=1}^{n} w_k = 1 \qquad (4)$$

P_k - Preference function
If the criterion is to be maximized then

$$P_k(a_i, a_j) = F_k\left[d_k(a_i, a_j)\right] \forall a_i, a_j \in A \qquad (5)$$

where,

$$d_k(a_i, a_j) = g_k(a_i) - g_k(a_j) \qquad (3)$$

and for which,

$$0 \leq P_k(a_i, a_j) \leq 1 \qquad (6)$$

If the criterion is to be minimized, then

$$P_k(a_i, a_j) = F_k\left[-d_k(a_i, a_j)\right] \forall a_i, a_j \in A \tag{7}$$

Appling the methodology two indicators are used to evaluate the preference relationship between alternatives (Brans & Mareschal, 2005), those indicators are generated by the computation of the preference index $\pi(a_i a_j)$ and $\pi(a_j, a_i)$ or each pair of alternatives

- the positive preference flow ɸ+(a) measures how much an action a is preferred to the other n-1 ones. It is a global measurement of the strengths of action a. The larger ɸ+(a) the better the action

$$\Phi^+(a) = \frac{1}{n-1} \sum_{a_j \neq a_i} \pi(a_i, a_j) \tag{8}$$

- the negative preference flow ɸ⁻(a) measures how much the other n-1 actions are preferred to action a. It is a global measurement of the weaknesses of action a. The smaller ɸ⁻(a) the better the action.

$$\Phi^-(a) = \frac{1}{n-1} \sum_{a_j \neq a_i} \pi(a_j, a_i) \tag{9}$$

The net preference flow ɸ(a) is the balance between the positive and negative preference flows:

$$\Phi(a) = \Phi^+(a) - \Phi^-(a) \tag{10}$$

It thus takes into account and aggregates both the strengths and the weaknesses of the action into a single score. Φ(a) can be positive or negative.
The larger the Φ(a) better the action (Mareschal, 2013).
Thus, so, two rankings will be generated:

- **PROMETHEE I** – partial ranking, is obtained from the positive and the negative outranking flows.

In some cases partial ranking will not decide which alternative is the best, assigning that responsibility to the decision maker, that's why (Brans, Jean-Pierre, De Smet, 2017) consider that the PROMETHEE I ranking as prudent.

- **PROMETHEE II** – complete ranking, is the balance between the positive and the negative outranking flows. The higher the net flow, the better the alternative.

    An alternative a_i will be preferred to a_j if $\Phi(a_i) > \Phi(a_j)$
    An alternative a_i will be indifferent to a_j if $\Phi(a_i) = \Phi(a_j)$

According to (Brans, Jean-Pierre, De Smet, 2017), when PROMETHEE II is considered, all the alternatives are comparable. No incomparability remains, but the resulting information can be more disputable because more information gets lost by considering the difference (10).

Based on (Mareschal, 2013) the PROMETHEE GAIA is used to minimize the loss of information, starting from a multidimensional representation of the decision problem. The objective is to graphically describe the main characteristics of the decision problems, among other aspects, determining if the alternatives are different or similar from each other, which criteria conflict, what is the impact of the weighting assigned to the criteria in the ranking obtained.

AHP - Analytic Hierarchy Process

According to (Saaty, 1990) a decision is defined by a structure which represents the elements of the problem: a goal, criteria, sub criteria and alternatives (options) and a set of judgements to establish relationships among them. The aim is to derive a scale of relative importance for the alternatives.

Developed by Thomas L. Saaty in the 1970s, the AHP, Analytic Hierarchy Process, uses hierarchy structures, matrices and linear algebra to formalize the decision process.

The method was built on three principles: the principle of constructing hierarchies, the principle of establishing priorities, and the principle of logical consistency (Badri & Abdulla, 2004).

AHP has been a popular approach for supplier selection and has been used in a wide variety of situations by a number of researchers (Perçin, 2006). According to (Levary, 2007), one advantage of the AHP is that forces the user to systematically and carefully evaluate the importance of each criterion in relation to the others in a hierarchical manner.

On supplier selection, with AHP the buyer is only required to give verbal, qualitative statements regarding the relative importance of one criterion versus another criterion and similarly regarding the relative preference for one supplier versus another on a criterion. (de Boer et al., 2001).

Pairwise comparisons were formulated to include all the combinations of criteria/sub-criteria/alternatives relationships. The decision-team compared the criteria and sub-criteria by assigning corresponding numerical values based on the relative importance of alternatives under consideration to their parent element in the decision hierarchy. Each supplier selection criteria have first been compared against other criteria (Perçin, 2006).

For the methodology application according to (T. L. Saaty, 1980) cited by (Pinho & Lopes, 2020) in the elaboration of the square matrices or decision matrices, where i represents the line number of the matrix, j the columns and a ij represents the comparison between criteria and alternatives A_i and A_j, the following rules must be respected:

$$A = \begin{bmatrix} a_{11} & \cdots & a_{1n} \\ \vdots & \ddots & \vdots \\ a_{n1} & \cdots & a_{nn} \end{bmatrix}$$

where, $a_{ij} = \dfrac{1}{a_{ji}}$ so, if $a_{ij}=k$ then $a_{ji} = \dfrac{1}{k}$ for all $k>0$ and $a_{ii}=1$ for all i - mean that in the fundamental scale each criterion or alternative compared to itself assumes equal importance.

The main principle of filling in the matrix is simple because an expert should indicate how much more important is a particular criterion than another. Saaty suggested a widely known 5-point scale (1-3-5-7-9) (Podvezko, 2009), known as the fundamental scale of Saaty (Table 1).

Table 1. Fundamental scale of Saaty (source:adapted from (Saaty, 1990))

Importance	Defenition	Explanation
1	Equal importance	Two atributes contribute identically to the objective
3	Moderate importance of one over the other	Experience and judgement slightly favors one attribute over another
5	Strong or essential importance	Experience and judgement strongly favors one attribute over another
7	Demosntrated dominance	An attribute's dominance is demosntrated in practice
9	Exrtreme dominance	The evidence favoring na attribute over another is affirmed to the highest possible
2,4,6,8	Intemediate values	Further subdivision or compromise is needed

The second step, in order to obtain the relative weights, the matrix has to be normalized and will be defined by

$$A' = \left[a'_{ij} \right]$$

Where $a'_{ij} = \dfrac{a_{ij}}{\sum_{k=1}^{n} a_{ik}}$ for $1 \leq i \leq n$ and $1 \leq j \leq n$

Once the matrix is normalized in each line is calculated the average value $W=[w_k]$ where,

$$w_k = \dfrac{\sum_{k=1}^{n} a'_{ij}}{n}$$ for $1 \leq i \leq n$, and $1 \leq j \leq n$

However, on the comparison process some inconsistency can be generated, especially when the problem has a considerable number of criteria.

In order to verify whether the evaluations were consistent or not, it is necessary to calculate the Consistency Ratio (*CR*) which correlates the Consistency Index (*CI*) with the Random Consistency Index (*RI*), and is given by the following expression:

$$CR = \dfrac{CI}{RI} \qquad (11)$$

The Consistency Index (*CI*) is obtained by the following formula (Saaty, 1990),

$$CI = \frac{\lambda_{max} - n}{n-1} \qquad (12)$$

and the values for the Random Consistency Index are obtained from Table 2.

Table 2. The RI values

Matrix size	1	2	3	4	5	6	7	8	9	10	11
RI	0	0	0,58	0,90	1,12	1,24	1,32	1,41	1,45	1,49	1,51

(adapted from (Podvezko, 2009))

According to (Saaty, 1990), the value of CR, to indicate consistency, can take as maximum value 10%.

RESULTS AND DISCUSSION

All the quantitative data were collected accessing the informatics system of the company. The qualitative ones were discussed in formal and informal meetings with different work streams used to deal with the material in daily bases.

The alternatives were indicated by purchasing and planning departments and the criterion, as previously mentioned were discussed with financial, production and procurement departments.

Application of AHP

For the methodology application the structure of *Figure 3* was considered.

The comparison of the 11 criteria was done using the fundamental scale of Saaty in order to establish the relative importance of each criterion. The matrix was normalized doing the sum of the rows and dividing the result for each matrix element.

Figure 3. Problem structure
(source: own)

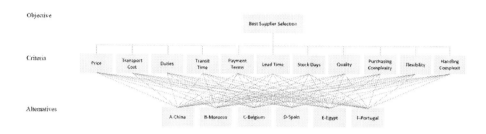

Table 3. Matrix normalized

Matrix size	1	2	3	4	5	6	7	8	9	10	11
RI	0	0	0,58	0,90	1,12	1,24	1,32	1,41	1,45	1,49	1,51

(Source: own)

According to the evaluation of the decision makers, the "Price" came as the criteria with the higher weight assigned, 25%, followed by "Transport cost" and "Duties" with the same importance, 19%, it is no surprise since the decision maker come from the financial department and obviously more focused on direct costs, the ones that he can easily percept. The "Stock days", the daily followed KPI, obtain the third place, 10%, and again the finance perspective it's clearly given the influence to this important criterion for the company.

Due the considerable number of criteria, inconsistency was expected, however it has not happened.

The consistency was calculated, manually and double checked using an online calculator on both obtaining a Consistency Ratio CR < 10 which represents the consistency of the comparisons.

In the case of the criterion comparison the CR was 7,94% which is more that acceptable.

The same procedure using the fundamental scale of Saaty was apply for the Alternatives on each criterion individually, all with CRs < 10. On this exercise some calculations were previously done to make easier the comparisons for the decision maker, again, showing the real differences of the values, was easier to apply the Satty scale.

"Purchasing complexity", "Flexibility" and "Handling complexity" were the criterion with the horst score, with the last one in the bottom of the evaluation. Actually, even understanding the impact on the cycle time, it's difficult to measure them and convert in cost, and when compared in a set of so many criteria it comes natural to be undervalued.

Finally, the weights obtained for the alternatives in each criterion will be weighted by the ones obtained for the criterion,

In order to obtain a ranking of the best suppliers, we calculate the weighted average of these parcels, which will allow to find the final value of importance of each supplier and establish priorities. *Table 4* presents a summary table with the global ranking obtained with "D-Spain" on the top of the ranking.

Table 4. Ranking

Matrix Normalized	Price Avg	Transport cost	Duties	Transit time	Payment terms	Lead time	Stock days	Quality	Purchsing complexity	Flexibility	Handling complexity	w*
Price Avg	0,30	0,37	0,37	0,18	0,22	0,21	0,27	0,24	0,19	0,18	0,17	24,7%
Transport cost	0,15	0,19	0,19	0,16	0,22	0,16	0,27	0,24	0,19	0,18	0,17	19,3%
Duties	0,15	0,19	0,19	0,16	0,22	0,21	0,27	0,24	0,17	0,16	0,15	19,0%
Transit time	0,04	0,03	0,03	0,02	0,01	0,01	0,02	0,01	0,01	0,01	0,04	2,1%
Payment terms	0,04	0,03	0,03	0,07	0,03	0,08	0,02	0,02	0,07	0,08	0,07	4,8%
Lead time	0,06	0,05	0,04	0,07	0,02	0,04	0,02	0,02	0,07	0,08	0,09	5,0%
Stock days	0,08	0,05	0,05	0,09	0,09	0,12	0,07	0,15	0,12	0,13	0,11	9,5%
Quality	0,06	0,04	0,04	0,11	0,09	0,12	0,02	0,05	0,12	0,08	0,11	7,7%
Purchsing complexity	0,04	0,02	0,03	0,05	0,09	0,01	0,01	0,01	0,02	0,05	0,04	3,5%
Flexibility	0,04	0,03	0,03	0,07	0,01	0,03	0,01	0,02	0,01	0,03	0,02	2,6%
Handling complexity	0,04	0,02	0,03	0,01	0,01	0,01	0,01	0,01	0,01	0,03	0,02	1,8%
Sum	1,00	1,00	1,00	1,00	1,00	1,00	1,00	1,00	1,00	1,00	1,00	100%

(Source: own)

"F-Portugal" was the second best classified alternative, very close to "B-Morocco". "E-Egypt" and "C-Belgium" obtain very similar results, and finally "A-China" was the alternative with the lower classification.

Application of PROMETHEE

The *Figure 4* shows the representation on Visual PROMETHEE software that was used to support the PROMETHEE Method where 6 alternatives have been considered and evaluated in 11 criteria chosen by de decision makers.

A weight was assigned to each criterion according to the relative importance that the financial manager perception. Independently of camming from finance is a decision maker very involved with all the company areas and with a global overview of the company.

Figure 4. Visual PROMETHEE software interface
(source: Visual PROMETHEE)

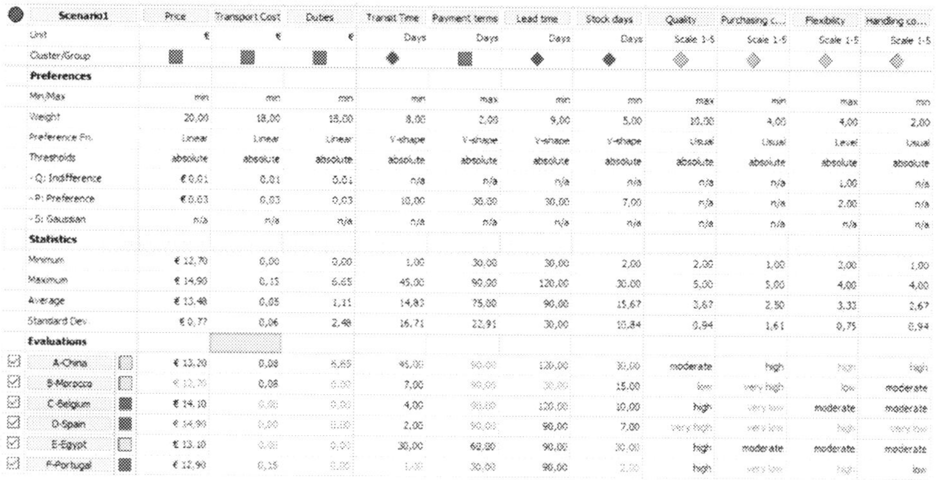

Scenario1	Price	Transport Cost	Duties	Transit Time	Payment terms	Lead time	Stock days	Quality	Purchasing c...	Flexibility	Handling co...
Unit	€	€	€	Days	Days	Days	Days	Scale 1-5	Scale 1-5	Scale 1-5	Scale 1-5
Cluster/Group											
Preferences											
Min/Max	min	min	min	min	max	min	min	max	min	max	min
Weight	20,00	18,00	15,00	8,00	2,00	9,00	5,00	10,00	4,00	4,00	2,00
Preference Fn.	Linear	Linear	Linear	V-shape	V-shape	V-shape	V-shape	Usual	Usual	Level	Usual
Thresholds	absolute	absolute	absolute	absolute	absolute	absolute	absolute	absolute	absolute	absolute	absolute
- Q: Indifference	€ 0,01	0,01	0,01	n/a	n/a	n/a	n/a	n/a	n/a	1,00	n/a
- P: Preference	€ 0,03	0,03	0,03	10,00	30,00	30,00	7,00	n/a	n/a	2,00	n/a
- S: Gaussian	n/a	n/a	n/a	n/a	n/a	n/a	n/a	n/a	n/a	n/a	n/a
Statistics											
Minimum	€ 12,70	0,00	0,00	1,00	30,00	30,00	2,00	2,00	1,00	2,00	1,00
Maximum	€ 14,90	0,15	6,65	45,00	90,00	120,00	30,00	5,00	5,00	4,00	4,00
Average	€ 13,48	0,05	1,11	14,83	75,00	90,00	15,67	3,67	2,50	3,33	2,67
Standard Dev.	€ 0,77	0,06	2,48	16,71	22,91	30,00	10,84	0,94	1,61	0,75	0,94
Evaluations											
A-China	€ 13,20	0,08	6,65	45,00	90,00	120,00	30,00	moderate	high	high	high
B-Morocco	€ 12,70	0,08	0,00	7,00	90,00	30,00	15,00	low	very high	low	moderate
C-Belgium	€ 14,10	0,00	0,00	4,00	90,00	120,00	10,00	high	very low	moderate	moderate
D-Spain	€ 14,90	0,00	0,00	2,00	90,00	90,00	7,00	very high	very low	high	very low
E-Egypt	€ 13,10	0,00	0,00	30,00	60,00	90,00	30,00	high	moderate	moderate	moderate
F-Portugal	€ 12,90	0,15	0,00	1,00	30,00	90,00	2,00	high	very low	high	low

The preference functions were chose taking in account the type of criteria and the range of the evaluation.

In a first approach it was difficult for the decision maker to decide some of the thresholds, to make the task easier, some calculations with different values were done, in order to give him the real impact in the BOM cost for small variations of the criteria value. Before the simulations he was not comfortable about what to define in order to generate preference or indifference, even understanding the importance of that for the model, instead showing him the real impact on BOM it came very easy to establish those thresholds.

PROMETHEE Rankings

As stated, the PROMETHEE II Complete Ranking (*Figure 5*) is based on the net preference flow (Phi) (Mareschal, 2013).

Multicriteria Decision Support Model for Selection of Fiberglass Suppliers

From the complete ranking of PROMETHEE II, where no incomparability remains, the upper half of the scale (green) corresponds to a positive Phi score and the bottom half (red) to negative score. Therefore, "D-Spain" is above all suppliers, which means that is the best option, followed by "F-Portugal", E-Egypt, B-Morroco, "C-Belgium" and finally with a considerable distance from the other options, "A-China" is the worst.

Figure 5. Complete ranking
(source: Visual PROMETHEE)

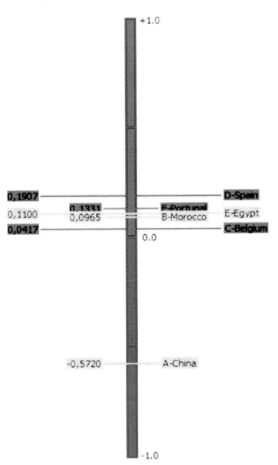

On the PROMETHEE Flow Table (*Figure 6*) we can see Phi, Phi+, Phi- score. Suppliers are ordered by PROMETHEE II complete ranking. The positive flow expresses how much an alternative is dominating the other ones, and the negative flow how much it is dominated by the other ones.

Multicriteria Decision Support Model for Selection of Fiberglass Suppliers

Hereupon the alternative with the larger Φ^+ is "B-Morocco" but the one with smaller Φ^- is "D-Spain" which is as well the one with the higher $\Phi(a)$ and so the best alternative according to PROMETHEE II.

The fact that alternative "B-Morocco" has a better Φ^+ but a horst Φ^- when compared to Spain, means that they may be incomparable. Same occurs between "B-Morocco" and "F-Portugal" and between "B-Morocco" and "C-Belgium". The result gives no doubts about the low performance of A-China, appearing with the worst Φ^+ and Φ^- presented.

Figure 6. PROMETHEE flow table
(source: Visual PROMETHEE)

Rank	action	Phi	Phi+	Phi-
1	D-Spain	0,1907	0,4175	0,2267
2	F-Portugal	0,1331	0,4151	0,2820
3	E-Egypt	0,1100	0,3800	0,2700
4	B-Morocco	0,0965	0,4260	0,3295
5	C-Belgium	0,0417	0,3239	0,2823
6	A-China	-0,5720	0,1600	0,7320

PROMETHEE Network

On The PROMETHEE Network (*Figure 7*) the alternatives (suppliers) are represented by nodes and arrows are drawn to indicate preferences. PROMETHEE Network which presents PROMETHEE I partial ranking. "D-Spain" is significantly preferred to other suppliers.

Figure 7. PROMETHEE network
(source: Visual PROMETHEE)

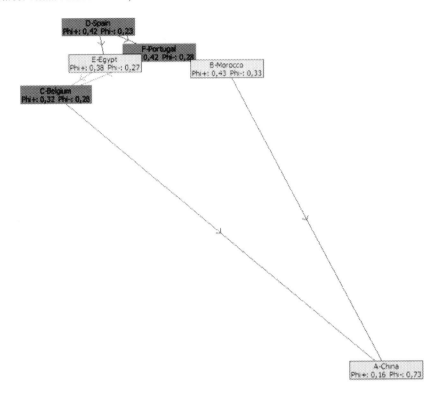

With this graphical representation the similarity between alternatives is easy to detect, for instance "F-Portugal" and "E-Egypt" are very close to each other showing their similarity, in the other hand it is possible to observe that "B-Morroco" is only comparable with "A-China". In fact, "A-China" is completely overstepped from all the other alternatives.

GAIA Plane

On the GAIA Plane (*Figure 8*), the alternatives (suppliers) are represented by points, the criteria are represented by axes, whose length indicates their importance in the problem.

Multicriteria Decision Support Model for Selection of Fiberglass Suppliers

Figure 8. GAIA plane
(source: Visual PROMETHEE)

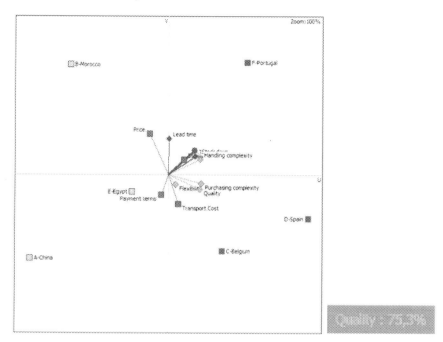

Clearly, we can observe that the "Price" is the criterion with the longer length.

Criteria expressing conflicting (opposite) preferences are represented by axes oriented in opposite directions. That is the case of "Price" and "Transport cost".

The position of the criteria indicates the similarity or conflict between them: the smaller the angle, the more similar two criteria are.

The angle between "Stock days" and "Transit time" is very small, showing their similarity, as long the transit time is, as much stock days the company has to cover.

Alternatives located near (far) have similar (dissimilar) performances; that is the case of "D-Spain" and "C-Belgium".

The 2D GAIA analysis presented on *Figure 8* is considered reliable when the quality level is above or close to 70%, which is the case as we got a result of 75,3%.

PROMETHEE Rainbow

The PROMETHEE Rainbow (*Figure 9*) is a disaggregated view of the PROMETHEE II complete ranking (Mareschal, 2013). It is a very easy way to understand how and how much each criterion is contributing for the alternative score.

Positive (upward) slices correspond to good features while negative (downward) slices correspond to weaknesses. This way, the balance between positive and negative slices is equal to the Phi score. Actions are ranked from left to right according to the PROMETHEE II Complete Ranking (Mareschal, 2013).

Figure 9. PROMETHEE rainbow
(source: Visual PROMETHEE)

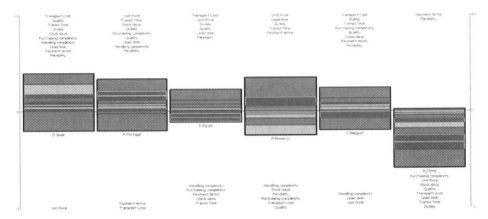

The alternative "D-Spain", the one on the top of the complete ranking only has the "Price" giving a negative contribute to the alternative but is also the one with the bigger slice, meaning that not even is the one with more negative contribute but as well the one with more intensity. All the remaining criteria have a positive contribution to this alternative with "Transport cost" and "Quality" with the best contributes.

"F-Portugal", the second on the Phi classification, has two criteria on which the contribution is negative, "Payment Terms" and "Transport Cost", this one with a big negative impact.

If no major differences between the slices on one alternative, that means that this is an average alternative, and that's the case of "C-Belgium" and "E-Egypt".

Walking Weights

It is clear, that PROMETHEE II is influenced by weights allocated to the criteria, thus it is essential to know how the ranking changes when the weights change. Thus, using a special feature of the software called "Walking Weights" (*Figure 10*), a sensitivity analysis is carried out to verify how sensitive the results are when the weights change.

Figure 10. Walking weights
(source: Visual PROMETHEE)

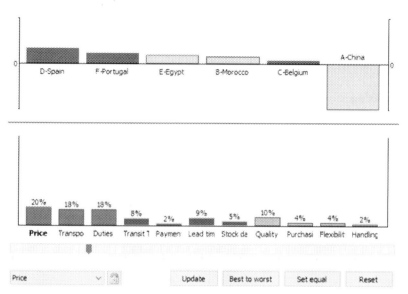

The walking weights feature of the Visual PROMETHEE software allows the weights of a particular criterion to be increased while proportionately decreasing the weights of the other criteria and see the impact on the Visual PROMETHEE analysis. Is especially useful when two alternatives are very closed to each other and in a simple and easy way, adjusting the weight of one criterion we can immediately observe the behaviour of the alternatives.

If, for instance we modify weights of the criterion "Price", increase the weight assigned to the criterion in 10%, from this analysis, it is clear that "D-Spain" will no longer be the best choice but "B-Morocco" (*Figure 11*), which means that most of the criteria (and their weights) have influence in the final ranking.

Therefore, changing the weights to the criteria allows us to simulate different scenarios, allowing us to quickly observe whether the ranking is changed or not.

Figure 11. Walking weights
(source: Visual PROMETHEE)

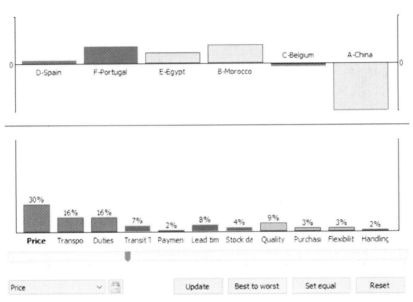

The walking weights can be used to interactively modify the weights of the criteria and immediately see the impact of the modification on the PROMETHEE II complete ranking and on the position of the decision axis in the GAIA plane. This can particularly useful when the decision-maker has no clear idea of the appropriate weighting of the criteria and wants to explore his space of freedom (J.-P. Brans & Mareschal, 2005).

CONCLUSION

With the application of both methods, we could establish a ranking of the suppliers, despite the differences between the two methodologies, especially on the way as the decision maker is invited to make the comparisons, the results are very similar, with the alternative "D-Spain" on the top of the ranking.

There is no objection on assuming that the way as weights were assigned, both in PROMETHEE method and AHP, was strongly influenced by the fact that the decision maker is from financial department and so more sensitive to criteria related with direct cost.

All the PROMETHEE and GAIA computations take place in real-time and any data modification is immediately reflected in the output windows. The PROMETHEE rankings, action profiles and GAIA are displayed in separate windows and can easily be compared. In which concerns PROMETHEE, the weight assignment was quite simple for the decision maker, the main difficulty was faced defining the preference function thresholds, to support on that, same calculations were made to give the impact on the BOM for some variations, with this exercise it came much easier to understand for each difference he considered important to prefer an alternative over the other or to up which value no preference should be generated.

The first interesting fact is that on both methods the supplier with higher evaluation was the one with the higher price, that shows that, even not directly realizing, the decision maker has token in account the relative importance of other criteria.

Making a comparison between the weight directly assigned by the decision maker when applying PROMETHEE method and the ones calculated trough AHP methodology, it was interesting to observe that they are very similar, especially the ones related with direct costs, actually, was on the ones which are not so familiar to the decision maker where we found some discrepancies.

Although, the decision maker was surprised with the results, due the fact that the alternative on the top of the ranking is actually the one with the higher price, despite being the criteria with the higher weight assigned, for sure that there was not transport costs or duties applied to this alternative, however, even so, if we due the sum of all the direct costs, "D-Spain" will be the alternative with the second higher value, so it was expected no to be the one on the top, but actually it was. The rainbow from Visual PROMETHEE is a good tool to understand why, the price was the only one with negative contribute and the positive contribute of all the other criteria were more than enough to compensate that, actually, during the interviews with the different work streams this alternative always had the best impression in terms of performance; no delivery failures, easy to handle, right documents, etc. Even with AHP, where the decision maker is given the preferences comparing criteria and alternatives by pairwaising, a more subjective way to assign weights, the result came the same with supplier D-Spain on the top as the best option.

As explained, the goal was to have 2 suppliers selected, and in both methods "F-Portugal" came in the second position on the ranking, with only two criteria not favourable, appears to be the second choice, however, the qualification is not yet completed, and despite that there's always a chance, even small, of not be qualified, in that case, the company will face a new challenge as the alternatives in third and four position are very close to each other and must be considered not comparable, they are average alternatives and it's difficult to understand which is the better.

The Gaia Plane, as the Rainbow, may support the new problematic, has it is easier to see where the straight and weaknesses are, as well as the walking weight with the simulation tool, moving the weight bar and "playing" with the weight distribution it's easy to identify the trade-offs and see how the alternatives behave.

A new element came during this study related with supplier "B-Morocco" which can suffer a change at medium term due an inquiry raised by the European Union to the fiberglass coming from Morocco due suspicion of anti-trust rules violation, if it is confirmed, antidumping rate will be applied, and this alternative will follow down in the ranking.

In that case the second supplier selected by PROMETHEE will be Egypt.

With Visual PROMETHEE the decision makers will have the opportunity to any time change or adjust the data in the software and run it again.

REFERENCES

Alves, M. A. (2018). *Proposta de Agregação Robusta de Múltiplos Métodos com Incertezas em Problemas de Tomada de Decisão Multicritério*. Academic Press.

Anand, G., & Kodali, R. (2008). Selection of lean manufacturing systems using the PROMETHEE. *Journal of Modelling in Management, 3*(1), 40–70. doi:10.1108/17465660810860372

Azadfallah, M. (2017). Evaluation and selection of suppliers in the supply chain using the extended group PROMETHEE I procedures. *International Journal of Supply Chain and Operations Resilience, 3*(1), 56. doi:10.1504/IJSCOR.2017.087161

Badri, M. A., & Abdulla, M. H. (2004). Awards of excellence in institutions of higher education: An AHP approach. *International Journal of Educational Management, 18*(4), 224–242. doi:10.1108/09513540410538813

Bayazit, O. (2006). Use of analytic network process in vendor selection decisions. *Benchmarking, 13*(5), 566–579. doi:10.1108/14635770610690410

Brans, J-P., & De Smet, Y. (2017). *PROMETHEE methods* (Vol. 3). doi:10.1007/978-1-4939-3094-4

Brans, J. P., & De Smet, Y. (2016). *PROMETHEE methods* (Vol. 233). International Series in Operations Research and Management Science. doi:10.1007/978-1-4939-3094-4_6

Brans, J.-P., & Mareschal, B. (2005). PROMETHEE methods. In *Multiple criteria decision analysis: state of the art surveys*. Springer. doi:10.1007/0-387-23081-5_5

Çebi, F., & Bayraktar, D. (2003). An integrated approach for supplier selection. *Logistics Information Management, 16*(6), 395–400. doi:10.1108/09576050310503376

Chen, C. T., Lin, C. T., & Huang, S. F. (2006). A fuzzy approach for supplier evaluation and selection in supply chain management. *International Journal of Production Economics*, *102*(2), 289–301. doi:10.1016/j.ijpe.2005.03.009

de Boer, L., Labro, E., & Morlacchi, P. (2001). A review of methods supporting supplier selection. *European Journal of Purchasing and Supply Management*, *7*(2), 75–89. doi:10.1016/S0969-7012(00)00028-9

Dias, E. M. P. da S. (2015). *Modelo de apoio à decisão multicritério para selecção de fornecedores de azeite*. Faculdade de Economia do Porto.

Jalalvand, F., Teimoury, E., Makui, A., Aryanezhad, M. B., & Jolai, F. (2011). A method to compare supply chains of an industry. *Supply Chain Management*, *16*(2), 82–97. doi:10.1108/13598541111115347

Katsikeas, C. S., & Leonidou, L. C. (1996). International Supplier Selection. *Journal of Global Marketing*, *9*(3), 23–45. doi:10.1300/J042v09n03_03

Levary, R. R. (2007). Ranking foreign suppliers based on supply risk. *Supply Chain Management*, *12*(6), 392–394. doi:10.1108/13598540710826317

Mareschal, B. (2013). *Visual PROMETHEE manual*. Academic Press.

Mareschal, B. (2018). *Preference functions and thresholds*. Academic Press.

Morais, D. C., & de Almeida, A. T. (2006). Modelo de decisão em grupo para gerenciar perdas de água. *Pesquisa Operacional*, *26*(3), 567–584. doi:10.1590/S0101-74382006000300007

Perçin, S. (2006). An application of the integrated AHP-PGP model in supplier selection. *Measuring Business Excellence*, *10*(4), 34–49. doi:10.1108/13683040610719263

Pinho, R. R., & Lopes, A. P. (2020). *Multicriteria Decision Support Model for Selection of Tinplate Suppliers*. doi:10.4018/978-1-7998-2216-5.ch006

Podvezko, V. (2009). Application of AHP technique. *Journal of Business Economics and Management*, *10*(2), 181–189. doi:10.3846/1611-1699.2009.10.181-189

Rae, E. (2020). *COVID-19 and impacts on global wind supply chain*. Retrieved from https://gwec.net/covid-19-and-impacts-on-global-wind-supply-chains/

Saaty, T. L. (1990). The analytic hierarchy process in conflict management. *International Journal of Conflict Management*, *1*(1), 47–68. doi:10.1108/eb022672

Chapter 7
Practice of Green Supply Chain Management and Organization Performance in the Manufacturing Industries of the Kathmandu Valley

Seeprata Parajuli
Research Management Cell, Quest International College, Pokhara University, Nepal

Ruby Shrestha
Quest International College, Pokhara University, Nepal

Niranjan Devkota
https://orcid.org/0000-0001-9989-0397
Research Management Cell, Quest International College, Pokhara University, Nepal

Sashi Rana Magar
Quest International College, Pokhara University, Nepal

Sharad Rajbhandari
Quest International College, Pokhara University, Nepal

Udaya Raj Poudel
Quest International College, Pokhara University, Nepal

EXECUTIVE SUMMARY

This chapter aims to analyze the practice of green supply chain management and organization performance in manufacturing industries of Kathmandu valley. This study uses descriptive research design. Two hundred and seven manufacturing industries in three industrial estates (Balaju, Bhaktapur, and Patan) of Kathmandu valley were taken as a sample for the study whereas all 245 operating industries were the population of the study. The findings revealed that 33.3% of industries are

DOI: 10.4018/978-1-7998-9140-6.ch007

Copyright © 2022, IGI Global. Copying or distributing in print or electronic forms without written permission of IGI Global is prohibited.

highly practicing green supply management chain whereas 23.7% and 19.6% are practicing it moderately and less, respectively. It was found that industries of all scale—large, medium, and low—are equally practicing green supply management chain to a greater extent. Thus, the study concludes that manufacturing industries ought to consider the systemic interaction between the internal and external facets of the application of the GSCM and to ensure that their respective operations are integrated in order to achieve improved environmental and organizational efficiency and consequently to achieve economic benefits.

INTRODUCTION

In today's world, environmental issues and the preservation of human life are more crucial than ever (Harper & Snowden, 2017). The main goals of a company's green management are the aspects in which businesses carry out operations that have no adverse effect on the local or world economy (Skibińska & Kott, 2015). Global warming and climate change are the major issues in the present world faced by humanity, caused by the various business activities such as huge energy generation and consumption, exploiting natural resources, disposal of toxic waste (Hernandez & Ona, 2015). Therefore, the concept of green management has arouse in order to cope with emerging business problems due to environmental issues (Rostamzadeh, Govindan, Esmaeili, & Sabaghi, 2015).

Likewise, supply chain is a channel of all actors (e.g. producer, maker, seller, wholesaler, consumer, client, etc.) directly or indirectly involved in the production and transfer of products or services to ultimate consumers, on both the upstream and downstream sides, through physical storage, information exchange and finance (Chin, Tat, & Sulaiman, 2015). Green supply chain management (GSCM) can be viewed as an alternative to this management theory, incorporating certain aspects of the supply chain that are seen as a truly ethical and inclusive method for organizations or also integrating environmental thinking to supply chain management (Rostamzadeh et al., 2015). Nowadays many organizations has initiated the agenda of green supply chain management as it motivates the managers to gain the potential benefits that they can achieve by implementing green practice.

Nepal, being a mountainous, forest-rich, least developed, landlocked country with political, social and economic changes and complexities, conspicuous social and gender disparities, increasing climate change and lack of good governance for which there are no strong or consistent hopes of a transition into a green economy at both national and local level (Karki, 2014). Most of the business organization in Nepal does not have a special person working with green issues, and many of them aren't conscious. Many manufacturing industries in Nepal even do not have particular team responsible for environmental issues and local industries only considers green issues in choosing the suppliers. The fact that Nepal is a small country, implementing such green practices and strategies is bit slow (Shrestha, 2017).

The nature of the economy and resource endowment plus existing geo-sociopolitical reality of Nepal demands green economy or green growth channel to explore inclusive and sustainable development intervention ahead (Bhuju, Thapaparajuli, Sharma, & Aryal, 2014). Talking about energy aspect, Nepal acquires a lot of hydropower potential but due to many problems it has not been able to use even its renewable energy as solar power. Promoting the use of renewable energy and demotivating them to use fossil fuel by the help of right policies, Nepal can contribute to the green economy by enhancing its alternate energy sector. Hence, further study seems to be required in the area. Thus, this research aims to analyze practice of green supply chain management and organizational practices in manufacturing industries of Kathmadu valley.

This study is further categorized into five sections. Second section includes review of literature whereas, third section includes methodology followed by result and discussion in fourth section and fifth section finally concludes the study.

LITERATURE REVIEW

Industries all around the world are seeking to apply green practices not just in their manufacturing processes, but also in their supply chains to reduce environmental effect (Sujatha & Kathikeyan, 2021). Green management is today's buzz word specially in business organizations (Ahmad, 2015) and supply chain is the process involved in manufacturing from acquiring raw materials to generating final product (Bhool & Narwal, 2013). Environmental issues and resource depletion have caused hurdles in the operation as well as regulation of the business enterprises (Zhu, Geng, Fujita, & Hashimoto, 2010; Zhu, Sarkis, & Lai, 2012). The rigorous attempt is shown by the government and organizations to reduce the impact of business activities on the environment worldwide. By bringing change in the whole supply chain activities, any of the major greening projects happening today will be successful. It is quite sad that, very few studies or researches have mentioned the issue of considering the green supply chain. We should be aware that considering the coordination among manufacturer and retailer in a supply chain for 'greening' their operations are important (Chin et al., 2015; Swami & Shah, 2013).

In order to obtain competitive advantage, business organizations are adopting variety of sustainability initiatives. Environmental sustainability application in the supply chain is considered as green supply chain management (GSCM). But the literature in this sector is not widely developed and GSCM practices are not understood well (Hazen, Cegielski, & Hanna, 2011). According (Swami & Shah, 2013), there are several benefits of GSCM such as mitigating risks and accelerating innovation, increased adaptability, promotes cooperation with suppliers and consumers which contributes to a better business process and values. Green et al. (2012) stated that practice of chain management in manufacturing industries resulted in improvement of environmental and economic performance thus resulting in positive impact on overall operational performance of the organization. Electronics manufacturers are benefited by implementing various green management practices as recycling the returned products, undertaking clean transportation practices to mitigate environmental pollution and also attract and retain those customers who are concerned about environment (Wong, Lai, Shang, Lu, & Leung, 2012). Marcus & Fremeth (2009) found that automobile industry has innovated new products as electric / solar powered automobile and hybrid automobile that is comparatively environment friendly. Taylor (1992) found that smart businesses are taking these pressures under consideration to boost operational efficiency, increase visibility, develop new markets and generate whole range of other benefits. By implementing environmental management standards industries are slowly starting to change the rule of competition. As there is global competition in today's world, environmental governance is not restricted to national.

Increasing social interest has been paid to environmental issues (Wang et al., 2013). Quality management (QM) is an essential precedent for the environmental management maturity (EMM) of a company, which in turn influences the adoption of GSCM practices that influence green performance (Jabbour, Jabbour, Latan, Teixeira, & de Oliveira, 2015). Hence, Green manufacturing can result in reduced cost of raw material, efficiency gains in production, reduced environmental and occupational safety costs, and improved corporate image (Sezen & Çankaya, 2013). In everyday life and business practice, environmental awareness has become increasingly important. Measures to reduce environmental impact of business activities have been branded as handling the sustainable supply chain of the business. According to Bhool and Narwal (2013) factors that drives green supply chain management are most to be considered by organizations and should be given significant importance. In china, significant relation between operational practices and performance in manufacturing industries were identified (Zhu & Sarkis, 2004). Further, in Malaysia as well the practice of green supply chain management is increasing and is assumed to be increased continuously (Rozar et al., 2015). Mathiyazhagan et al. (2013) mentioned that SMEs in India are focused in adoption of green supply chain management however they are struggling to implement the process. Moreover we also consider that sum of the supplier and retailer's optimum greening activities is equivalent to the combination of their green tolerance and greening expenses level (Swami & Shah, 2013).

According to Large & Thomsen (2011) green supply management capabilities, strategic level of purchasing department, level of environmental commitment, degree of green supplier assessment and the degree of green collaboration with suppliers are five major drivers of green supply chain management in Germany. According to managers in German automotive companies on the one hand need of green supply management is felt however, problems were identified in terms of resources (Thun & Muller, 2010). The most influential and significant factor is the increase in cost for obtaining environmentally friendly materials, whereas the most successful criterion is pollution control activities as seen in manufacturing industries (Lin et al., 2011). Similarly, Elbarkouky & Abdelazeem (2013) revealed that construction companies in Egypt indicates that key incentives for GSCM implementation in Egypt are ISO 14001 certification and market competitiveness, while the main impediments are a lack of rules, government backing, and social pressure.

In the firms of Malaysia according to Suryanto et al. (2018) three GSCM factors are considered; external relationship, eco-design and IR factors and in Malaysia GSCM is a novel eco-friendly approach management that focuses on supply chains rather than specific plants. In India, Firms are compelled to embrace GSCM practices as a result of GSCM demands, which have a substantial impact on environmental and economic performance (Sujatha & Karthikeyan, 2021). However, as mentioned by Tumpa et al. (2019) low demand of green products and financial constraints are major barriers of green supply chain management in textile industries of Bangladesh. Al-Mujaini & Walke (n.d.) stated that although there has been significant effort in the oil and gas industry to use green supply chain methods, there is still work to be done to boost adoption. Environmental performance was positively impacted by GSCM procedures, which resulted in environmental gains. However, it appears that GSCM was less effective than planned in influencing social and, in particular, economic performance (Cankaya & Sezen, 2019).

Also, implementation of green supply chain management is considered as expense which would increase overall cost of the product thus decision makers should be very careful and aware while implement the process (Diabat & Govindan, 2011). However, Srivastava (2007) indicated that no abundant research is conducted in the field of green supply chain management despite of it being an emerging issue. Further, Seman et al. (2012) also discussed that proper study on adoption and implementation of green supply chain management is lacking especially in developing nations. Therefore, the importance of the study related to green supply management has come up. This study will further help to analyze the status of green practice by manufacturers of Kathmandu valley.

RESEARCH METHOD

Study Area and Population

Nepal has 77 districts, and from the 77 district, 3 districts include in Kathmandu valley (Kathmandu, Bhaktapur and Lalitpur) situated in Bagmati province were taken as the study area. Kathmandu valley is the center for major industries such as carpets, garments, finance, tourism, health, educational services as well as banking services. According to Economic Survey 2018, a total of 7,832 industries were registered in Nepal out of which two-thirds are in Bagmati province. Due to the lack of infrastructural development and services in other part of Nepal, Kathmandu valley is becoming a hub for many business and service activities.

Figure 1. Study area

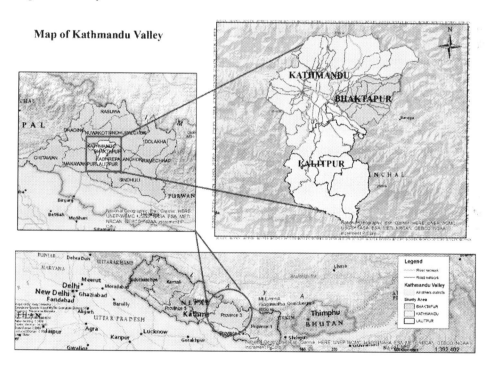

In present context, the number of manufacturing companies are more in the valley as there are three industrial areas that are located in Balaju, Patan and Bhaktapur because of this reason these three industrial areas are considered as population for this study. The total land area owned by Bhaktapur industrial estate was 71,28 ropanies, and all of the property was fully developed, with 36 out of 35 industries working. The total land area of the industrial state of Patan was 293 ropanies, of which 293 were well developed. Likewise the area of activity contained 73 ropanies. Inside the district there were actually 118 factories, of which 113 were working and Balaju Industrial estate has 670 ropanies of which 540 fully established ropanies of land. The area currently comprised 141 industries, of which 134 were active industries. These three industrial estates contain 295 companies, of which 282 work. As this study only focuses on the manufacturing industries total 220 manufacturing industries are currently operating which are considered as population for this study.

Sample Size Determination

Since population of the study were three industrial estate of Kathmandu valley. These three industrial estates together covers 220 manufacturing companies. Therefore, the population number for my research is 220. Thus, data were then collected from 207 industries which were in operation in three industrial estates (Bhaktapur, Balaju and Patan Industrial estates).

Research Instrument

A questionnaire has been prepared and implemented for the data collection. Self-administrative questionnaire has been used for collecting the data. Questionnaire were made in such a manner that all the objectives of the research were met. The data has been collected from the industrial areas of Kathmandu Valley which is located in Balaju, Patan and Bhaktapur. Data were collected with the help of Kobo Kollect, data collection tool further analyzed and presented with the help of data, charts and tables.

RESULTS AND DISCUSSION

Industries Profile

For this study three industrial estates inside Kathmandu valley (Kathmandu, Bhaktapur and Patan) is chosen. Among 296 industries 207 manufacturing industries are taken into consideration for this study among which 101 industries are from Balaju industrial estate, 81 from Patan industrial estate and remaining 25 from Bhaktapur industrial estate. As maximum number of industries are located in Balaju industrial estate this study as well covers higher percentage of industries from Balaju industrial estate.

Figure 2. Scale of industry

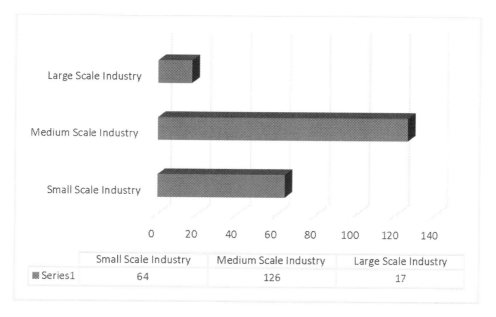

Likewise, those industrial estates are categorized into three scales: small, medium and large scale industries. Scale of the industry are categorized in accordance to the amount of capital invested in the industry. Among 207 industries considered for this study 64 were small scale industries, 126 were medium scale industry and 17 were large scale industry as presented in figure 1.

Respondents Profile

Among respondents in 207 industries, 83% were male and 17% were female respondents as presented in table 1. All respondents were the workers working in the industry in various position which indicates there are more male employees in comparison to females in manufacturing industries which also shows the gender gap between employees in industries.

Majority of the respondents (57%) were from management team members and only 1.4% of board members were accessible for the interview. However, information could be gathered from 14.5% executive directors/CEO. Similarly, more than 50% employees had work experience of 5-10 years and only 2.4% had experience of above 25 years. 11.6% respondents had experience below 5 years. From the data it can be analyzed that most of the employees are of new generation which would ease them in adoption of GSCM.

Table 1. Respondents profile

	Number	%
Sex		
Male	172	83
Female	35	17
Job Title		
Board President	4	1.9
Board Member	3	1.4
Executive Director/CEO	30	14.5
Management Team Member	118	57
Other	52	25.2
Working Experience		
Below 5 years	24	11.6
5-10 years	105	50.7
11-15 years	43	20.7
16-20 years	18	18.6
21-25 years	12	5.7
Above 25 years	5	2.4

GSCM Practiced Level

Findings of the study revealed that 33.3% industries are highly practicing GSCM whereas 23.7% and 19.62% are practicing it moderately and less respectively.

Figure 3. Scale of industry and practiced level

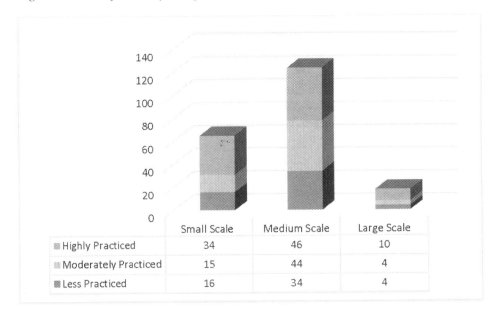

From this data it can be depicted that industries are slowly and gradually adopting GSCM in Kathmandu valley as well. As male employees were found to be in higher number compared to female employees it was obvious result that GSCM was found to be actively practiced to greater extent by male employees in the manufacturing industries. Moreover, figure 1 shows the Scale of industry and the GSCM practiced Level which shows industries of all scale (large, medium and small) are highly practicing the GSCM notion in their organization. The data reflects that no matter the size or the scale of the organization the GSCM are practiced are highest level.

Factors Affecting the Organizational Performance in Relation to the Practice of GSCM

Under this section various factors affecting organizational performance in relation to practice of GSCM are discussed. Five variables are mentioned below for the further analysis and they include: GSCM implementation, employee job satisfaction, operational efficiency, relational efficiency and business performance. These variables are measured in five scale under Likert scale (1= Strongly Disagree, 2= Disagree, 3=Neutral, 4=Agree, 5=Strongly Agree).

GSCM in the emerging concept in the industrial world of today's era. In Nepalese context also the GSCM implementation seems to be followed by various organizations. In reference to table 5 it can be seen that majority of industries stated that they agree that they have implemented GSCM practice, they adopt operational

Figure 4. Factors affecting GSCM practice

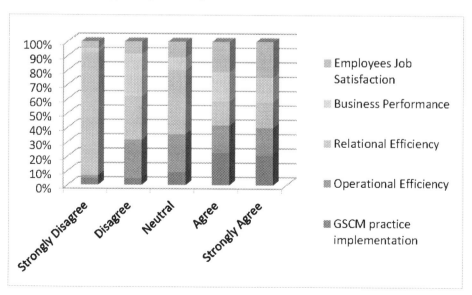

efficiency, GSCM affects relational efficiency. Business efficiency has also been increased due to GSCM practice and increased employee job satisfaction. Therefore, it can be stated that the factors impact GSCM practice to greater level.

Green Supply Chain Management Index

Green supply chain management index is determined with the help of three constructs namely; technology context, organizational and environmental context as displayed in table 2. Under technological context 76.32% industries thinks that they are capable of implementing green supply chain management and there are adequate technologies which could aid this process. However, almost 73% industries agreed that decision making is affected to greater extent when complexity arises in GSCM adoption. This shows lack of solid decision making power in manufacturing industries. Likewise, 76.2% industries revealed that product performance plays greater role in decision making process to adopt GSCM.

Similarly, another construct in regards to organizational context states that adoption of GSCM and incorporating them in organization will help in sustainability of industries and maintain proper CSR as mentioned by 77.7% industries of Kathmandu valley. Majority of industries (81.1%) agrees to the fact that top management supports them in adoption of GSCM and majority (69.5%) of them also agrees that financial

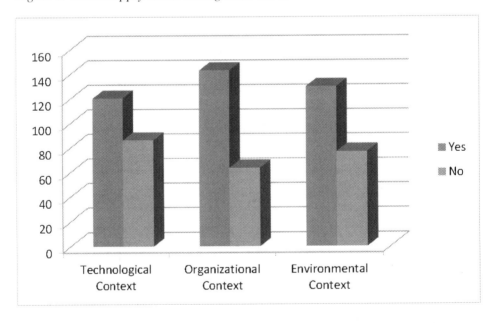

Figure 5. Green supply chain management index

budget have been allocated for the adoption of GSCM. On the similar note 51.69% denied that it was challenging to adopt GSCM due to centralization.

In addition, under environmental context it was witnessed that maximum number of industries i.e. 63.28% have not got any support for government for the adoption of GSCM. But, industries are inclining towards adoption of GSCM on their own and 71% of them think their competitors have started GSCM process. As the awareness of environmental issues have increased among customers, customers also demands industries to use GSCM due to which 69.5% industries were pressurized by customers for adoption of GSCM and 74% feels that suppliers also coordinate with them to meet the environmental standards and the environmental footprints have been reduced.

Challenges in Green Supply Chain Management Practice

While asking industries regarding challenges in implementation of GSCM practice it was found that more than two third (i.e. 86%) of industries faces challenges while practicing GSCM. Upon analyzing major challenges that they were facing it was found that major challenge was pressure from the local government on the manufacturers of industrial property without prior notice (31%) followed by unnecessary obstacles or threats generated by different groups or unions that ultimately affect the implementation of GSCM and the operation of the company (21%), the high costs of controlling and maintaining green SCM activities (20%), not all businesses find GSCM appealing, particularly for industries with branches in many locations, Shortage of experienced human resources required to implement

Figure 6. Challenges faced by industries

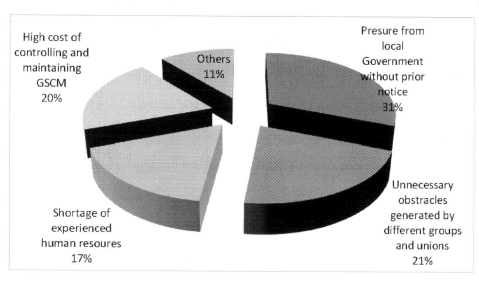

the GSCM policies effectively in the organization (17%) and other minor challenges (11%). From these challenges we can conclude that industries were facing several challenges that must be address by concern authorities so that GSCM practice in industries will implement more efficiently.

Managerial Solution for Green Supply Chain Management Practice

By putting GSCM programs in operation, prospects arise for substantial economic development. It needs government action on a global scale, though. Governments typically need to set ambitious and national goals for the average corporate fuel economy of oceangoing shipping, aircraft, and other types of transport (Jaggernath & Khan, 2015). This study identified there are several hurdles while adopting GSCM practice within an organization but 89% of the industries believes that those hurdles can be managed through various strategies if they are adopted and implemented well. Other think it is not manageable because of unstable or unclear policy of government, government role as regulator more than facilitator, nature of business etc.

However, some of the managerial solution suggested by industries personnel that could be implemented and would help to achieve better organizational performance. Some of the major solutions that respondents emphasized are highlighted in figure

Figure 7. Managerial solutions

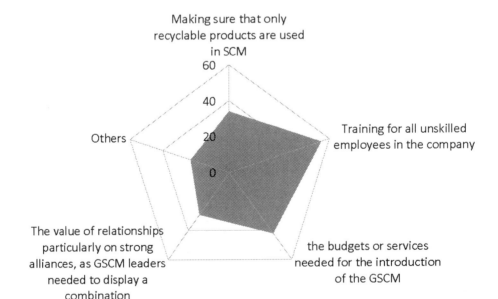

3. Industries mainly suggest the following solutions making sure that only recyclable products are used in supply chain management will have enormous consequences; manufacturers down the chain are then accelerated to turn their processes into greener ones, whether by enhancing packaging or by including environmentally friendly products in their practices, training for all unskilled employees in the company should be given in order to make the introduction of the GSCM better and more efficient, the budgets or services needed for the introduction of the GSCM should be allocated in organizations, value of relationships particularly on strong alliances, as GSCM leaders needed to display a combination of vision while displaying reality and competence through the implementation of GSCM and others minor solutions to improve the efficiency of GSCM practices in industries.

CONCLUSION AND RECOMMENDATIONS

This study was a first study that examines the practice of GSCM and organization performance in manufacturing industries in Nepal. It analyzed that 33.3% industries are highly practicing GSCM whereas 23.7% and 19.6% are practicing it moderately and less respectively. Talking about GSCM index, industries were found to have positive prospect on all three (technological, organizational and environmental context). However, 86% of the industries are still facing challenges in the implementation of GSCM and majority of the respondents suggested that providing trainings for unskilled employees and awaring those employees about GSCM could minimize the challenges. Thus, the study concludes that industries should analyze the awareness level of their employees in regards to GSCM and provide them skills and training as per their necessity which would help to enhance industrial practice of GSCM and make the process effective and efficient.

Further, this study recommends that for effective GSCM practice industries should mandatorily allocate the budget in the name of GSCM, conduct trainings for the needy employees, and make surveillance for GSCM practice. Also, government should provide special facilities to the firms practicing GSCM. Though this study has tried to cover greater aspect in GSCM practice in manufacturing industries this field still requires more investigation. Further research can be conducted considering all the manufacturing industries of the country which this study could not cover due to various limitations. As this is descriptive study future study incorporating inferential analysis could serve the purpose to a greater and better extent.

REFERENCES

Ahmad, S. (2015). Green human resource management: Policies and practices. *Cogent Business and Management, 2*(1), 1–13. doi:10.1080/23311975.2015.1030817

Al Mujaini, S., & Walke, S. (n.d.). *Identification and assessment of innovative green supply chain practices in the oil and gas industry of the Gulf Cooperation Council (GCC) countries*. Academic Press.

Bhool, R., & Narwal, M. S. (2013). An analysis of drivers affecting the implementation of green supply chain management for the Indian manufacturing industries. *International Journal of Research in Engineering and Technology, 2*(11), 2319–1163.

Bhuju, D., Thapa-parajuli, R., Sharma, P., & Aryal, P. (2014). *Nepal's green economy initiative and framework proposed Nepal's green economy initiative and framework proposed*. Academic Press.

Chin, T. A., Tat, H. H., & Sulaiman, Z. (2015). Green supply chain management, environmental collaboration and sustainability performance. *Procedia CIRP, 26*, 695–699. doi:10.1016/j.procir.2014.07.035

Diabat, A., & Govindan, K. (2011). An analysis of the drivers affecting the implementation of green supply chain management. *Resources, Conservation and Recycling, 55*(6), 659–667. doi:10.1016/j.resconrec.2010.12.002

Elbarkouky, M. M. G., & Abdelazeem, G. (2013). A green supply chain assessment for construction projects in developing countries. *WIT Transactions on Ecology and the Environment, 179*, 1331–1341. doi:10.2495/SC131132

Green, K. W. Jr, Zelbst, P. J., Meacham, J., & Bhadauria, V. S. (2012). Green supply chain management practices: Impact on performance. *Supply Chain Management, 17*(3), 290–305. doi:10.1108/13598541211227126

Harper, C. L., & Snowden, M. (2017). *Environment and society: Human perspectives on environmental issues*. Routledge. doi:10.4324/9781315463254

Hazen, B. T., Cegielski, C., & Hanna, J. B. (2011). Diffusion of green supply chain management: Examining perceived quality of green reverse logistics. *International Journal of Logistics Management, 22*(3), 373–389. doi:10.1108/09574091111181372

Hernandez, A. A., & Ona, S. (2015). A Qualitative study of green it adoption within the philippines business process outsourcing industry: A multi-theory perspective. *International Journal of Enterprise Information Systems, 11*(4), 28–62. doi:10.4018/IJEIS.2015100102

Jabbour, A. B. L. de S., Jabbour, C. J. C., Latan, H., Teixeira, A. A., & de Oliveira, J. H. C. (2015). Reprint of "Quality management, environmental management maturity, green supply chain practices and green performance of Brazilian companies with ISO 14001 certification: Direct and indirect effects.". *Transportation Research Part E, Logistics and Transportation Review*, *74*, 139–151. doi:10.1016/j.tre.2014.12.011

Jaggernath, R., & Khan, Z. (2015). Green supply chain management. *World Journal of Entrepreneurship, Management and Sustainable Development*, *11*(1), 37–47. doi:10.1108/WJEMSD-06-2014-0018

Karki, M. (2014). Green economy for sustainable development in Nepal: Role of forestry sector. *The Initiation*, *5*, 96–109. doi:10.3126/init.v5i0.10259

Large, R. O., & Thomsen, C. G. (2011). Drivers of green supply management performance: Evidence from Germany. *Journal of Purchasing and Supply Management*, *17*(3), 176–184. doi:10.1016/j.pursup.2011.04.006

Lin, R. J., Chen, R. H., & Nguyen, T. H. (2011). Green supply chain management performance in automobile manufacturing industry under uncertainty. *Procedia: Social and Behavioral Sciences*, *25*, 233–245. doi:10.1016/j.sbspro.2011.10.544

Marcus, A. A., & Fremeth, A. R. (2009). Green management matters regardless. *The Academy of Management Perspectives*, *23*(3), 17–26. doi:10.5465/amp.2009.43479261

Mathiyazhagan, K., Govindan, K., NoorulHaq, A., & Geng, Y. (2013). An ISM approach for the barrier analysis in implementing green supply chain management. *Journal of Cleaner Production*, *47*, 283–297. doi:10.1016/j.jclepro.2012.10.042

Rostamzadeh, R., Govindan, K., Esmaeili, A., & Sabaghi, M. (2015). Application of fuzzy VIKOR for evaluation of green supply chain management practices. *Ecological Indicators*, *49*, 188–203. doi:10.1016/j.ecolind.2014.09.045

Rozar, N. M., Mahmood, W. H. W., Ibrahim, A., & Razik, M. A. (2015). A study of success factors in green supply chain management in manufacturing industries in Malaysia. *J Econ Bus Manag*, *3*(2), 287–291. doi:10.7763/JOEBM.2015.V3.196

Sezen, B., & Çankaya, S. Y. (2013). Effects of green manufacturing and eco-innovation on sustainability performance. *Procedia: Social and Behavioral Sciences*, *99*, 154–163. doi:10.1016/j.sbspro.2013.10.481

Shrestha, S. S. (2017). Strengthening supply chains for a sustainable housing sector in Nepal : Factors influencing the organization, management, relationships and the adoption and use of green practices, products and services. *International Journal of Managing Value and Supply Chains, 8*(1), 1–22. doi:10.5121/ijmvsc.2017.8101

Skibińska, W., & Kott, I. (2015). Green management in companies policies and activities. In *WEI International Academic Conference Proceedings* (pp. 220-226). WEI.

Sujatha, R., & Karthikeyan, M. S. (2021). Investigating green supply chain management practices and performance among apparel manufacturing firms. *International Journal of Integrated Supply Management, 14*(3), 271–290. doi:10.1504/IJISM.2021.117239

Suryanto, T., Haseeb, M., & Hartani, N. H. (2018). The correlates of developing green supply chain management practices: Firms level analysis in Malaysia. *International Journal of Supply Chain Management, 7*(5), 316.

Swami, S., & Shah, J. (2013). Channel coordination in green supply chain management. *The Journal of the Operational Research Society, 64*(3), 336–351. doi:10.1057/jors.2012.44

Taylor, S. R. (1992). Green management: The next competitive weapon. *Futures, 24*(7), 669–680. doi:10.1016/0016-3287(92)90075-Q

Thun, J. H., & Müller, A. (2010). An empirical analysis of green supply chain management in the German automotive industry. *Business Strategy and the Environment, 19*(2), 119–132.

Tumpa, T. J., Ali, S. M., Rahman, M. H., Paul, S. K., Chowdhury, P., & Khan, S. A. R. (2019). Barriers to green supply chain management: An emerging economy context. *Journal of Cleaner Production, 236,* 117617. doi:10.1016/j.jclepro.2019.117617

Wang, Y. F., Chen, S. P., Lee, Y. C., & Tsai, C. T. (2013). Developing green management standards for restaurants: An application of green supply chain management. *International Journal of Hospitality Management, 34*(1), 263–273. doi:10.1016/j.ijhm.2013.04.001

Wong, C. W. Y., Lai, K. H., Shang, K. C., Lu, C. S., & Leung, T. K. P. (2012). Green operations and the moderating role of environmental management capability of suppliers on manufacturing firm performance. *International Journal of Production Economics, 140*(1), 283–294. doi:10.1016/j.ijpe.2011.08.031

Zhu, Q., & Sarkis, J. (2004). Relationships between operational practices and performance among early adopters of green supply chain management practices in Chinese manufacturing enterprises. *Journal of Operations Management, 22*(3), 265–289. doi:10.1016/j.jom.2004.01.005

Chapter 8
Rating Risk Factors Related to Dangerous Goods Transportation and Selecting an Ideal Warehouse Location

Çağlar Karamaşa
Anadolu University, Turkey

Selçuk Korucuk
Giresun University, Turkey

Ezgi Demir
Gebze Technical University, Turkey

EXECUTIVE SUMMARY

Considering the environment and human life, the importance of dangerous goods transportation should be carefully considered. Preventing damages during this transportation, anticipating the dangers, and minimizing the risks are vital components for businesses, human life, and the environment. Therefore, reducing/minimizing risks in dangerous goods transportation is a critical element of vital importance. This chapter is aimed to rate the risk factors related to dangerous goods transportation and select the most ideal warehouse locations due to the their importance for human and environmental health. There are a number of factors for that purpose. There are six provinces in the Eastern Black Sea region having the strategic function and structure. According to the decision makers' views and judgments, three provinces are determined in terms of dangerous goods transportation. Picture fuzzy sets-based AHP-TOPSIS methodology was used to analyze the problem of dangerous goods transportation and the most ideal warehouse location selection.

DOI: 10.4018/978-1-7998-9140-6.ch008

Copyright © 2022, IGI Global. Copying or distributing in print or electronic forms without written permission of IGI Global is prohibited.

INTRODUCTION

The emergence, in December 2019, of acute respiratory disease, called Coronavirus-2 and declared a pandemic by the World Health Organization (WHO) in March 2020, sent us into a state of unprecedented global demand (Acar, 2020). During the pandemic, many businesses faced problems such as lack of raw material inventory, an insufficient workforce, lack of working capital, and increased freight rates. The pandemic negatively impacted the efficiency of transportation and port unloading, which led to a sharp decline in export orders and almost ran the global export trade of industrial products to a halt. The increase in the risk due to the pandemic also brought uncertainty to companies regarding the maintenance of production and cash flow. The decrease in total factor productivity caused by the closure of businesses and their production played an important role in reducing the average production of the sector by 1.78%. The decline in labor productivity caused by the gradual resumption of work has reduced the industry's average output by 0.55% (WHO, 2020)

However, even during the pandemic, the rapid increasing of industrialization with the globalizing world has increased dependence on dangerous substances, and the use of these substances has become widespread. Using dangerous substances became compulsory in almost all areas of our lives and has become one of the issues to be considered. Dangerous goods have usually transported by road; it consists of humans, animals, the environment, in short, substances that threaten the living space. These substances' effects are sudden and emerge as the safety of life and property and environmental disasters. It requires adequate transportation and risk management understanding in the transportation of these substances (Korucuk, 2018).

Work and the nature of the workplace have changed drastically during the pandemic due to the changes experienced in the workforce and the labor market, new forms of employment. This poses new risks and challenges for the safety and health of workers. These must be anticipated and addressed to ensure safe and healthy workplaces in the future. Risks should be addressed in a timely and effective manner, especially in global epidemic situations, and the emerging occupational health and safety risks should be supported with reliable, high-quality data (Prem et al., 2020).

Because in particular, to positioning such materials separately; the detailing of the relocation processes, ranging from the scope and extent of the content, arise from the specific transports that concern many different stakeholders to the harmony between operations and political unions.

A hazardous substance is a concept; They are substances that can endanger general safety, order, life, and society due to their composition (Korucuk, 2018). Oggero et al. (2006),

hazardous materials have been defined as substances in solid, liquid, or gaseous form that may endanger or damage the environment and human safety as a result of carelessness/accidents during production, use, handling, storage, or transportation. The US Occupational Health and Safety Administration (OSHA) has divided hazardous materials into physical hazards and health hazards. Physical hazards have been defined as flammable, explosive, flammable, unstable reagents or reactive water and chemicals that emit dust, gas, smoke, fog during normal handling, oxidizing, and pyrophoric substances use or storage. On the other hand, health hazards have been identified as toxic agents, irritants, abrasives, sensitizers affecting the lungs, skin, eyes, or mucous membrane, factors affecting the hematopoietic system, and carcinogens (OSHA., 2017).

The transportation of the dangerous substances listed above threatens the human, animal, briefly the whole environment, and brings along effective logistics practices. According to Daimonlogistics (2017), as an essential issue within the scope of adequate logistics and transportation applications, it has been emphasized that packaging, marking, handling, transportation, and storage functions should be implemented and managed effectively according to the transport mode. Responsibilities for the transport of dangerous substances have been distributed in different ways. In this context, the shipper, loader, transporter, vehicle driver, and other vehicle officers, the recipient, and the tank/container/warehouse operators have various responsibilities. Possible negligence that may occur in any of these listed stakeholders and stages is reflected in all other stakeholders and may cause unavoidable negativity (Ministry of Transport, 2008). Erdal (2018) stated keeping the costs under control while protecting the living and non-living environment in the transportation of dangerous goods, and therefore it is crucial to determine the route that creates the least risk and cost.

It is necessary to take various precautions during the movement of dangerous substances. During transportation, transport containers should be protected from impacts and knocks and should not be dropped. The speed of the vehicle should be kept at a level that does not pose a danger according to visibility, road, weather and traffic conditions, so as not to exceed the speed limits for vehicles carrying dangerous goods (Ministry of Transport, 2008).

With sight on the sustainability of industries, many efficiency-oriented studies have been carried out in Supply Chain Management and management approaches such as lean production and Just-in-time production have been adopted. These approaches represent production strategies that cushion organizations from bearing the costs arising from excess stock (Sert and Kesen, 2019).

Some of the basic factors that lead organizations to lose their flexibility in adapting to rapidly changing conditions are the location of establishment and the selection of the warehouse location (Johnson & McGinnis, 2011). As such, the approach that reduces the cost of warehouse and inventory should be adopted (Pisuchpen, 2012). These issues have only increased in significance during the Covid 19 pandemic.

Dangerous goods transportation includes many risk factors arising from the goods transported. Although it is vital to keep the risk factors related to living and non-living assets under control, it is also crucial to carry out works and processes with the least cost. Chen et al. (2007) grouped dangerous goods transport risk factors into five groups. These factors are hazardous materials, vehicles, personnel, road and environment, security monitoring, and emergency rescue. However, in another study, these factors are divided into management reasons, vehicles, packaging, equipment, traffic conditions, environment, illegal or wrong movements (Liu, 2005).

According to Demirci and Arıkan (2021), for example, the high demand for the coronavirus vaccine produced by Pfizer and BioNTech and the lack of existing stock necessitated the production of vast amounts within a short time. To meet the high demand, the two organizations entered into a production partnership with Novartis. This situation here shows that if the vaccines had been stocked in the right locations, this level of rapid and high production would not be needed and it would be possible to meet the demands without the need for any news partnerships (Demirci and Arıkan, 2021). The same can be said for the selection of a location of hazardous materials, and meeting demand.

The sender, loader, transporter, vehicle driver, and other officers in the vehicle, the recipient, the tank/container/ warehouse operator have various responsibilities. Any negligence that may occur in any of them may cause unavoidable negative consequences by reflecting on all other units. Therefore, the decisions to be made regarding the transportation of dangerous goods are of vital importance. These decisions should be taken scientifically so that their irreversible effects on both society and the environment should be avoided.

Also firms can produce value added goods and services via efficient storage decisions. Besides the benefits and outputs of storage decisions on production, and efficiency level need to be determined especially for manufacturing firms. Because efficient and productive storage decisions provide cost reduction, competitive advantage and customer satisfaction (Demirdöğen & Korucuk, 2017).

The presence of warehouses positioned in the right positions is considered to positively affect the distribution processes and stock management (WHO World Health Report, 2010). The need to meet rising demand and reach consumers has increased the emphasis on the right stocking plan and correctly positioned warehouses The COVID-19 global epidemic has also brought to the fore the necessity of having stocks and the advantage associated with being able to reach the final consumer even when production comes to a standstill (Demirci and Arıkan, 2021).

Furthermore, the most ideal warehouse location selection as a critical alternative needs to be considered as an essential parameter with respect to the effects and content of dangerous goods. To prevent disruptions in the supply chain, especially in the era of Covid 19, distribution, transportation and the selection of the right location have become even more important in logistics. Similarly, the need to avoid the disruption of production during the pandemic period, to ensure customer satisfaction, and to maintain competitiveness has also put emphasis on the transportation of dangerous goods. In light of all these, more focus is needed on understaing the risk factors associated with transportation of dangerous goods and the problem of choosing a suitable warehouse for dangerous goods in order to prevent disruptions in the supply chain, continue production and ensure customer satisfaction during the Covid 19 period.

Therefore criteria and alternatives need to be determined in order to achieve the conditions of warehouse location selection problem. This problem is considered as a Multi Criteria Decision Making (MCDM) problem due to having a number of criteria and alternative (Ustasüleyman & Perçin, 2007).

In this regard this study aims to determine dangerous goods transportation risk factors and select the most ideal warehouse location for companies having corporate identity that transport dangerous goods in the Eastern Black Sea Region during Covid 19 pandemic. In this study, the picture fuzzy sets based AHP-TOPSIS methodology was used among multi-criteria decision-making methods. The following part of the study includes a comprehensive literature review on hazardous material transportation, risk factors in dangerous goods transportation and warehouse location selection for dangerous goods. In the third part, information about picture fuzzy sets, picture fuzzy AHP and picture fuzzy TOPSIS have been presented. Application of case study has been given in the forth part. In the last section, conclusion and future suggestions are given too.

LITERATURE REVIEW

Studies for dangerous goods, dangerous goods transportation risk factors and warehouse location selection have been presented as below:

Korpela and Tuominen (1996), Hale and Moberg (2005), Zhidong et al. (2012), Erbaş et al. (2014) and Oral et al. (2021) examined the selection of the storage of hazardous material storage location and its importance.

Bonvicini et al. (1998) Lazar et al. get. (2001), Fabiano et al. (2002), Liu et al. (2005), Huang (2006), Özyağcı (2008), Batarliene and Jarasuniene (2014), Kabir and Sumi (2015), Obricovic and Milaradov(2016), Erdal (2018), Popek (2019), Batarliene (2020) and Mert and Çetinyokuş (2020) investigated the risk factors arising from uncertainty in the transportation of dangerous goods, and highlighted their importance for nature, environment, business and people.

Lahdelma et al. (2002) evaluated four alternative for waste treatment plant in terms of seventeen criteria via SMAA-O method in Finland.

Chen et al. (2003) made overall evaluation related to transportation risks in radioactive substance and waste under normal and accident conditions.

Xin et al. (2007) evaluated routing, inventory, planning, management organization and external factors under logistic risks context.

Mete and Zabinsky (2009) developed a probabilistic programming approach for planning of distribution and storage of emergency medical care kits.

Huo and Hua and Xiong(2010) evaluated the safety-oriented study with the AHP method to evaluate hazardous chemical sources in their research.

Demirel et al. (2010) and Gül and Eren (2017) considered the problem of the selection of a storage location.

Rodríguez-Espíndola et al. (2017), developed an emergency readiness system by considering resource management from different organizations via GIS.

Szeto et al. (2017) tried to determine the probability of accidents in the transport of fuel oil and flammable substances by road with the route-flow emission algorithm and the recursive dynamic algorithm.

Korucuk (2018) conducted a literature review on using multi-criteria decision-making methods in dangerous goods transportation.

Korucuk and Erdal (2018) examined the logistics risk criteria of companies dealing in cold chain transportation.

Loree and Aros-Vera (2018) formed a model that integrates deprivation cost functions into the site of establishment decisions in order to minimize social costs and providing the most suitable distribution points and strategies.

Bęczkowska (2019) proposed a model for the optimum route selection method in the road transport of dangerous goods.

Özder et al. (2019), applied ANP method in order to determine the competence level for personnel scheduling problem in energy sector.

Memiş et al. (2020) rated the risk factors of road transport according to the logistical functions in Giresun via fuzzy PIPRECIA.

Ergün et al. (2020) evaluated the criterion for ideal disaster storage selection in Giresun by using MCDM methods.

According to the literature review there is not any study that proposes to rate the risk factors related to dangerous good transportation and select the most ideal warehouse location in Eastern Black Sea region during Covid 19 process. That shows the novelty and originality of manuscript. Also study differs from others by used methodology and application area.

METHODOLOGY

This section consists of picture fuzzy sets, picture fuzzy AHP and picture fuzzy TOPSIS respectively.

Picture Fuzzy Sets

Picture fuzzy sets (PFS) firstly proposed by Cuong (2014) are defined as extension of intuitionistic fuzzy sets (IFS).

A PFS $\tilde{B}_P$ on a universe of discourse X can be defined as (Gündoğdu et al., 2021):

$$\tilde{B}_P = \left\{ x, \left(\mu_{\tilde{B}_P}(x), \eta_{\tilde{B}_P}(x), v_{\tilde{B}_P}(x) \right) \big| x \in X \right\} \tag{1}$$

where $\mu_{\tilde{B}_P}(x): X \to [0,1], \eta_{\tilde{B}_P}(x): X \to [0,1], v_{\tilde{B}_P}(x): X \to [0,1]$ are called the degree of positive membership, the degree of neutral membership and the degree of negative membership of x in X by satisfying the following condition:

$$0 \leq \mu_{\tilde{B}_P}(x) + \eta_{\tilde{B}_P}(x) + v_{\tilde{B}_P}(x) \leq 1 \quad \forall x \in X \tag{2}$$

The degree of refusal of x in $\tilde{B}_P$ can be obtained by $\rho_{\tilde{B}_P} = 1 - \left(\mu_{\tilde{B}_P}(x) + v_{\tilde{B}_P}(x) + \eta_{\tilde{B}_P}(x) \right)$ that shows reflection of commitment or uncertainty related with positive, neutral and negative membership degrees or all in $\tilde{B}_P$ (Gündoğdu et al., 2021; Dutta, 2018).

Basic operations for single valued Picture fuzzy sets can be stated as follows (Gündoğdu et al., 2021; Ashraf et al. 2019):

$$\tilde{B}_P \oplus \tilde{C}_P = \left\{ \mu_{\tilde{B}_P} + \mu_{\tilde{C}_P} - \mu_{\tilde{B}_P} \mu_{\tilde{C}_P}, \eta_{\tilde{B}_P} \eta_{\tilde{C}_P}, v_{\tilde{B}_P} v_{\tilde{C}_P} \right\} \tag{3}$$

$$\tilde{B}_P \otimes \tilde{C}_P = \left\{ \mu_{\tilde{B}_P} \mu_{\tilde{C}_P}, \eta_{\tilde{B}_P} \eta_{\tilde{C}_P}, v_{\tilde{B}_P} + v_{\tilde{C}_P} - v_{\tilde{B}_P} v_{\tilde{C}_P} \right\} \tag{4}$$

$$\lambda \cdot \tilde{B}_P = \left\{ \left(1-\left(1-\mu_{\tilde{B}_P}\right)^{\lambda}\right), \eta_{\tilde{B}_P}^{\lambda}, v_{\tilde{B}_P}^{\lambda} \right\} \text{ for } \lambda > 0 \tag{5}$$

$$\tilde{B}_P^{\lambda} = \left\{ \mu_{\tilde{B}_P}^{\lambda}, \eta_{\tilde{B}_P}^{\lambda}, \left(1-\left(1-v_{\tilde{B}_P}\right)^{\lambda}\right) \right\} \text{ for } \lambda > 0 \tag{6}$$

Single valued picture fuzzy weighted geometric (PFWG) and arithmetic (PFWA) operators can be calculated as below (Gündoğdu et al. 2021; Ashraf et al., 2019; Wei, 2017):

$$PFWG_w\left(\tilde{B}_1,........,\tilde{B}_n\right) = \left\{ \prod_{j=1}^{n} \mu_{\tilde{B}_j}^{w_j}, \prod_{j=1}^{n} \eta_{\tilde{B}_j}^{w_j}, 1 - \prod_{j=1}^{n} \left(1-v_{\tilde{B}_j}\right)^{w_j} \right\} \tag{7}$$

$$PFWA_w\left(\tilde{B}_1,........,\tilde{B}_n\right) = \left\{ 1 - \prod_{j=1}^{n} \left(1-\mu_{\tilde{B}_j}\right)^{w_j}, \prod_{j=1}^{n} \eta_{\tilde{B}_j}^{w_j}, \prod_{j=1}^{n} v_{\tilde{B}_j}^{w_j} \right\} \tag{8}$$

where $w=(w_1,w_2,…,w_n)$, $w_j \hat{I}[0,1]$; and $\sum_{j=1}^{n} w_j = 1$.

Score and accuracy functions are used for the purpose of defuzzifying and sorting picture fuzzy numbers and given as below (Gündoğdu et al. 2021):

$$Score_1\left(\tilde{B}_P\right) = \frac{1}{2}\left(1 + 2\mu_{\tilde{B}_P} - v_{\tilde{B}_P} - \frac{\eta_{\tilde{B}_P}}{2}\right) \tag{9}$$

$$Score_2\left(\tilde{B}_P\right) = \left(2\mu_{\tilde{B}_P} - v_{\tilde{B}_P} - \frac{\eta_{\tilde{B}_P}}{2}\right) \tag{10}$$

$$Score_3\left(\tilde{B}_P\right) = \left(\mu_{\tilde{B}_P} - v_{\tilde{B}_P}\right) \tag{11}$$

$$Accuracy(\tilde{B}_P) = \mu_{\tilde{B}_P} + v_{\tilde{B}_P} + \eta_{\tilde{B}_P} \tag{12}$$

The condition of $\tilde{B}_P < \tilde{C}_P$ is possible if and only if;

(i) $Score(\tilde{B}_P) < Score(\tilde{C}_P)$ or

(ii) $Score(\tilde{B}_P) = Score(\tilde{C}_P)$ and $Accuracy(\tilde{B}_P) < Accuracy(\tilde{C}_P)$

For any two picture fuzzy number $(\tilde{B}_P, \tilde{C}_P)$ some distance measures can be used given as below (Gündoğdu et al. 2021; Dutta, 2018):

1-The Hamming distance:

$$D_H(\tilde{B}_P, \tilde{C}_P) = \frac{1}{2}\sum_{i=1}^{n}\left[\begin{array}{l}\left|\mu_{\tilde{B}_P}(x_i) - \mu_{\tilde{C}_P}(x_i)\right| + \left|v_{\tilde{B}_P}(x_i) - v_{\tilde{C}_P}(x_i)\right| \\ + \left|\eta_{\tilde{B}_P}(x_i) - \eta_{\tilde{C}_P}(x_i)\right| + \left|\rho_{\tilde{B}_P}(x_i) - \rho_{\tilde{C}_P}(x_i)\right|\end{array}\right] \tag{13}$$

2-The normalized Hamming distance:

$$D_{NH}(\tilde{B}_P, \tilde{C}_P) = \frac{1}{2n}\sum_{i=1}^{n}\left[\begin{array}{l}\left|\mu_{\tilde{B}_P}(x_i) - \mu_{\tilde{C}_P}(x_i)\right| + \left|v_{\tilde{B}_P}(x_i) - v_{\tilde{C}_P}(x_i)\right| \\ + \left|\eta_{\tilde{B}_P}(x_i) - \eta_{\tilde{C}_P}(x_i)\right| + \left|\rho_{\tilde{B}_P}(x_i) - \rho_{\tilde{C}_P}(x_i)\right|\end{array}\right] \tag{14}$$

3-The Euclidean distance:

$$D_E(\tilde{B}_P, \tilde{C}_P) = \sqrt{\frac{1}{2}\sum_{i=1}^{n}\left[\begin{array}{l}\left(\mu_{\tilde{B}_P}(x_i) - \mu_{\tilde{C}_P}(x_i)\right)^2 + \left(v_{\tilde{B}_P}(x_i) - v_{\tilde{C}_P}(x_i)\right)^2 \\ + \left(\eta_{\tilde{B}_P}(x_i) - \eta_{\tilde{C}_P}(x_i)\right)^2 + \left(\rho_{\tilde{B}_P}(x_i) - \rho_{\tilde{C}_P}(x_i)\right)^2\end{array}\right]} \tag{15}$$

4-The normalized Euclidean distance:

$$D_{NE}(\tilde{B}_P,\tilde{C}_P) = \sqrt{\frac{1}{2n}\sum_{i=1}^{n}\begin{bmatrix}\left(\mu_{\tilde{B}_P}(x_i)-\mu_{\tilde{C}_P}(x_i)\right)^2 + \left(v_{\tilde{B}_P}(x_i)-v_{\tilde{C}_P}(x_i)\right)^2 \\ +\left(\eta_{\tilde{B}_P}(x_i)-\eta_{\tilde{C}_P}(x_i)\right)^2 + \left(\rho_{\tilde{B}_P}(x_i)-\rho_{\tilde{C}_P}(x_i)\right)^2\end{bmatrix}}$$

(16)

Picture Fuzzy AHP

Steps of picture fuzzy AHP can be summarized as below (Gündoğdu et al. 2021):

1- Pairwise comparison matrices for criteria evaluations are formed based on linguistic terms of importance shown as Table 1.

Table 1. Linguistic terms for picture fuzzy sets

Linguistic terms	Picture fuzzy numbers (μ,η,v)	Intensity of importance
Very high importance	(0.9,0.0,0.05)	7
High importance	(0.75,0.05,0.1)	5
Slightly more importance	(0.6,0.0,0.3)	3
Equally importance	(0.5,0.1,0.4)	1
Slightly low importance	(0.3,0.0,0.6)	1/3
Low importance	(0.25,0.05,0.6)	1/5
Very low importance	(0.1,0.0,0.85)	1/7

Source: Gündoğdu et al. (2021)

Following the procedure of AHP consistency ratio (CR) of each pairwise comparison matrix are computed. For this purpose, the linguistic terms in the examined matrix are transferred to their corresponding score indices shown as Table 1. Then, classical consistency check ratio formula is applied. If the consistency ratio is less than 0.1, pairwise comparison matrices can be considered as tolerably inconsistent.

2- Decision makers' judgments are aggregated via picture fuzzy aggregation operators. In order to obtain Picture fuzzy global weights for each criterion, pairwise comparison matrices obtained from each decision maker are aggregated by using picture fuzzy weighted geometric (PFWG) mean operator seen as Eq.(7).

3-Final picture fuzzy criteria weights are converted into crisp ones via one of the score functions given in Eqs. (9),(10) and (11).

Picture Fuzzy TOPSIS

Steps of picture fuzzy TOPSIS are stated as below (Gündoğdu et al. 2021):

1-Decision matrices are constructed by evaluating alternatives with respect to criteria according to the decision makers' judgments. For that purpose a linguistic scale given in Table 1 was used.

2-Different decision matrices are aggregated by picture fuzzy weighted geometric (PFWG) mean operator given in Eq.(7). Then aggregated decision matrix is obtained and given in Eq. (17):

$$\tilde{b}_{ij} = \left(C_j(\tilde{Z}_i)\right)_{mxn} = \begin{pmatrix} (\mu_{11};\eta_{11};v_{11}) & (\mu_{12};\eta_{12};v_{12}) & \cdots & (\mu_{1n};\eta_{1n};v_{1n}) \\ (\mu_{21};\eta_{21};v_{21}) & (\mu_{22};\eta_{22};v_{22}) & \cdots & (\mu_{2n};\eta_{2n};v_{2n}) \\ \vdots & \vdots & & \vdots \\ (\mu_{m1};\eta_{m1};v_{m1}) & (\mu_{m2};\eta_{m2};v_{m2}) & \cdots & (\mu_{mn};\eta_{mn};v_{mn}) \end{pmatrix}$$
(17)

3-Weighted aggregated decision matrix is computed by multiplying crisp criteria weights obtained from picture fuzzy AHP and aggregated decision matrix according to the Eq.(5).

4-Crisp values of weighted aggregated decision matrix is handled via using Eq.(18) in terms of score functions and seen as follows:

$$Score\left(C_j(Z_{ij})\right) = \frac{1}{2}\left(1 + 2\mu_{Z_{ij}} - v_{Z_{ij}} - \frac{\eta_{Z_{ij}}}{2}\right) \tag{18}$$

5-Positive and negative ideal solutions are obtained by taking score functions into the account according to Eqs. (19) and (20).

$$Z^+ = \{C_j, maxScore(C_j(Z_{ij})) \mid j=1,2,\ldots n\} \tag{19}$$

$$Z^- = \{C_j, minScore(C_j(Z_{ij})) \mid j=1,2,\ldots n\} \tag{20}$$

6- Distance of each alternative to positive and negative ideal solutions can be computed via Eqs. (17) and (18) in terms of normalized Euclidean distance:

$$D_{NE}\left(\tilde{Z}^+,\tilde{Z}_i\right)=\sqrt{\frac{1}{2n}\sum_{i=1}^{n}\left[\begin{array}{c}\left(\mu_{\tilde{Z}^+}(x_i)-\mu_{\tilde{Z}_i}(x_i)\right)^2+\left(v_{\tilde{Z}^+}(x_i)-v_{\tilde{Z}_i}(x_i)\right)^2\\+\left(\eta_{\tilde{Z}^+}(x_i)-\eta_{\tilde{Z}_i}(x_i)\right)^2+\left(\rho_{\tilde{Z}^+}(x_i)-\rho_{\tilde{Z}_i}(x_i)\right)^2\end{array}\right]} \qquad (21)$$

$$D_{NE}\left(\tilde{Z}^-,\tilde{Z}_i\right)=\sqrt{\frac{1}{2n}\sum_{i=1}^{n}\left[\begin{array}{c}\left(\mu_{\tilde{Z}^-}(x_i)-\mu_{\tilde{Z}_i}(x_i)\right)^2+\left(v_{\tilde{Z}^-}(x_i)-v_{\tilde{Z}_i}(x_i)\right)^2\\+\left(\eta_{\tilde{Z}^-}(x_i)-\eta_{\tilde{Z}_i}(x_i)\right)^2+\left(\rho_{\tilde{Z}^-}(x_i)-\rho_{\tilde{Z}_i}(x_i)\right)^2\end{array}\right]} \qquad (22)$$

7- Closeness coefficient is calculated via Eq.(19) and alternatives are ranked according to descending coefficient values.

$$\tau_i=\frac{D_{NE}\left(\tilde{Z}^-,\tilde{Z}_i\right)}{D_{NE}\left(\tilde{Z}^-,\tilde{Z}_i\right)+D_{NE}\left(\tilde{Z}^+,\tilde{Z}_i\right)} \qquad (23)$$

Analysis

In this study, the criteria were determined as Human Originated Factors, Factors Associated with the Business, Factors Related to Material and Packaging, Factors Related to Vehicles, Factors Regarding Environment and Traffic, Factors Related to Physical and Legal Infrastructure, Factors Related to Lack of Control and Lack of Service Standards according to the depth literature review (Fabiano et al. 2002; Liu, 2005; Huang, 2006; Chen et al.2007;

Shang et al. 2008; Batarliene & Jarasuniene 2014; Korucuk, 2018; Bęczkowska, 2019). For this purpose evaluations of 6 decision makers (2 academicians, 4 logistics managers) are taken into the account. Criteria related to risk factors for dangerous goods transportation is given in Table 2.

Table 2. Criteria related to risk factors for dangerous goods transportation

Criteria	Mark
Human originated factors	C1
Factors associated with the business	C2
Factors related to material and packaging	C3
Factors related to vehicles	C4
Factors regarding environment and traffic	C5
Factors related to physical and legal infrastructure	C6
Factors related to lack of control	C7
Lack of service standards	C8

Additionally three provinces are determined for selection of the most ideal warehouse location and given in Table 3.

Table 3. Alternatives for the most ideal warehouse location selection

Alternatives	Mark
Trabzon	A1
Ordu	A2
Artvin	A3

Picture fuzzy set based evaluation matrix in terms of criteria considered for dangerous goods transportation is constructed through decision makers' linguistic judgments which are seen as Table 1. Picture fuzzy set based evaluation matrix consisting views of decision maker 1 (DM1) for criteria can be shown as Table 4.

Table 4. Picture fuzzy set based evaluation matrix for criteria

DM1	C1	C2	C3	C4	C5	C6	C7	C8
C1	(0.5,0.1,0.4)	(0.6,0,0,0.3)	(0.75,0.05,0.1)	(0.6,0,0,0.3)	(0.6,0,0,0.3)	(0.9,0,0,0.05)	(0.5,0.1,0.4)	(0.75,0.05,0.1)
C2	(0.3,0,0,0.6)	(0.5,0.1,0.4)	(0.1,0,0,0.85)	(0.9,0,0,0.05)	(0.9,0,0,0.05)	(0.9,0,0,0.05)	(0.9,0,0,0.05)	(0.5,0.1,0.4)
C3	(0.25,0.05,0.6)	(0.9,0,0,0.05)	(0.5,0.1,0.4)	(0.9,0,0,0.05)	(0.75,0.05,0.1)	(0.5,0.1,0.4)	(0.5,0.1,0.4)	(0.25,0.05,0.6)
C4	(0.3,0,0,0.6)	(0.1,0,0,0.85)	(0.1,0,0,0.85)	(0.5,0.1,0.4)	(0.75,0.05,0.1)	(0.75,0.05,0.1)	(0.5,0.1,0.4)	(0.6,0,0,0.3)
C5	(0.3,0,0,0.6)	(0.1,0,0,0.85)	(0.25,0.05,0.6)	(0.25,0.05,0.6)	(0.5,0.1,0.4)	(0.9,0,0,0.05)	(0.5,0.1,0.4)	(0.75,0.05,0.1)
C6	(0.1,0,0,0.85)	(0.1,0,0,0.85)	(0.5,0.1,0.4)	(0.25,0.05,0.6)	(0.1,0,0,0.85)	(0.5,0.1,0.4)	(0.3,0,0,0.6)	(0.75,0.05,0.1)
C7	(0.5,0.1,0.4)	(0.1,0,0,0.85)	(0.5,0.1,0.4)	(0.5,0.1,0.4)	(0.5,0.1,0.4)	(0.6,0,0,0.3)	(0.5,0.1,0.4)	(0.75,0.05,0.1)
C8	(0.25,0.05,0.6)	(0.5,0.1,0.4)	(0.75,0.05,0.1)	(0.3,0,0,0.6)	(0.25,0.05,0.6)	(0.25,0.05,0.6)	(0.25,0.05,0.6)	(0.5,0.1,0.4)

After that picture fuzzy set based evaluation matrix for six decision makers is aggregated by using PFWG as Eq.(7). Then evaluation matrix is transformed to crisp one by using Eq. (9). Then normalization process is applied and normalized evaluation matrix is obtained as Table 5.

Table 5. Normalized evaluation matrix for criteria

Criteria	C1	C2	C3	C4	C5	C6	C7	C8
C1	0.15851	0.19245	0.11325	0.17419	0.16838	0.11065	0.19382	0.15104
C2	0.07536	0.09943	0.14238	0.11564	0.08192	0.10254	0.09617	0.09166
C3	0.15943	0.08137	0.11372	0.15934	0.11625	0.10537	0.09568	0.09255
C4	0.11753	0.11467	0.09431	0.13358	0.15392	0.15283	0.13583	0.14252
C5	0.11828	0.15348	0.12974	0.10463	0.12738	0.23144	0.14768	0.06738
C6	0.16125	0.11253	0.12974	0.09758	0.06485	0.11539	0.15752	0.12835
C7	0.08665	0.11253	0.12974	0.10463	0.09243	0.07848	0.10834	0.21143
C8	0.10858	0.11468	0.13068	0.09758	0.19285	0.09365	0.05371	0.10528

Priorities for criteria are computed by taking the overall row averages and seen as Table 6:

Table 6. Weights of criteria

Criteria	Weights
C1	0.15778
C2	0.10063
C3	0.11546
C4	0.13064
C5	0.13500
C6	0.12090
C7	0.11552
C8	0.11212

According to the Table 6 while human based factors (C1) was found as the most important criterion having the value of 0.15778, business based factors (C2) was obtained as the least important one having the value of 0.10063. Besides decision makers' evaluations are found as consistent because of having CR value (0.012) smaller than 0.1.

Following that decison matrix consisting picture fuzzy numbers for evaluating alternatives in terms of criteria is formed. Decision matrix consisting judgments of DM1 can be seen as Table 7.

Table 7. Decision matrix for evaluating alternatives in terms of criteria

DM1	C1	C2	C3	C4	C5	C6	C7	C8
A1	(0.75,0.05,0.1)	(0.1,0,0,0.85)	(0.9,0,0,0.05)	(0.5,0.1,0.4)	(0.6,0,0,0.3)	(0.25,0.05,0.6)	(0.75,0.05,0.1)	(0.5,0.1,0.4)
A2	(0.6,0,0,0.3)	(0.3,0,0,0.6)	(0.75,0.05,0.1)	(0.25,0.05,0.6)	(0.9,0,0,0.05)	(0.3,0,0,0.6)	(0.75,0.05,0.1)	(0.5,0.1,0.4)
A3	(0.9,0,0,0.05)	(0.1,0,0,0.85)	(0.6,0,0,0.3)	(0.5,0.1,0.4)	(0.75,0.05,0.1)	(0.1,0,0,0.85)	(0.6,0,0,0.3)	(0.3,0,0,0.6)

After applying other steps of picture fuzzy TOPSIS weighted aggregated decision matrix consisting crisp values are shown in Table 8.

Table 8. Weighted aggregated decision matrix consisting crisp values

Alternatives	C1	C2	C3	C4	C5	C6	C7	C8
A1	0.92	0.63	1.15	0.94	0.86	1.08	0.74	1.13
A2	0.84	0.58	0.83	0.76	0.84	0.95	0.66	1.05
A3	0.81	0.43	0.72	0.71	0.62	0.73	0.61	0.94

Closeness coefficients and ranking of alternatives are given in Table 9.

Table 9. Closeness coefficients and ranking of alternatives

Alternatives	$D_{NE}(\tilde{Z}^+, \tilde{Z}_i)$	$D_{NE}(\tilde{Z}^-, \tilde{Z}_i)$	τi	Ranking
A1	0.145	0.128	0.468	1
A2	0.206	0.092	0.308	2
A3	0.278	0.083	0.229	3

According to the Table 9 while Trabzon (A1) was found as the most ideal warehouse location for dangerous goods transportation, Artvin (A3) was obtained as the least ideal one.

CONCLUSION

In this study the risk factors related to the transportation dangerous goods are determined by deep literature review process are weighted by using picture fuzzy AHP. Then warehouse location alternatives are ranked via picture fuzzy TOPSIS method. Picture fuzzy sets are preferred compared to fuzzy, interval-valued and intuitionistic sets due to efficiency, flexibility and easiness for explaining decision makers' views and judgments. The results of the study corrspond to those found by Lazar et. al. (2001), Fabiano et al. (2002), Huang (2006), Kabir and Sumi (2015), Korucuk and Memiş, (2018), Popek (2019) and Batarliene (2020).

A review of the relevant literatüre found no similar study. In this respect, the study can be considered as an example for comparison concerning the Covid 19 pandemic, and the transportation of dangerous goods and their risk factors. Even though the study considered the opinions of experts, the number of experts considered in the group was limited by time constraints. Another constraint could be the Covid 19 pandemic itself. The study may also have been limited by the fact that neither the opinions of the expert group nor the literature review found any criteria set for the theme of risk factors in the transportation of dangerous goods.

The findings of the study were found to support the expectations of the decision-maker, based on interviews with the expert group. However, modeling the real situation is both very difficult and very complex, since human decisions, expectations, and judgments are uncertain and cannot be precisely numerically expressed.

The findings of this study have established that the selection of the storage location in the transportation of dangerous goods during the Covid 19 pandemic is a critical issue that should be emphasized. To obtain more accurate results, the study suggests comparing the results obtained using more than one method.

For further researches, risk factors related to dangerous goods transportation and warehouse locations related to that can be expanded and results can be compared with different MCDM methods. Also, various hybrid techniques can be proposed and applied for real-world complex decision-making problems.

REFERENCES

Acar, Y. (2020). Yeni Koronavirüs (COVID-19) Salgını ve Turizm Faaliyetlerine Etkisi. *Güncel Turizm Araştırmaları Dergisi*, 4(1), 7–21. doi:10.32572/guntad.703410

Ashraf, S., Mahmood, T., Abdullah, S. & Khan, Q. (2019). Different approaches to multicriteria group decision making problems for picture fuzzy environment. *Bull. Braz. Math. Soc. (N.S.)*, 50(2), 373–397.

Batarliene, N., & Jarasuniene, A. (2014). *Analysis of The Accidents and Incidents Occurring During The Transportation of Dangerous Goods By Railway Transport*. Academic Press.

Baterline, N. (2020). Improving Safety of Transportation of Dangerous Goods by Railway Transport. *Infrastructures*, 5(7), 1–12.

Bęczkowska, S. (2019). The method of optimal route selection in road transport of dangerous goods. *Transportation Research Procedia*, 40, 1252–1259. doi:10.1016/j.trpro.2019.07.174

Bonvicini, S., Leonelli, P., & Spadoni, G. (1998). Risk analysis of hazardous materials transportation: Evaluating uncertainty by means of fuzzy logic. *Journal of Hazardous Materials*, 1(62), 59–74. doi:10.1016/S0304-3894(98)00158-7

Çetinyokuş, S., & Mert, A. (2020). Denizyolu tehlikeli madde taşımacılığına yönelik kazaların analizi. *Journal of Humanities and Tourism Research*, 10(1), 41–54.

Chen, Y. S., Biwer, Y. M., Monette, A. F., Luna, R., Yoshimura, R., Detrick, C., Dunn, T., Maheras, S., Bhatnagar, S., & Kapoor, K. (2003). Resource Handbook On Transport Risk Assessment. *International Journal of Radioactive Materials Transport*, 14(1), 29–38. doi:10.1179/rmt.2003.14.1.29

Chen, Z., Chen, Z. G., & Tian, H. (2007). Assessment on Road Transportation System for Dangerous Goods. *Industrial Safety and Environmental Protection*, 33, 51–53.

Cuờng, B. C. (2014). Picture fuzzy sets. *J. Comput. Sci. Cybern.*, 30(4), 409–420.

Daimonlogistics. (2017). *Tehlikeli Madde Lojistiği*. http://daimonlogistics.com/26-tehlikelimadde-tasimaciligi/

Demirci, A., & Arıkan, Ö. U. (2021). COVID-19 döneminde ilaç deposu yeri seçimi: Mersin örneği. *Uluslararası İktisadi ve İdari Bilimler Dergisi*, 7(1), 5–27.

Demirdöğen, O., & Korucuk, S. (2017). Depolama Ve Satın Alma Kararlarının Üretime Etkisi: Tra1 Bölgesi İmalat İşletmelerinde Bir Uygulama. *Dumlupınar Üniversitesi Sosyal Bilimler Dergisi*, 54, 56–76.

Demirel, T., Demirel, N. Ç., & Kahraman, C. (2010). Multicriteria warehouse location selection using choquet integral. *Expert Systems with Applications, 37*(5), 3943–3952. doi:10.1016/j.eswa.2009.11.022

Dutta, P. (2018). Medical diagnosis based on distance measures between picture fuzzy sets. *International Journal of Fuzzy System Applications, 7*(4), 15–36. doi:10.4018/IJFSA.2018100102

Erbaş, M., Bali, Ö., & Durğut, T. (2014), Tehlikeli madde depo yeri seçiminin coğrafi bilgi sistemleri açısından incelenmesi. Uzaktan Algılama- CBS Sempozyumu, İstanbul, Turkey.

Erdal, H. (2018). Tehlikeli Madde Taşımacılığı Güzergâh Seçimi Problemi İçin Stokastik Bir Risk Analizi. *Anemon Muş Alparslan Üniversitesi Sosyal Bilimler Dergisi, 6*(6), 935–943.

Ergün, M., Korucuk, S., & Memiş, S. (2020). Sürdürülebilir Afet Lojistiğine Yönelik İdeal Afet Depo Yeri Seçimi. *Giresun İli Örneği, Çanakkale Onsekiz Mart Üniversitesi Fen Bilimleri Enstitüsü Dergisi, 6*(1), 144–165. doi:10.28979/comufbed.686301

Eroğlu, Ö., Bali, Ö., & Ağdaş, M. (2013). Criteria evaluation model for third party logistics provider selection ın fuel transportation. *XI Logistics and Supply Chain Congress*, 451-470.

Fabiano, B., Curro, F., Palazzi, E., & Pastorino, R. (2002). A framework for risk assessment and decision-making strategies in dangerous good transportation. *Journal of Hazardous Materials, 93*(1), 1–15. doi:10.1016/S0304-3894(02)00034-1 PMID:12062950

Gül, E., & Eren, T. (2017). Lojistik dağıtım ağ problemlerinde analitik hiyerarşi prosesi yöntemi ve hedef programlama ile depo seçimi. *Harran Üniversitesi Mühendislik Dergisi, 2*(1), 1–13.

Gündoğdu, F. K., Duleba, S., Moslem, S., & Aydın, S. (2021). Evaluating public transport service quality using picture fuzzy analytic hierarchy process and linear assignment model. *Applied Soft Computing, 100*, 106920. doi:10.1016/j.asoc.2020.106920

Hale, T., & Moberg, C. R. (2005). Improving supply chain disaster preparedness: A decision process for secure site location. *International Journal of Physical Distribution & Logistics Management, 35*(3), 195–207. doi:10.1108/09600030510594576

Huang, B. (2006). GIS-based route planning for hazardous material transportation. *Journal of Environmental Informatics, 8*(1), 49–57. doi:10.3808/jei.200600076

Huo, H., & Xiong, Z. Y. (2010). Study on the Application of Safety Assessment Model about Source of Hazardous Chemicals. *Advanced Materials Research, 113-116*, 1925–1929. doi:10.4028/www.scientific.net/AMR.113-116.1925

Johnson, A., & McGinnis, L. (2011). Performance Measurement in The Warehousing Industry. *IIE Transactions, 43*(3), 220–230. doi:10.1080/0740817X.2010.491497

Kabir, G., & Sumi, R. S. (2015). Hazardous Waste Transportation Firm Selection Using Fuzzy Analytic Hierarchy and PROMETHEE Methods. *International Journal of Shipping and Transport Logistics, 7*(2), 115. doi:10.1504/IJSTL.2015.067847

Korpela, J., & Tuominen, M. (1996). A decision aid in warehouse site selection. *International Journal of Production Economics, 45*(1-3), 169–180. doi:10.1016/0925-5273(95)00135-2

Korucuk, S. (2018). *Tehlikeli Madde Taşımacılığında Çok Kriterli Karar Verme Yöntemlerinin Kullanımına İlişkin Literatür Taraması*. SOSCON Congress, Antalya.

Korucuk, S., & Memiş, S. (2018). Tedarik Zinciri Yönetimindeki Risk Faktörlerinin AHP İle Ölçülmesi: Erzurum İli Örneği. *Bitlis Eren Üniversitesi Sosyal Bilimler Enstitüsü Dergisi, 7*(2), 1036–1051.

Korucuk, S., & Erdal, H. (2018). AHP-VIKOR Bütünleşik Yaklaşımıyla Lojistik Risk Faktörlerinin ve Risk Yönetimi Araçlarının Sıralanması: Samsun İli Örneği. *İşletme Araştırmaları Dergisi, 10*(3), 282-305.

Lahdelma, R., Salminen, R. P., & Hokkanen, J. (2002). Locating a waste treatment facility by using stochastic multicriteria acceptability analysis with ordinal criteria. *European Journal of Operational Research, 142*(2), 345–356. doi:10.1016/S0377-2217(01)00303-4

Lazar, R. E., Dumitrescu, M., & Stefanescu, I. (2001). Risk Assessment Of Hazardous Waste Transport. Perspectives of GIS Application, 808.1-808.8.

Liu, J. J., Xu, X. H., & Xu, K. (2005). Discussion and analysis of dangerous cargo's road transport. *Journal of Safety Science and Technology, 1*(1), 74–77.

Loree, N., & Aros-Vera, F. (2018). Points of distribution location and inventory management model for postdisaster humanitarian logistics. *Transportation Research Part E, Logistics and Transportation Review, 116*, 1–24. doi:10.1016/j.tre.2018.05.003

Memiş, S., Demir, E., Karamaşa, Ç., & Korucuk, S. (2020). Prioritization Of Road Transportation Risks: An Application in Giresun Province. *Operational Research in Engineering Sciences: Theory and Applications, 3*(2), 111–126.

Mete, H. O., & Zabinsky, Z. B. (2010). Stochastic optimization of medical supply location and distribution in disaster management. *International Journal of Production Economics*, *126*(1), 76–84. doi:10.1016/j.ijpe.2009.10.004

Ministry of Transportation. (2008, June 15). Tehlikeli Maddelerin Karayoluyla Taşınması Hakkında Yönetmelik. *Sayılı Resmi Gazete*.

Obricovic, S., & Milaradov, M. (2016). Multi-Criteria Selection of Municipal Waste Treatment System Using VIKOR Method. *International Journal of Environment and Waste Management*, *18*(1), 43. doi:10.1504/IJEWM.2016.080261

Oggero, A., Darbra, R. M., Munoz, M., Planas, E., & Casal, J. (2006). A survey of accidents occurring during the transport of hazardous substances by road and rail. *Journal of Hazardous Materials*, *133*(1), 1–7. doi:10.1016/j.jhazmat.2005.05.053 PMID:16298045

Oral, N., Yumuşak, R., & Eren, T. (2021). AHP ve ANP yöntemleri kullanılarak tehlikeli madde depo yeri seçimi: Kırıkkale ilinde bir uygulama. *NOHU J. Eng. Sci.*, *10*(1), 115–124.

Özder, E. H., Özcan, E., & Eren, T. (2019). Staff task-based shift scheduling solution with an ANP and goal programming method in a natural gas combined cycle power plant. *Mathematics*, *7*(2), 192–218. doi:10.3390/math7020192

Özyağcı, S. (2008). *Tehlikeli Maddelerin Karayolu İle Taşınması* (Unpublished Master Thesis). İstanbul Technical University Graduate School of Science.

Pisuchpen, R. (2012). Integration of JIT Flexible Manufacturing, Assembly and Disassembly Using a Simulation Approach. *Emerald Insight*, *32*(1), 51–61. doi:10.1108/01445151211198719

Popek, M. (2019). Factors influencing on the environment during hazardous goods transportation by the sea. *IOP Conf. Series: Earth and Environmental Science*, *214*, 1-8.

Prem, K., Liu, Y., Russell, T. W., Kucharski, A. J., Eggo, R. M., Davies, N., & Abbott, S. (2020). The effect of control strategies to reduce social mixing on outcomes of the COVID-19 epidemic in Wuhan, China: A modelling study. *The Lancet. Public Health*, *5*(5), e261–e270. doi:10.1016/S2468-2667(20)30073-6 PMID:32220655

Rodríguez-Espíndola, O., Albores, P., & Brewster, C. (2018). Disaster preparedness in humanitarian logistics: A collaborative approach for resource management in floods. *European Journal of Operational Research*, *264*(3), 978–993. doi:10.1016/j.ejor.2017.01.021

Sert, M., & Kesen, S. E. (2019). Tam Zamanında Üretim Felsefine Dayalı Bir Seri Üretim Hattının Simülasyon Tekniğiyle Performans Analizi. *Selçuk Üniversitesi Mühendislik, Bilim Ve Teknoloji Dergisi*, 7(1), 115–134. doi:10.15317/Scitech.2019.186

Shang, H., Dong, D., Wang, X. & Wu, X. (2008). The Risk Evaluation for Hazardous Materials Transportation. *Service Operations and Logistics, and Informatics*, 1553–1558.

Szeto, W. Y., Farahani, R. Z., & Sumalee, A. (2017). Linkbased multi-class hazmat routing-scheduling problem: A multiple demon approach. *European Journal of Operational Research*, 261(1), 337–354. doi:10.1016/j.ejor.2017.01.048

Ustasüleyman, T., & Perçin, S. (2007). Analitik ağ süreci yaklaşımıyla kuruluş yeri seçimi. *Gazi Üniversitesi İktisadi ve İdari Bilimler Fakültesi Dergisi*, 9(3), 37–55.

WHO. (2010). The world health report: health systems financing: The path to universal coverage. WHO Library,

World Health Organization. (2020). *Coronavirus disease 2019 (COVID-19): Situation report 72*. WHO.

Xin, C., Cui, Y., & Zhao, J. (2007). Research on Some Problems in The Exploration of Project Logistics. *China Water Transport*, 5, 206–208.

Zhidong, Y., Xitang, Z. & Xiang, Y. (2012), Research on the Safety Evaluation of Oil-gas Storage and Transportation Systems Based on AHP. *Guangdong Chemical Industry*, 14.

Chapter 9
The Significant Impact of the COVID-19 Pandemic on Supply Chains

Ana Paula Lopes
https://orcid.org/0000-0003-1603-6959
Polytechnic of Porto, Portugal

EXECUTIVE SUMMARY

As the COVID-19 pandemic has spread across the world, the existence of disruptions in demand and supply have become more severe, conducted by containment measures taken by countries and affecting different sectors around the world. Although businesses and workplaces are restarting activities in some countries, with containment measures gradually being lifted, overall consumer demand is expected to remain low, also determined by the loss of jobs and income. Therefore, the scale of the impact on supply chains exceeded anything most companies had anticipated. This study aims to understand how companies were affected and identify some lessons learned about their vulnerabilities and the possible ways to address them in the long term. On the other hand, it is intended to reveal some of the impacts of COVID-19 and make some practical suggestions that can help in political and operational decisions to strengthen and build additional resilience in supply chains in the future.

INTRODUCTION

Coronavirus disease (COVID-19), is an infectious disease caused by a newly discovered coronavirus, emerged in Wuhan, China, at the end of 2019 (Hui et al.,

DOI: 10.4018/978-1-7998-9140-6.ch009

2020). COVID-19 is an acute, sometimes severe, respiratory illness caused by a novel coronavirus SARS-CoV-2. The clinical spectrum of SARS-CoV-2 infection appears to be wide, encompassing asymptomatic infection, mild upper respiratory tract illness, and severe viral pneumonia with respiratory failure and even death, with many patients being hospitalised with pneumonia in Wuhan and it soon became clear that efficient person-to-person transmission was occurring (Huang et al., 2020; Wang et al., 2020). In a short period of months, the disease went beyond the boundaries of China and spread quickly to other countries worldwide. On March 11 of 2020, World Health organization (WHO) declared COVID 19 a global pandemic (World Health Organization, 2020). The COVID-19 pandemic has caused a collapse in consumer demand forcing governments to implement containment measures, including the closure of jobs. Supply chains play an important role in spreading economic impact across sectors and countries (OIT, 2020b). To limit the spread of COVID-19, governments were forced to implement measures of confinement, which severely affected companies and workers from all over the world. The international interconnectivity of production across global Supply Chains implies that measures of confinement adopted by a particular country can have a significant impact on production and employment in other countries. Supply Chains are particularly complex and extend across multiple countries and sectors, playing a very important role in propagating the economic impacts of containment measures not only in internal markets, but also across borders (Barakat, Ali, Abdelbary, & Haroun, 2020).

There are some main factors that impact production and jobs: on the one hand, the lack of consumer confidence, the decrease in purchasing power resulting from the loss of jobs and income, and the introduction of containment measures, such as the closure of stores or travel restrictions, contributed to a sharp decline in global demand for consumers. On the other hand, the local closure of activities has disrupted the supply of factors of production across borders, causing a lack of vital inputs for industrial production of at least some companies.

In general, when talking about Supply Chain management, there are two very important concepts to take into account, efficiency and resilience. While these concepts are often in conflict with each other, it is the right balance between them that makes supply chains effective.

THE RISK FOR SUPPLY CHAINS

According to (S. Y. Ponomarov, 2012), from the beginning of the 2000s onwards, "as a result of globalization of supply chains, the use of outsourcing, the use of lean methodologies, attacks terrorists committed and of various threats", the theme of risk management in the supply chain wins relevance. However, according to the available literature, the concepts of management and management of risks are still under construction.

On the other hand, some authors have established indications that suggest that the term risk management "relates to coordination between members of a supply chain in order to reduce the

vulnerability throughout the chain" (Jüttner & Maklan, 2011; Jüttner, Peck, & Christopher, 2003). Thus, management would be how the chain is strategically organized to manage risks, referring to its architecture and action planning, in order to avoid unwanted situations, while management is intrinsically linked to the structure and processes within the chain. Also according to (Jüttner et al., 2003), a risk management model is based on four phases, namely the identification of risk sources, risk assessment, strategy proposition and risk mitigation. (Tummala & Schoenherr, 2011) propose in their study the "Supply Chain Risk Management Process (SCRMP)", a model composed of three phases and the treatment of risks effectively and efficiently, as described below:

Phase 1 - Risk Identification
- **Identification** of affected areas and understanding of consequences, aiming to implement mitigation strategies. The identified threats (forces that can produce adverse results) can affect the chain's resources (assets, people, earnings);
- **Risk classification** to determine its consequences and impact magnitude. They can be classified as catastrophic, critical, marginal or despicable. Consequences are the manner or extent to which a threat manifests its effects on resources and may include loss or damage to assets, cost overruns, schedule delays, disruption of service levels, etc.;
- **Risk assessment** refers to the assessment of uncertainties and relates to determining the probability of each risk factor. Each risk has a probability category, that is, the probability index proposed by the model will help to identify the risk. can be considered as very common (occurs 1 x per week), frequent (occurs 1 x per month), rare (occurs 1 x per year), and very rare (occurs 1 x every 10 years).

Phase 2 - Supply Chain Risk Management Process - (SCRMP)
- **Risk estimation** refers to the classification, or ranking, based on the "value assigned to risk exposure (VER)". In this context, the risk is calculated based on the formula below, and the higher the calculated risk value, the greater the attention required in relation to it. The risk it may also be classified as tolerable, acceptable or unacceptable.
- **Risk mitigation and contingency** plans to contain or control risks. Plans are evaluated and the best course of action determined. This step

also considers the analysis of the possible costs involved to mitigate the identified risks, which are classified as: substantial, medium, low and trivial.
- **Risk Totem Pole Analysis** refers to a diagram designed to combine dimensions of risk, allowing the determination of a probability of occurrence rating, severity of consequence and the cost of implementing an action plan in response to an identified risk in the supply chain.

Phase 3 - Supply Chain Risk Management Process - (SCRMP)

In this phase, of control and monitoring of risks, it is possible to check the progress made in relation to the implementation of action plans to respond to risks, determine preventive measures and suggest improvements. Deviations, abnormal cases and interruptions are reported. If the expected results are not achieved, the risk management process must return to Phase 1 for re-analysis.

According to Sheffi & Rice (2005) an interruption will inevitably have a negative effect on the company performance. The authors define the rupture profile and the response dynamics in eight phases, these being:

- Preparation - It refers to the first moment of disruption and, according to the authors, in some cases it can be predicted, giving the company time to prepare, thus minimizing its effects, such as, for example, when there is a strike movement, which aims to halt production. This phase lasts until the moment of rupture, in fact;
- Disruption event - It refers to the disruptive event itself, such as a weather event, a supplier closing the deal, the beginning of a strike. The existence of capabilities, such as redundancy, which presupposes the maintenance of some resources in reserve to be used in the event of an interruption, can serve to mitigate the event;
- Initial response - It refers to the attempt to control the disruptive event and the prevention of further damage;
- Initial impact - It may be noticed immediately or it may take time to affect the business, depending on the magnitude of the disruption. In this case, the available redundancy and the level of resilience inherent in your supply chain can mitigate the effects of the event;
- Total impact - It is noticed when the effects of the event reach their greatest level and the company's performance drops drastically. Objectively, the performance drop starts with the disturbing event. It is at this stage that actions to prepare for recovery begin to manifest themselves;
- Preparation for recovery - It occurs parallel to the first response or even before the response, if it was anticipated. According to the authors, this step

considers the qualification of new suppliers or the redirection of suppliers' resources;
- Recovery - It can be done with the use of loss of production compensation. Companies make use of overtime, producing at a higher than normal level, seeking to recover losses;
- Long-term impact - It has extensive effects. The impact will be greater if it reaches the end of the chain, that is, the customers.

According to Scholten, Scott, & Fynes (2014) and Sheffi & Rice (2005), it is observed that the preparation phase occurs when the company is strategically directed towards prevention behaviours in relation to disruptive events, while the immediate response refers to actions taken immediately after the break. The recovery phase can start still in the response phase and consists of the implementation of actions. Mitigation is linked to risk management and continuous improvement processes. The details of the phases according to (Scholten et al., 2014):

Mitigation
- Establish planning team;
- Analyse supply chain resources and risks;
- Develop a communication plan for preparedness, response and recovery;
- Develop continuous improvement and supply chain risk mitigation plans.

Preparation
- Implement preparedness plan: translate strategic investments into issues operational with the creation of new forms of delivery;
- Evaluate, based on measurements and metrics, the impacts of the interruption;
- Establish routines through training and simulation in the main links in the chain.

Response
- Implement the response plan, measurements and metrics;
- Evaluate directions and controls;
- Evaluate communication throughout the supply chain;
- Assess the extent of supply chain disruption.

Recovery
- Review and implement a recovery plan;
- Ensure continued risk management and resilience;
- Maintain support for employees.

The available literature shows that several risk management models have been developed. However, it is clear that the models have emphasis on a particular aspect and that they differ little from each other. However, the models show, in general, that companies must anticipate the threat of risks, through the prevention and construction of consistent and appropriate plans for the business profile, as well as selecting the best strategy for each type of risk, from in order to reduce the probability of the occurrence of an event and/or reduce its impact, if the rupture materializes.

The COVID-19 pandemic is not the first calamity that unexpectedly damaged supply chains. More than a few other natural catastrophes, such as the 2011 earthquake and tsunami in Fukushima-Japan and extensive flooding in Thailand, the 2003 SARS outbreak in China, the 2004 tsunami in Indonesia (Kraude, Narayanan, Talluri, Singh, & Kajiwara, 2018; Tan & Enderwick, 2006), the 2005 hurricane Katrina barreled ashore in New Orleans (Irwin, 2012), have led to absences of products. But, it can be pointed out here that the production is recovered from these events in a matter of weeks. However, based on range and dimension, the impacts caused by COVID-19 are different from all previous disasters. Most of the disasters, like earthquakes, tsunamis, nuclear accidents, diseases and wars, are frequently restricted to precise geographic areas over quite small periods.

With the virus spreading rapidly to the planet, sending billions of people into lockdown and total confinement, and contributing to the partial or total shutdown of several countries and economies, the disruption of supply chains has become serious (Inoue & Todo, 2020). Furthermore, it is not possible to predict when this pandemic will be contained; any infected area on the planet is undoubtedly a high risk area for a new outbreak, as well as the presence of new variants (Xu, Elomri, Kerbache, & El Omri, 2020).

Supply chains have become fundamental to getting goods and services quickly and safely to all those who are at risk of infection or who are working on the frontlines of the medical response. Therefore, business leaders had to make quick decisions and take immediate action to sustain business operations, serve consumers, customers and communities, as well as to protect and support their employees. COVID-19 not only disrupted the Supply Chains, but it deeply affected Supply Chains at all stages, from the supply sources to the final customers. Has shown that businesses are connected through complex networks of Supply Chains in which the actors at the upstream of a supply chain are seriously affected by the almost "erratic" behavior of downstream actors, essentially large companies, who experience disruptions and very sharp variations in demand (Leonard, 2020).

According to (Sherman, 2020), 94% of companies experienced supply chain disruptions caused by COVID-19, 75% of companies have already suffered negative or extremely negative impacts on their business and 55% of companies intend to lower their growth goals (or have already done so). Thus, the impact of the crisis caused by COVID-19 had repercussions on economies and on the labor market, saving few companies and workers. But, its degree, has varied consonant to the qualities of the company and the worker, not only but also through the countries, depending on their levels of income and economy.

Figure 1 presents a scheme in order to visualize different ways in which workers and companies were and continue to be affected by the crisis caused by COVID-19. It is important to be aware of these mechanisms so that better responses can be designed and projected.

Figure 1. COVID-19: the impact of a global crisis on workers and companies
Source: World Employment and Social Outlook (ILO, 2021b)

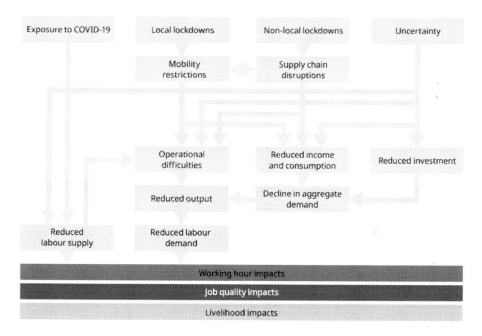

Restrictions in each country, in particular the closure have greatly affected the performance of companies, leading to a snowball effect on global supply chains, international trade and foreign direct investment (ILO, 2020b). In addition, it is necessary to highlight the change in consumer behavior during the pandemic with regard to the types of goods and services acquired as well as the buying methods used by consumers. During home confinement due to lockdown, there was an increase in reliance on the Internet to buy basic goods such as food, particularly in countries with high- and middle-income economies. On the other hand, spending on services such as tourism and restaurants fell abruptly (ILO, 2021a).

Consumer confidence fell across the board at the fastest speed in recent history in March and April 2020. Based on available data, average confidence fell sharply in March and April, reaching the lowest levels measured during the 2008-09 financial crisis (Figure 2). During this latest crisis, it took 20 months for consumer confidence to decline so much, highlighting the extraordinary pace and scale of the crisis related to COVID-19. This graph illustrates the monthly unweighted average of a normalized index for consumer confidence from May 2005 to April 2020 across a sample of 40 countries. Normalization resizes the distance consumer confidence indices expressed in standard deviations around their mean. On April 8, 2020, the World Trade Organization estimated that global trade would fall between 13 and 32 percent by 2020: https://www.wto.org/english/news_e/pres20_e/pr855_e.htm

Figure 2. Consumer confidence dropped dramatically in 2020
Source: Adaptation of COVID-19 and global supply chains (Stefan Kühn, 2020)

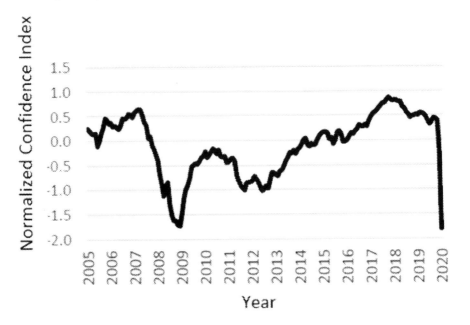

The collapse of retail sales endangers the livelihoods of both those working in the retail sector and those producing the processed products. But not all processed products suffered an equal drop in demand during the COVID-19 crisis, food and pharmaceutical products, for example, are essential goods and have not suffered any declines. The decrease in demand also depended on the strict application of the imposed containment measures, and it was greater when the trade was closed and the physical distance rules were strictly applied. This policy summary classifies

The Significant Impact of the COVID-19 Pandemic on Supply Chains

industrial sectors according to risk (low, medium or high) considering a decrease in demand for their products as a reflection of the crisis, depending on the country where consumers make their purchases. This risk assessment is based on data relating to retail sales, sector indices of stock exchanges, as well as the strictness levels of the containment measures. This risk assessment is based on data retail sales data, sector indices of stock exchanges, as well as the strictness levels of the containment measures.

From 3 June 2020, 292 million jobs in production supply chains were found to be at risk due to falling consumer demand, and another 63 million jobs were at medium risk (Figure 3) (OIT, 2020b). In total, more than one in two jobs in production supply chains, and more than one in seven of all jobs, are currently at medium to high risk, despite the recent relaxation of containment measures in some countries. Most of these workers are subject to losing their job, reduced income, reduced working hours or other pressures of deteriorating working conditions and non-compliance with the provisions established in international standards, while their employers may suffer financial problems or even insolvencies, leading to cutbacks in investments and layoffs. Among the jobs that are at high risk, 167 million jobs belong to the manufacturing sector or other productive sectors. And 29 million of these jobs are in agriculture and 96 million in services, whose activities are responsible for providing inputs. Service workers are directly suffering from the crisis due to many factors, such as the drastic decline in tourism or the closure of trade and other businesses. Thus, the impact on service sector professionals through reduced demand for goods is considerable.

Figure 3. The drop in consumption related to COVID-19 puts jobs in production supply chains at risk (millions)
Source: Estimates based on data from 64 countries that represent 74 percent of the world's workforce, adapted from (Stefan Kühn, 2020)

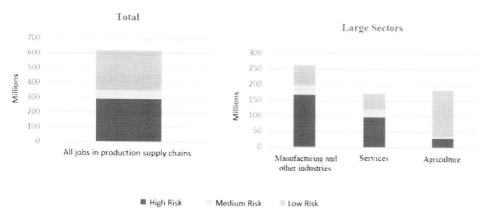

By 2020, there were 73 million high-risk jobs in the textile and apparel supply chains, representing one in four high-risk jobs (OIT, 2020b). The cancellations of orders and the inability to pay those in production, due to the lack of demand from consumers for clothing, threatened, in some cases, the ability of companies in these supply chains to pay the salaries of their staff, mostly women, from low- and middle-income countries. In addition, an estimated 54 million jobs in motor vehicle supply chains were at high risk (OIT, 2020a). The complete collapse of consumer demand for these goods, regardless of the levels of containment measures in a given country, means that jobs in these supply chains have automatically been at high risk.

Although some countries have recently started to relieve containment measures, people have not yet returned to pre-pandemic consumption patterns: in a survey conducted in the United States of America, 56% of consumers said they were cutting back on spending and 48% reported that economic uncertainty was constraining the purchases they planned to make. In China, where more than 90% of clothing stores have reopened, clothing sales, at least initially, remained 50 to 60 percent lower than in the pre-crisis period (AMED et al., 2020). In Germany, more than half of respondents reported not having purchased non-essential items, despite the reopening of stores (Thomasson, 2020).

The dramatic drop in consumer demand, such as for clothes, has had a devastating impact on international fashion brands, with the global fashion industry estimated to have shrunk by up to 30%, in 2020 (AMED et al., 2020). Fashion brands canceled orders for clothing and, in some cases, were unable to pay those already in production, affecting Asian suppliers and their workers. A survey of Bangladeshi employers found that one million people were laid off or made redundant. In many cases, they went home without any pay (Anner, 2020). The call to Action COVID 19 "Action in the Global garment industry" is a joint effort, endorsed by brands and manufacturers, trade unions and the ILO, to catalyze the entire international garment industry's support for business and protect income, health and clothing sector employment (International Labour Organization, 2020). This support is of utmost importance as clothing and textiles constitute a significant part of the exported goods in several Asian economies: 91% in Bangladesh, 67% in Cambodia, 27% in Myanmar and 14% in Vietnam in 2018 (OEC, 2020). In Cambodia, for one in five families the clothing sector is their source of income (OIT, 2019). Globally, 91 million people were employed in the textile and clothing sector in 2019, of which 50 million are women, or 55 percent. In Asia and the Pacific, more than 5 percent of women worked in this sector, making it the largest employer among all industrial sectors, and the fourth largest in the world. Furthermore, considering the total value of jobs in the textile and apparel supply chain in the 64 countries with available estimates, 82 percent are located in Asia and the Pacific (International Textile Manufacturers Federation, 2020).

The closure of activities in one country has potentially serious repercussions in other countries if the supply of production inputs from one country to another is interrupted. Disruptions to supply become even more impactful when many countries close down workplaces as a result of the pandemic. Once stocks are depleted, this can be a serious obstacle for companies to maintain their production and workers to earn income.

At the height of the first wave of the COVID-19 pandemic, nearly 60 percent of all imported inputs were disrupted due to the mandatory closure of all economic activities except those deemed essential. The ILO survey of SCORE Program (Sustainable Competitive and Responsible Enterprises) participants corroborates these estimates, finding that 67 percent of companies experienced supply shortages between February and April (ILO, 2020a).

In June 2020, companies in the manufacturing sector and their workers continued to experience an average decrease of 35 percent in the supply of imported inputs due to the closure of all activities, except essential ones, below the almost 60 percent recorded in early April, as we can see in Figure 4.

Figure 4. Level of disturbances in the supply of imported inputs due to the mandatory closure of activities
Source: This graph presents the weighted average share of jobs relative to the supply of imported intermediate inputs, from countries with necessary closure of all activities except essential ones. The calculations are based on data from 64 countries that represent 74 percent of the world's working population, adapted from (OECD, 2020).

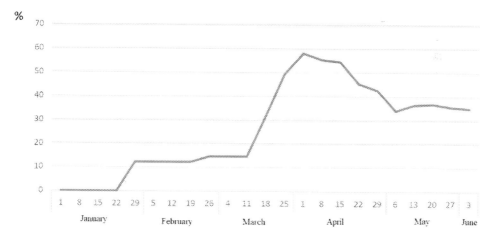

This disruption of input supply chains is likely to contain the recovery of economic activities in countries that can open workplaces, all the more so as suppliers will need time to adapt to new circumstances before they can return to pre-existing levels of activity. crisis, once closures in the workplace are lifted. Moreover, the lack of just one essential input can disrupt the entire supply chain. Given this evidence, it is not surprising that 55% of companies surveyed by the ILO have estimated that supply shortages would continue throughout 2020 (ILO, 2020a).

RESILIENCE IN SUPPLY CHAINS

The concept of resilience was studied from the perspectives of different fields of knowledge, such as ecological, social, physiological, economic, organizational and risk in supply chains (S. Y. Ponomarov, 2012). Although there is, to date, no consensus on the definition of the term "resilience", it appears that several definitions, more or less comprehensive, were created over time. However, it is possible to verify that, in the context of supply chain risk management, several recent studies have adopted the definition described below:

(...) "the adaptive capacity of the supply chain to prepare for unexpected events, respond to interruptions and recover from them, maintaining the continuity of operations at the level of connectivity and control over the desired structure and function (Serhiy Y. Ponomarov & Holcomb, 2009)

According to Scholten et al. (2014), resilience, in the context of the supply chain, is defined as "the adaptive capacity to prepare for unexpected events, respond to interruptions and recover from them, maintaining the continuity of operations at the same level. connectivity and control over structures and functions". Resilience is also addressed as a characteristic of the company or the chain, based on capabilities. The authors discuss, in their article, the existence and relationship of the different capabilities that form resilience, from the perspective of the phases of a rupture, in order to correlate the importance and role of each capability according to the different moments or phases from the rupture to the resumption, in fact, of the operation.

For Christopher & Peck (2004) and (Tukamuhabwa, Stevenson, Busby, & Zorzini, 2015), the resilience of a supply chain is a network phenomenon resulting from connectivity and interdependence between companies.

In turn, the resilience of a company is determined, then, by the resilience of its network, since strategies implemented in specific actors (links), individually, can be harmful and not contribute to the formation of a strong chain. Furthermore, the strategy to be adopted to make a supply chain resilient is intrinsically linked to the types of risks it is exposed to (Sheffi & Rice, 2005).

(Hub, 2020) suggests that a resilient supply chain should be able to detect warning signs about the risks of an interruption, while also responding to these risks by shifting production or service provision to alternative sources, in addition to having a contingency plan that allows the use of substitute suppliers and logistical means.

Likewise, (Ambulkar, Blackhurst, & Grawe, 2015) understand that, when facing an interruption, a company must be able to assess what resources it has, identify which of them are available, where they are, etc., and be able to to add new, recombine, or rearrange existing resource sets. In short, to achieve resilience, companies must be able to reconfigure their resources in the face of disruption. The authors also defend that significant importance, at a strategic level, must be given to the risk of interruption, which is the starting point for decision-making by managers, with regard to the establishment and reconfiguration of critical resources.

LESSONS LEARNED FROM COVID-19 AND THE FUTURE

The chaos caused by the COVID-19 pandemic created the perfect environment for a revolution in the supply chain. Fluctuating demand, unpredictable consumer behavior and commercial vulnerabilities, but they have also created a unique opportunity for business leaders to make smarter and bolder decisions in terms of their supply chains.

This is not a typical risk event and its impact surpasses anything most supply chain leaders would have anticipated. The exponential growth of this virus required continuous evaluation, optimization and monitoring. Therefore, companies needed to respond quickly and confidently, defining and executing a short-term tactical plan that mitigates human health risks and protects the functioning of global supply chains.

The COVID-19 pandemic is not just a short-term crisis. It has lasting implications for how people work and how supply chains work. There is a pressing need for organizations to build long-term resilience into their value chains to deal with future challenges. This requires a holistic approach to managing the supply chain. Organizations must create enough flexibility to protect themselves against future disruptions. Companies should also consider developing a robust framework that includes responsiveness and resilience in risk management operations. This capability must be technology-based, leveraging platforms that support applied analytics, artificial intelligence and machine learning. They must also ensure end-to-end transparency across the entire supply chain. In the long run, risk response will need to become an integral part of business protocols.

Around the world, organizations that have embraced innovation, change and development have realized the short-term competitive advantages and lasting value of more efficient supply chains. It's no wonder, then, that 75% of organizations are planning to adapt to build more resilient supply chains, according to recent surveys exploring how companies around the world have navigated the turmoil of

COVID-19. So what have business leaders learned from 2020 on? And what will the supply chains of the future look like?

CONCLUSION

The best response to emerging challenges sometimes begins with lessons learned, lessons from past facts. In this line, from the verified, rather than a "return to the future", it is important to follow a logic of "moving into the past", recalling areas of strategic potential for the world, as it was in the past and as it will continue to be, the economy, in order to be well prepared for the "next day" of the post-crisis.

The COVID-19 pandemic is not just a short-term crisis. It has lasting implications for how people work and how supply chains work. There is a pressing need for organizations to build long-term resilience into their value chains to deal with future challenges. This requires a holistic approach to managing the supply chain. Organizations must create enough flexibility to protect themselves against future disruptions. Companies should also consider developing a robust framework that includes responsiveness and resilience in risk management operations. This capacity should be based on technology, taking advantage of platforms that support applied analytics, artificial intelligence and machine learning. They must also ensure transparency throughout the supply chain. In the long run, risk response will need to become an integral part of business protocols.

This pandemic and other disruptions have changed the priorities of many supply chain leaders. Now, more than ever, they need to balance cost and operational efficiency with greater supply chain resilience to protect their networks. As John (2014), said "Disruptions to supply chain operations have intensified in the past few years. This means that the cost of retaining multiple supply locations must be seen more as a cost of doing business, rather than an inefficiency".

It will be in the capacity of the various countries to respond to the strategic challenges presented that future global resilience will lie. A more developed, stronger and more protected planet will be more likely to better resist threats and risks, whether they are presented in a microscopic, environmental or other form, for which the right, preventive, responsible and sustained investments must be promoted, knowing, however, that financial resources are always scarce. In the XIX century, the French physicist and mathematician, Laplace, considered that the future could be foreseen if he had enough information and time to develop the necessary calculations; today, we know that this will not be possible, not even in the most precise sciences, much less in economics (Samuelson, P. A. & Northaus, 1988), even more because of the countless variables and uncertainties brought about by the current pandemic. However, this does not imply that proper planning is not done, in a coherent and articulated manner. One thing is certain: a fragile economic health makes the country more vulnerable and subject to the worsening of its state, while a timely prophylaxis, with adequate and appropriate measures planned, will help to face emerging diseases, whether in the form of risks or threats.

REFERENCES

Ambulkar, S., Blackhurst, J., & Grawe, S. (2015). Firm's resilience to supply chain disruptions: Scale development and empirical examination. *Journal of Operations Management*, *33-34*(1), 111–122. Advance online publication. doi:10.1016/j.jom.2014.11.002

Amed, I., Berg, A., Balchandani, A., Hedrich, S., Rölkens, F., Young, R., ... Rolkens, F. (2020). The State of Fashion 2020: Coronavirus Update. McKinsey & Company.

Anner, M. (2020). *Abandoned? The Impact of Covid-19 on Workers and Businesses at the Bottom of Global Garment Supply Chains*. Penn State Center for Global Rights (CGWR).

Barakat, M., Ali, A., Abdelbary, I., & Haroun, M. (2020). *The impact of supply chain integration on operational performance through resilience under COVID-19 pandemic*. doi:10.24264/icams-2020.III.2

Christopher, M., & Peck, H. (2004). Building the Resilient Supply Chain. *International Journal of Logistics Management*, *15*(2), 1–14. Advance online publication. doi:10.1108/09574090410700275

Huang, C., Wang, Y., Li, X., Ren, L., Zhao, J., Hu, Y., Zhang, L., Fan, G., Xu, J., Gu, X., Cheng, Z., Yu, T., Xia, J., Wei, Y., Wu, W., Xie, X., Yin, W., Li, H., Liu, M., ... Cao, B. (2020). Clinical features of patients infected with 2019 novel coronavirus in Wuhan, China. *Lancet*, *395*(10223), 497–506. Advance online publication. doi:10.1016/S0140-6736(20)30183-5 PMID:31986264

Hub. (2020). *How Coronavirus will affect the global supply chain*. Author.

Hui, D. S., & Azhar, I. (2020, February). The continuing 2019-nCoV epidemic threat of novel coronaviruses to global health— The latest 2019 novel coronavirus outbreak in Wuhan, China. *International Journal of Infectious Diseases*, *91*, 264–266. Advance online publication. doi:10.1016/j.ijid.2020.01.009 PMID:31953166

ILO. (2020a). *ILO SCORE Global Covid-19 Enterprise Survey*. Retrieved from https://www.ilo.org/wcmsp5/groups/public/---ed_emp/---emp_ent/documents/presentation/wcms_745097.pdf

ILO. (2020b). *Working from Home: Estimating the worldwide potential*. International Labour Organization Policy Brief.

ILO. (2021a). *World Employment And Social Outlook: The role of digital labour platforms in transforming the world of work International*. International Labour Organization.

ILO. (2021b). *World Employment And Social Outlook: Trends 2021*. ILO.

Inoue, H., & Todo, Y. (2020). The Propagation of the Economic Impact through Supply Chains: The Case of a Mega-City Lockdown against the Spread of COVID-19. SSRN *Electronic Journal*. doi:10.2139/ssrn.3564898

International Labour Organization. (2020). *COVID-19 : Action in the Global Garment Industry*. Author.

International Textile Manufacturers Federation. (2020). *2nd ITMF-Survey about the Impact of the Corona-Pandemic on the Global Textile Industry*. ITMF Press Release.

Irwin, N. (2012). Why Hurricane Katrina Should Make Us Optimistic About Economic Impact of Sandy. *Washington Post*.

John, G. (2014). *Innovative Approaches to Supply Chain Risk (SCM World)*. Report.

Jüttner, U., & Maklan, S. (2011). Supply chain resilience in the global financial crisis: An empirical study. *Supply Chain Management, 16*(4), 246–259. Advance online publication. doi:10.1108/13598541111139062

Jüttner, U., Peck, H., & Christopher, M. (2003). Supply chain risk management: outlining an agenda for future research. *International Journal of Logistics Research and Applications*. doi:10.1080/13675560310001627016

Kraude, R., Narayanan, S., Talluri, S., Singh, P., & Kajiwara, T. (2018). Cultural Challenges in Mitigating International Supply Chain Disruptions. *IEEE Engineering Management Review, 46*(1), 98–105. Advance online publication. doi:10.1109/EMR.2018.2809910

Leonard, M. (2020). *What procurement managers should expect from a 'bullwhip on crack*. Retrieved from https://www.supplychaindive.com/

OEC. (2020). *Exports of textiles for selected countries*. Author.

OECD. (2020). *International trade — OECD Statistics on International Trade in Services Publication*. OECD.

OIT. (2019). *Promoting decent work in garment sector global supply chains: Highlights and insights from the ILO project.* OIT.

OIT. (2020a). *A COVID-19 e a indústria automóvel.* Retrieved from https://www.ilo.org/lisbon/publicações/WCMS_754378/lang--pt/index.htm

OIT. (2020b). *The effects of COVID-19 on trade and global supply chains.* Research Brief.

Ponomarov, S. Y. (2012). *Antecedents and consequences of supply chain resilience: a dynamic capabilities perspective.* Doctoral Dissertations University.

Ponomarov, S. Y., & Holcomb, M. C. (2009, May 22). Understanding the concept of supply chain resilience. *International Journal of Logistics Management, 20*(1), 124–143. Advance online publication. doi:10.1108/09574090910954873

Samuelson, P. A., & Northaus, W. D. (1988). Economia (12th ed.). New York: McGraw-Hill.

Scholten, K., Scott, P. S., & Fynes, B. (2014). Mitigation processes - antecedents for building supply chain resilience. *Supply Chain Management, 19*(2), 211–228. Advance online publication. doi:10.1108/SCM-06-2013-0191

Sheffi, Y., & Rice, J. B. (2005). A supply chain view of the resilient enterprise. *MIT Sloan Management Review.*

Sherman, E. (2020). *94% of the Fortune 1000 are seeing coronavirus supply chain disruptions: Report.* Fortune.

Stefan Kühn, C. V. (2020). *A COVID-19 e as cadeias globais de abastecimento: Como a crise no emprego se propaga além-fronteiras.* Academic Press.

Tan, W. J., & Enderwick, P. (2006). Managing threats in the Global Era: The impact and response to SARS. *Thunderbird International Business Review, 48*(4), 515–536. Advance online publication. doi:10.1002/tie.20107

Thomasson, E. (2020). *Brands See an Uptick in Online Sales During the Covid-19 Crisis.* Retrieved from https://www.businessoffashion.com/articles/retail/brands-see-an-uptick-in-online-sales-during-the-covid-19-crisis

Tukamuhabwa, B. R., Stevenson, M., Busby, J., & Zorzini, M. (2015). Supply chain resilience: Definition, review and theoretical foundations for further study. *International Journal of Production Research, 53*(18), 5592–5623. Advance online publication. doi:10.1080/00207543.2015.1037934

Tummala, R., & Schoenherr, T. (2011). Assessing and managing risks using the Supply Chain Risk Management Process (SCRMP). *Supply Chain Management*, *16*(6), 474–483. Advance online publication. doi:10.1108/13598541111171165

Wang, D., Hu, B., Hu, C., Zhu, F., Liu, X., Zhang, J., Wang, B., Xiang, H., Cheng, Z., Xiong, Y., Zhao, Y., Li, Y., Wang, X., & Peng, Z. (2020). Clinical Characteristics of 138 Hospitalized Patients with 2019 Novel Coronavirus-Infected Pneumonia in Wuhan, China. *Journal of the American Medical Association*, *323*(11), 1061. Advance online publication. doi:10.1001/jama.2020.1585 PMID:32031570

World Health Organization. (2020). *Coronavirus disease 2019 (COVID-19). Situation Report, 32*. WHO.

Xu, Z., Elomri, A., Kerbache, L., & El Omri, A. (2020). Impacts of COVID-19 on Global Supply Chains: Facts and Perspectives. *IEEE Engineering Management Review*, *48*(3), 153–166. Advance online publication. doi:10.1109/EMR.2020.3018420

Compilation of References

Acar, Y. (2020). Yeni Koronavirüs (COVID-19) Salgını ve Turizm Faaliyetlerine Etkisi. *Güncel Turizm Araştırmaları Dergisi*, *4*(1), 7–21. doi:10.32572/guntad.703410

Acemoglu, D., Chernozhukov, V., Werning, I., & Whinston, M. D. (2020). *Optimal Targeted Lockdowns in a Multi-Group SIR Model*. NBER Working Papers 27102, National Bureau of Economic Research, Inc.

Adabalı, M. M. (2020). Konya İlinde Faaliyet Gösteren 4 ve 5 Yıldızlı Otel İşletmelerinde Kapasite Yönetimi Stratejilerinin Belirlenmesi ve Bir Uygulama. *International Journal of Arts and Social Studies*, *3*(4), 34–49.

Adenso-Diaz, B., Mena, C., García-Carbajal, S., & Liechty, M. (2012). The impact of supply network characteristics on reliability. *Supply Chain Management*, *17*(3), 263–276. doi:10.1108/13598541211227108

Agrawal, M., Eloot, K., Mancini, M., & Patel, A. (2020). Industry 4.0: Reimagining manufacturing operations after COVID-19. *McKinsey Insights*, (July), 1–18.

Ahmad, S. (2015). Green human resource management: Policies and practices. *Cogent Business and Management*, *2*(1), 1–13. doi:10.1080/23311975.2015.1030817

Akçakanat, Ö., Eren, H., Aksoy, E., & Ömürbek, V. (2017). Bankacılık Sektöründe Entropı Ve Waspas Yöntemleri İle Performans Değerlendirmesi. *Süleyman Demirel Üniversitesi İktisadi ve İdari Bilimler Fakültesi Dergisi*, *22*(2), 285–300.

Akturk, M. S., Ketzenberg, M., & Yıldız, B. (2021). Managing consumer returns with technology-enabled countermeasures. *Omega*, *102*, 102337. doi:10.1016/j.omega.2020.102337

Al Mujaini, S., & Walke, S. (n.d.). *Identification and assessment of innovative green supply chain practices in the oil and gas industry of the Gulf Cooperation Council (GCC) countries*. Academic Press.

Alarçin, M., & Kırçova, İ. (2020). A Conceptual Study On car-sharing Services Based On Sharing Economy. *Business & Management Studies: An International Journal*, *8*(5), 4521–4545.

Compilation of References

Ali, A., Mahfouz, A., & Arisha, A. (2017). Analysing supply chain resilience: Integrating the constructs in a concept mapping framework via a systematic literature review. *Supply Chain Management*, 22(1), 16–39. doi:10.1108/SCM-06-2016-0197

Alves, M. A. (2018). *Proposta de Agregação Robusta de Múltiplos Métodos com Incertezas em Problemas de Tomada de Decisão Multicritério*. Academic Press.

Ambulkar, S., Blackhurst, J., & Grawe, S. (2015). Firm's resilience to supply chain disruptions: Scale development and empirical examination. *Journal of Operations Management*, 33-34(1), 111–122. Advance online publication. doi:10.1016/j.jom.2014.11.002

Amed, I., Berg, A., Balchandani, A., Hedrich, S., Rölkens, F., Young, R., ... Rolkens, F. (2020). The State of Fashion 2020: Coronavirus Update. McKinsey & Company.

Anand, G., & Kodali, R. (2008). Selection of lean manufacturing systems using the PROMETHEE. *Journal of Modelling in Management*, 3(1), 40–70. doi:10.1108/17465660810860372

Anderson, E. T., Hansen, K., & Simester, D. (2009). The option value of returns: Theory and empirical evidence. *Marketing Science*, 28(3), 405–423. doi:10.1287/mksc.1080.0430

Anner, M. (2020). *Abandoned? The Impact of Covid-19 on Workers and Businesses at the Bottom of Global Garment Supply Chains*. Penn State Center for Global Rights (CGWR).

Anupindi, R., & Jiang, L. (2008). Capacity investment under postponement strategies, market competition, and demand uncertainty. *Management Science*, 54(11), 1876–1890. doi:10.1287/mnsc.1080.0940

Arashpour, M., Bai, Y., Aranda-mena, G., Bab-Hadiashar, A., Hosseini, R., & Kalutara, P. (2017). Optimizing decisions in advanced manufacturing of prefabricated products: Theorizing supply chain configurations in off-site construction. *Journal of Automation in Construction*, 84, 146–153. doi:10.1016/j.autcon.2017.08.032

Aria, M., & Cuccurullo, C. (2017). Bibliometrix: An R-tool for comprehensive science mapping analysis. *Journal of Informetrics*, 11(4), 959–975. doi:10.1016/j.joi.2017.08.007

Arslan, M. (2020). Corporate social sustainability in supply chain management: A literature review. *Journal of Global Responsibility*, 11(3), 233–255. doi:10.1108/JGR-11-2019-0108

Asdecker, B., Karl, D., & Sucky, E. (2017). Examining drivers of consumer returns in e-tailing with real shop data. In *Proceedings of the 50th Hawaii International Conference on System Sciences* (pp. 4192-4201). University of Hawaii. 10.24251/HICSS.2017.507

Ashraf, S., Mahmood, T., Abdullah, S. & Khan, Q. (2019). Different approaches to multicriteria group decision making problems for picture fuzzy environment. *Bull. Braz. Math. Soc. (N.S.)*, 50(2), 373–397.

Azadfallah, M. (2017). Evaluation and selection of suppliers in the supply chain using the extended group PROMETHEE I procedures. *International Journal of Supply Chain and Operations Resilience*, 3(1), 56. doi:10.1504/IJSCOR.2017.087161

Compilation of References

Badri, M. A., & Abdulla, M. H. (2004). Awards of excellence in institutions of higher education: An AHP approach. *International Journal of Educational Management*, *18*(4), 224–242. doi:10.1108/09513540410538813

Banerjee, A. (2016). Agile Supply Chain Mangement. In Handbook of Research on Strategic Supply Chain Management in the Retail Industry (pp. 55-152). IGI Global.

Barakat, M., Ali, A., Abdelbary, I., & Haroun, M. (2020). *The impact of supply chain integration on operational performance through resilience under COVID-19 pandemic.* doi:10.24264/icams-2020.III.2

Baranov, D. (2019). *How 3D printers reshape retail business.* https://blog.dataart.com/how-3d-printers-reshape-retail-business

Barkho, G. (2020). *How the coronavirus changed retailers' returns policies.* https://www.modernretail.co/retailers/how-the-coronavirus-changed-retailers-returns-policies/

Batarliene, N., & Jarasuniene, A. (2014). *Analysis of The Accidents and Incidents Occurring During The Transportation of Dangerous Goods By Railway Transport.* Academic Press.

Baterline, N. (2020). Improving Safety of Transportation of Dangerous Goods by Railway Transport. *Infrastructures*, *5*(7), 1–12.

Bayazit, O. (2006). Use of analytic network process in vendor selection decisions. *Benchmarking*, *13*(5), 566–579. doi:10.1108/14635770610690410

Bęczkowska, S. (2019). The method of optimal route selection in road transport of dangerous goods. *Transportation Research Procedia*, *40*, 1252–1259. doi:10.1016/j.trpro.2019.07.174

Bektaş, T., Crainic, T. G., & Van Woensel, T. (2017). From Managing Urban Freight to Smart City Logistics Networks. In Network Design and Optimization for Smart Cities (143-188). Academic Press.

Bell, D. R., Gallino, S., & Moreno, A. (2014). How to win in an omnichannel world. *MIT Sloan Management Review*, *56*(1), 45–53.

Bello, W. (2013). *Capitalism's Last Stand? Deglobalization in the Age of Austerity.* Zed Books. doi:10.5040/9781350218895

Bernon, M., Cullen, J., & Gorst, J. (2016). Online retail returns management: Integration within an omni-channel distribution context. *International Journal of Physical Distribution & Logistics Management*, *46*(6/7), 584–605. doi:10.1108/IJPDLM-01-2015-0010

Bhool, R., & Narwal, M. S. (2013). An analysis of drivers affecting the implementation of green supply chain management for the Indian manufacturing industries. *International Journal of Research in Engineering and Technology*, *2*(11), 2319–1163.

Bhuju, D., Thapa-parajuli, R., Sharma, P., & Aryal, P. (2014). *Nepal's green economy initiative and framework proposed Nepal's green economy initiative and framework proposed.* Academic Press.

Blackburn, J. D., Guide, V. D. R. Jr, Souza, G. C., & Van Wassenhove, L. N. (2004). Reverse supply chains for commercial returns. *California Management Review*, *46*(2), 6–22. doi:10.2307/41166207

Blome, C., Schoenherr, T., & Eckstein, D. (2013). The impact of knowledge transfer and complexity on supply chain flexibility: A knowledge-based view. *International Journal of Production Economics*, *147*, 307–316. doi:10.1016/j.ijpe.2013.02.028

Blondel, V. D., Guillaume, J. L., Lambiotte, R., & Lefebvre, E. (2008). Fast unfolding of communities in large networks. *Journal of Statistical Mechanics*, *2008*(10), P10008. doi:10.1088/1742-5468/2008/10/P10008

Blos, M. F., Mohammed Quaddus, H. M. W., & Watanabe, K. (2009). Supply Chain Risk Management (SCRM): A Case Study on the Automotive and Electronic Industries in Brazil. *Supply Chain Management*, *14*(4), 247–252. doi:10.1108/13598540910970072

Bonacini, L., Gallo, G., & Scicchitano, S. (2021). Working from home and income inequality: Risks of a 'new normal' with COVID-19. *Journal of Population Economics*, *34*(1), 303–360. doi:10.100700148-020-00800-7

Bonifield, C., Cole, C., & Schultz, R. L. (2010). Product returns on the internet: A case of mixed signals? *Journal of Business Research*, *63*(9-10), 1058–1065. doi:10.1016/j.jbusres.2008.12.009

Bonvicini, S., Leonelli, P., & Spadoni, G. (1998). Risk analysis of hazardous materials transportation: Evaluating uncertainty by means of fuzzy logic. *Journal of Hazardous Materials*, *1*(62), 59–74. doi:10.1016/S0304-3894(98)00158-7

Bozarth, C. C., Donald, P. W., Barbara, B. F., & Flynn, E. J. (2009). The impact of Supply Chain Complexity on manufacturing plant performance. *Journal of Operations Management*, *27*(1), 78–93. doi:10.1016/j.jom.2008.07.003

Brannen, S., Ahmed, H., & Newton, H. (2020). *Covid-19 Reshapes the Future*. Center for Strategic and International Studies.

Brans, J-P., & De Smet, Y. (2017). *PROMETHEE methods* (Vol. 3). doi:10.1007/978-1-4939-3094-4

Brans, J. P., & De Smet, Y. (2016). *PROMETHEE methods* (Vol. 233). International Series in Operations Research and Management Science. doi:10.1007/978-1-4939-3094-4_6

Brans, J.-P., & Mareschal, B. (2005). PROMETHEE methods. In *Multiple criteria decision analysis: state of the art surveys*. Springer. doi:10.1007/0-387-23081-5_5

Briggs, C. A. (2010). *Risk Assessment in the Up Stream Crude Oil Supply Chain: Leveraging Analytic Hierarchy Process* (Unpublished Ph.D. thesis). North Dakota University.

Brindley, C. (Ed.). (2004). Supply Chain Risks. Ashgate Publishing.

Browne, B. J., & Dubois, D. (1984). Classification of flexible manufacturing systems. *The FMS Magazine*, 114–117.

Compilation of References

BSI. (2014). *Supply Chain Impact of 2014 Ebola Outbreak.* Retrieved April 20, 2021, from https://www.bsigroup.com/globalassets/localfiles/aaa/Whitepaper%20Ebola_10.14_7.pdf

Bulut, Z. A. (2004). İşletmeler Açısından Kapasite Planlaması ve Kapasite Planlamasına Etki Eden Faktörler. *Mevzuat Dergisi, 7*(80), 1–13.

Cai, M., & Luo, J. (2020). Influence of COVID-19 on Manufacturing Industry and Corresponding Countermeasures from Supply Chain Perspective. *Journal of Shanghai Jiaotong University (Science), 25*(4), 409–416. doi:10.100712204-020-2206-z PMID:32834699

Çakır, E. & Kutlu Karabıyık, B. (n.d.). Bütünleşik SWARA - COPRAS Yöntemi Kullanarak Bulut Depolama Hizmet Sağlayıcılarının Değerlendirilmesi. *Bilişim Teknolojileri Dergisi, 10*, 417-434.

Çakır, S., & Perçin, S. (2013). Çok Kriterli Karar Verme Teknikleriyle Lojistik Firmalarında Performans Ölçümü. *Ege Akademik Bakış, 13*(4), 449–459. doi:10.21121/eab.2013418079

Çalışkan, A. Ö. (2012). *İşletmelerde Sürdürülebilirlik ve Muhasebe Mesleği İlişkisi.* In Mali Çözüm Dergisi. İSMMMO.

Calnan, M., Gadsby, E. W., Kondé, M. K., Diallo, A., & Rossman, J. S. (2018). The response to and impact of the Ebola epidemic: Towards an agenda for interdisciplinary research. *International Journal of Health Policy and Management, 7*(5), 402–411. doi:10.15171/ijhpm.2017.104 PMID:29764104

Çebi, F., & Bayraktar, D. (2003). An integrated approach for supplier selection. *Logistics Information Management, 16*(6), 395–400. doi:10.1108/09576050310503376

Çetinyokuş, S., & Mert, A. (2020). Denizyolu tehlikeli madde taşımacılığına yönelik kazaların analizi. *Journal of Humanities and Tourism Research, 10*(1), 41–54.

Chakraborty, S., Bhattacharyya, O., Zavadskas, E. K., & Antucheviciene, J. (2015). Application of WASPAS Method as an Optimization Tool in Non-Traditional Machining Processes. *Information Technology and Control, 44*(1), 77–88.

Chakraborty, S., & Zavadskas, E. K. (2014). Applications of WASPAS Method in Manufacturing Decision Making. *Informatica (Vilnius), 25*(1), 1–20. doi:10.15388/Informatica.2014.01

Chang, W., Ellinger, A. E., & Blackhurst, J. (2015). A contextual approach to supply chain risk mitigation. *International Journal of Logistics Management, 26*(3), 642–656. doi:10.1108/IJLM-02-2014-0026

Chatterjee, P., & Chakraborty, S. (2012). Material Selection Using Preferential Ranking Methods. *Materials & Design, 35*, 384–393. doi:10.1016/j.matdes.2011.09.027

Chen, C. T., Lin, C. T., & Huang, S. F. (2006). A fuzzy approach for supplier evaluation and selection in supply chain management. *International Journal of Production Economics, 102*(2), 289–301. doi:10.1016/j.ijpe.2005.03.009

Chen, J. I., & Paulraj, A. (2004). Towards A Theory Of Supply Chain Management: The Constructs And Measurements. *Journal of Operations Management*, *22*(2), 119–150. doi:10.1016/j.jom.2003.12.007

Chen, Y. S., Biwer, Y. M., Monette, A. F., Luna, R., Yoshimura, R., Detrick, C., Dunn, T., Maheras, S., Bhatnagar, S., & Kapoor, K. (2003). Resource Handbook On Transport Risk Assessment. *International Journal of Radioactive Materials Transport*, *14*(1), 29–38. doi:10.1179/rmt.2003.14.1.29

Chen, Z., Chen, Z. G., & Tian, H. (2007). Assessment on Road Transportation System for Dangerous Goods. *Industrial Safety and Environmental Protection*, *33*, 51–53.

Chiaramonti, D., & Maniatis, K. (2020). Security of supply, strategic storage and Covid19: Which lessons learnt for renewable and recycled carbon fuels, and their future role in decarbonizing transport? *Applied Energy*, *271*, 115216. doi:10.1016/j.apenergy.2020.115216

Chin, T. A., Tat, H. H., & Sulaiman, Z. (2015). Green supply chain management, environmental collaboration and sustainability performance. *Procedia CIRP*, *26*, 695–699. doi:10.1016/j.procir.2014.07.035

Chou, J., Kuo, N. F., & Peng, S. L. (2004). Potential impacts of the SARS outbreak on Taiwan's economy. *Asian Economic Papers*, *3*(1), 84–99. doi:10.1162/1535351041747969

Chowdhury, P., Paul, S. K., Kaisar, S., & Moktadir, M. A. (2021). COVID-19 pandemic related supply chain studies: A systematic review. *Transportation Research Part E, Logistics and Transportation Review*, *148*, 102271. doi:10.1016/j.tre.2021.102271 PMID:33613082

Christopher, M., & Peck, H. (2004). Building the Resilient Supply Chain. *International Journal of Logistics Management*, *15*(2), 1–14. doi:10.1108/09574090410700275

Christopher, M., & Towill, D. R. (2001). An Integrated Model for The Design of Agile Supply Chains. *International Journal of Physical Distribution & Logistics Management*, *31*(4), 235–246. doi:10.1108/09600030110394914

Cleophas, C., Cottrill, C., Ehmke, J. F., & Tierney, K. (2019). Collaborative urban transportation: Recent advances in theory and practice. *European Journal of Operational Research*, *273*(3), 801–816. doi:10.1016/j.ejor.2018.04.037

Çotur, Ö. K., & Öztürkoğlu, Y. (2016). Partnerships in supply chain management. In *Handbook of Research on Global Supply Chain Management* (pp. 161–185). IGI Global. doi:10.4018/978-1-4666-9639-6.ch010

Cường, B. C. (2014). Picture fuzzy sets. *J. Comput. Sci. Cybern.*, *30*(4), 409–420.

Cycleon. (2021). *Consumer returns during and after COVID-19*. https://cycleon.com/wp-content/uploads/2021/06/how-consumer-return-whitepaper-.pdf

Daimonlogistics. (2017). *Tehlikeli Madde Lojistiği*. http://daimonlogistics.com/26-tehlikelimadde-tasimaciligi/

Compilation of References

Darchambeau, M. (2020). *Covid-19 and The Last Mile*. Retrieved April 20, 2021, from https://postandparcel.info/120509/podcasts/covid-19-and-the-outbound-logistics/

Daugherty, P. J., Richey, R. G., Genchev, S. E., & Chen, H. (2005). Reverse logistics: Superior performance through focused resource commitments to information technology. *Transportation Research Part E, Logistics and Transportation Review*, 41(2), 77–92. doi:10.1016/j.tre.2004.04.002

Davis, S., Gerstner, E., & Hagerty, M. (1995). Money back guarantees in retailing: Matching products to consumer tastes. *Journal of Retailing*, 71(1), 7–22. doi:10.1016/0022-4359(95)90010-1

Davis, S., Hagerty, M., & Gerstner, E. (1998). Return policies and the optimal level of "hassle". *Journal of Economics and Business*, 50(5), 445–460. doi:10.1016/S0148-6195(98)00013-7

de Araújo, A. C., Matsuoka, E. M., Ung, J. E., Massote, A., & Sampaio, M. (2018). An exploratory study on the returns management process in an online retailer. *International Journal of Logistics Research and Applications*, 21(3), 345–362. doi:10.1080/13675567.2017.1370080

de Boer, L., Labro, E., & Morlacchi, P. (2001). A review of methods supporting supplier selection. *European Journal of Purchasing and Supply Management*, 7(2), 75–89. doi:10.1016/S0969-7012(00)00028-9

de Borba, J. L. G., de Magalhães, M. R., Filgueiras, R. S., & Bouzon, M. (2020). Barriers in omnichannel retailing returns: A conceptual framework. *International Journal of Retail & Distribution Management*, 49(1), 121–143. doi:10.1108/IJRDM-04-2020-0140

De, P., Hu, Y., & Rahman, M. S. (2013). *Product-oriented web technologies and product returns: An exploratory study*. https://cycleon.com/wp-content/uploads/2021/06/how-consumer-return-whitepaper-.pdfm doi:10.1287/isre.2013.0487

Demirci, A., & Arıkan, Ö. U. (2021). COVID-19 döneminde ilaç deposu yeri seçimi: Mersin örneği. *Uluslararası İktisadi ve İdari Bilimler Dergisi*, 7(1), 5–27.

Demirdöğen, O., & Korucuk, S. (2017). Depolama Ve Satın Alma Kararlarının Üretime Etkisi: Tra1 Bölgesi İmalat İşletmelerinde Bir Uygulama. *Dumlupınar Üniversitesi Sosyal Bilimler Dergisi*, 54, 56–76.

Demirel, T., Demirel, N. Ç., & Kahraman, C. (2010). Multicriteria warehouse location selection using choquet integral. *Expert Systems with Applications*, 37(5), 3943–3952. doi:10.1016/j.eswa.2009.11.022

Dey, I. (1993). *Qualitative Data Analysis*. Routledge.

Dey, M., & Loewenstein, M. (2020). How many workers are employed in sectors directly affected by COVID-19 shutdowns, where do they work, and how much do they earn? *Monthly Labor Review*, (April), 1–19. doi:10.21916/mlr.2020.6

Diabat, A., & Govindan, K. (2011). An analysis of the drivers affecting the implementation of green supply chain management. *Resources, Conservation and Recycling*, 55(6), 659–667. doi:10.1016/j.resconrec.2010.12.002

Dias, E. M. P. da S. (2015). *Modelo de apoio à decisão multicritério para selecção de fornecedores de azeite*. Faculdade de Economia do Porto.

Difrancesco, R. M., Huchzermeier, A., & Schröder, D. (2018). Optimizing the return window for online fashion retailers with closed-loop refurbishment. *Omega*, *78*, 205–221. doi:10.1016/j.omega.2017.07.001

Doganay, A., & Ergun, S. (2017). The effect of supply chain collaboration on supply chain performance. *Journal of Management Marketing and Logistics*, *4*(1), 30–39. doi:10.17261/Pressacademia.2017.377

Dohale, V., Ambilkar, P., Gunasekaran, A., & Verma, P. (2021). Supply chain risk mitigation strategies during COVID-19: exploratory cases of "make-to-order" handloom saree apparel industries. *International Journal of Physical Distribution & Logistics Management*.

Dorgham, K., Nouaouri, I., Nicolas, J. C., & Goncalves, G. (2020). A Collaborative Supply Chain Network Design within a Territory Hospital Group. In *13ème Conference Internationale De Modelisation*. AGADIR.

Downes, H. (2021). *Coronavirus: Extended returns policies and your rights to a refund*. https://www.which.co.uk/news/2021/02/coronavirus-extended-returns-policies-and-your-rights-to-a-refund/

Dun & Bradstreet. (2020). *Blindsided on the Supply Side*. Retrieved March 20, 2021, from https://foreignpolicy.com/2020/03/04/blindsided-on-the-supply-side/

Dutta, P. (2018). Medical diagnosis based on distance measures between picture fuzzy sets. *International Journal of Fuzzy System Applications*, *7*(4), 15–36. doi:10.4018/IJFSA.2018100102

Elbarkouky, M. M. G., & Abdelazeem, G. (2013). A green supply chain assessment for construction projects in developing countries. *WIT Transactions on Ecology and the Environment*, *179*, 1331–1341. doi:10.2495/SC131132

Erbaş, M., Bali, Ö., & Durğut, T. (2014), Tehlikeli madde depo yeri seçiminin coğrafi bilgi sistemleri açısından incelenmesi. Uzaktan Algılama- CBS Sempozyumu, İstanbul, Turkey.

Erdal, H. (2018). Tehlikeli Madde Taşımacılığı Güzergâh Seçimi Problemi İçin Stokastik Bir Risk Analizi. *Anemon Muş Alparslan Üniversitesi Sosyal Bilimler Dergisi*, *6*(6), 935–943.

Ergün, M., Korucuk, S., & Memiş, S. (2020). Sürdürülebilir Afet Lojistiğine Yönelik İdeal Afet Depo Yeri Seçimi. *Giresun İli Örneği, Çanakkale Onsekiz Mart Üniversitesi Fen Bilimleri Enstitüsü Dergisi*, *6*(1), 144–165. doi:10.28979/comufbed.686301

Eroğlu, Ö., Bali, Ö., & Ağdaş, M. (2013). Criteria evaluation model for third party logistics provider selection ın fuel transportation. *XI Logistics and Supply Chain Congress*, 451-470.

Ersöz, F., & Kabak, M. (2010). Savunma Sanayi Uygulamalarında Çok Kriterli Karar Verme Yöntemlerinin Literatür Araştırması. *Savunma Bilimleri Dergisi*, *9*(1), 97–125.

Compilation of References

Fabiano, B., Curro, F., Palazzi, E., & Pastorino, R. (2002). A framework for risk assessment and decision-making strategies in dangerous good transportation. *Journal of Hazardous Materials*, *93*(1), 1–15. doi:10.1016/S0304-3894(02)00034-1 PMID:12062950

Fan, Y., & Stevenson, M. (2018). A review of supply chain risk management: Definition, theory, and research agenda. *International Journal of Physical Distribution & Logistics Management*, *48*(3), 205–230. doi:10.1108/IJPDLM-01-2017-0043

FAO. (2020). *COVID-19 pandemic – impact on food and agriculture*. Retrieved March 25, 2021, from https://www.fao.org/2019-ncov/q-and-a/impact-on-food-and-agriculture/en/

Farahani, R. Z., Lotfi, M. M., & Rezapour, S. (2020). Mass casualty management in disaster scene: A systematic review of OR&MS research in humanitarian operations. *European Journal of Operational Research*, *287*(3), 787–819. doi:10.1016/j.ejor.2020.03.005

Fayezi, S., Zutshi, A., & O'Loughlin, A. (2017). Understanding and Devolopment of Supply Chain Agillity and Flexibility A Structured Literature Review. *International Journal of Management Reviews*, *19*(4), 379–407. doi:10.1111/ijmr.12096

Fazli, A., Sayedi, A., & Shulman, J. D. (2018). The effects of autoscaling in cloud computing. *Manage.Scence*, *64*(11), 5149–5163. doi:10.1287/mnsc.2017.2891

Ferguson, M., Guide, V. D. R. Jr, & Souza, G. C. (2006). Supply chain coordination for false failure returns. *Manufacturing & Service Operations Management*, *8*(4), 376–393. doi:10.1287/msom.1060.0112

Fiksel, J., Polyviou, M., Croxton, K. L., & Pettit, K. J. (2015). From risk to resilience: Learning to deal with disruption. *MIT Sloan Management Review*, *56*, 79–86.

Findlay, R., & O'Rourke, K. (2008). *Power and Plenty: Trade, War, and the World Economy in the Second Millennium*. Princeton University Press.

Fortune. (2020). *94% of the Fortune 1000 are seeing coronavirus supply chain disruptions: Report*. Retrieved April 10, 2021, from https://fortune.com/2020/02/21/fortune-1000-coronavirus-china-supply-chain-impact/

Furtado, V., Kolaja, T., Mueller, C., & Salguero, J. (2020, Apr.). Managing a manufacturing plant through the coronavirus crisis. *McKinsey & Company Insights*.

Gallino, S., & Moreno, A. (2018). The value of fit information in online retail: Evidence from a randomized field experiment. *Manufacturing & Service Operations Management*, *20*(4), 767–787. doi:10.1287/msom.2017.0686

Gao, F., & Su, X. (2017). Online and offline information for omnichannel retailing. *Manufacturing & Service Operations Management*, *19*(1), 84–98. doi:10.1287/msom.2016.0593

Garavelli, A. C. (2003). Flexibility Configurations for the Supply Chain Management. *International Journal of Production Economics*, *85*(2), 141–153. doi:10.1016/S0925-5273(03)00106-3

Gerschberger, M., Nowitzki, C. E., & Kummer, S. (2012). A model to determine complexity in supply networks. *Journal of Manufacturing Technology Management, 23*(8), 1015–1037. doi:10.1108/17410381211276853

Giannakis, M., & Louis, M. (2010). A multi-agent based framework for supply chain risk management. *Journal of Purchasing and Supply Management, 17*(1), 23–31. doi:10.1016/j.pursup.2010.05.001

Gonzalez-Feliu, J., & Morana, J. (2011). Collaborative transportation sharing: from theory to practice via a case study from France. In *Technologies for Supporting Reasoning Communities and Collaborative Decision Making: Cooperative Approaches* (pp. 252–271). IGI Global. doi:10.4018/978-1-60960-091-4.ch014

Goyal, M., & Netessine, S. (2007). Strategic technology choice and capacity investment under demand uncertainty. *Management Science, 53*(2), 192–207. doi:10.1287/mnsc.1060.0611

Green, K. W. Jr, Zelbst, P. J., Meacham, J., & Bhadauria, V. S. (2012). Green supply chain management practices: Impact on performance. *Supply Chain Management, 17*(3), 290–305. doi:10.1108/13598541211227126

Griffis, S. E., Rao, S., Goldsby, T. J., & Niranjan, T. T. (2012). The customer consequences of returns in online retailing: An empirical analysis. *Journal of Operations Management, 30*(4), 282–294. doi:10.1016/j.jom.2012.02.002

Grunwald, J., & Flamm, K. (1985). The global factory: Foreign assembly in international trade, Brookings Institution. *Washington D., C*, 1985.

Guide, V. D. R. Jr, Souza, G. C., Van Wassenhove, L. N., & Blackburn, J. D. (2006). Time value of commercial product returns. *Management Science, 52*(8), 1200–1214. doi:10.1287/mnsc.1060.0522

Gül, E., & Eren, T. (2017). Lojistik dağıtım ağ problemlerinde analitik hiyerarşi prosesi yöntemi ve hedef programlama ile depo seçimi. *Harran Üniversitesi Mühendislik Dergisi, 2*(1), 1–13.

Gunasekaran, A., Patel, C., & Tirtirogu, E. (2001). Performance Measures and Metrics in A Supply Chain Environment. *International Journal of Operations & Production Management, 21*(1/2), 71–87. doi:10.1108/01443570110358468

Gündoğdu, F. K., Duleba, S., Moslem, S., & Aydın, S. (2021). Evaluating public transport service quality using picture fuzzy analytic hierarchy process and linear assignment model. *Applied Soft Computing, 100*, 106920. doi:10.1016/j.asoc.2020.106920

Guo, S., Choi, T. M., & Shen, B. (2020). Green product development under competition: A study of the fashion apparel industry. *European Journal of Operational Research, 280*(2), 523–538. doi:10.1016/j.ejor.2019.07.050

Gupta, S., & Gentry, J. W. (2019). 'Should I Buy, Hoard, or Hide?'-Consumers' responses to perceived scarcity. *International Review of Retail, Distribution and Consumer Research, 29*(2), 178–197. doi:10.1080/09593969.2018.1562955

Compilation of References

Hale, T., & Moberg, C. R. (2005). Improving supply chain disaster preparedness: A decision process for secure site location. *International Journal of Physical Distribution & Logistics Management*, *35*(3), 195–207. doi:10.1108/09600030510594576

Harper, C. L., & Snowden, M. (2017). *Environment and society: Human perspectives on environmental issues*. Routledge. doi:10.4324/9781315463254

Hazen, B. T., Cegielski, C., & Hanna, J. B. (2011). Diffusion of green supply chain management: Examining perceived quality of green reverse logistics. *International Journal of Logistics Management*, *22*(3), 373–389. doi:10.1108/09574091111181372

Heckmann, I., Comes, T., & Nickel, S. (2015). A critical review on supply chain risk – definition, measure and modeling. *Omega*, *52*, 119–132. doi:10.1016/j.omega.2014.10.004

Hernandez, A. A., & Ona, S. (2015). A Qualitative study of green it adoption within the philippines business process outsourcing industry: A multi-theory perspective. *International Journal of Enterprise Information Systems*, *11*(4), 28–62. doi:10.4018/IJEIS.2015100102

Hess, J. D., Chu, W., & Gerstner, E. (1996). Controlling product returns in direct marketing. *Marketing Letters*, *7*(4), 307–317. doi:10.1007/BF00435538

Hobbs, J. E. (2020). Food supply chains during the COVID-19 pandemic. *Canadian Journal of Agricultural Economics/Revue canadienne d'agroeconomie*, *68*(2), 171-176.

Hong, Y., & Pavlou, P. A. (2014). Product fit uncertainty in online markets: Nature, effects, and antecedents. *Information Systems Research*, *25*(2), 328–344. doi:10.1287/isre.2014.0520

Huang, B. (2006). GIS-based route planning for hazardous material transportation. *Journal of Environmental Informatics*, *8*(1), 49–57. doi:10.3808/jei.200600076

Huang, C., Wang, Y., Li, X., Ren, L., Zhao, J., Hu, Y., Zhang, L., Fan, G., Xu, J., Gu, X., Cheng, Z., Yu, T., Xia, J., Wei, Y., Wu, W., Xie, X., Yin, W., Li, H., Liu, M., ... Cao, B. (2020). Clinical features of patients infected with 2019 novel coronavirus in Wuhan, China. *Lancet*, *395*(10223), 497–506. Advance online publication. doi:10.1016/S0140-6736(20)30183-5 PMID:31986264

Huang, M., & Jin, D. (2020). Impact of buy-online-and-return-in-store service on omnichannel retailing: A supply chain competitive perspective. *Electronic Commerce Research and Applications*, *41*, 100977. doi:10.1016/j.elerap.2020.100977

Hub. (2020). *How Coronavirus will affect the global supply chain*. Author.

Hui, D. S., & Azhar, I. (2020, February). The continuing 2019-nCoV epidemic threat of novel coronaviruses to global health— The latest 2019 novel coronavirus outbreak in Wuhan, China. *International Journal of Infectious Diseases*, *91*, 264–266. Advance online publication. doi:10.1016/j.ijid.2020.01.009 PMID:31953166

Huo, H., & Xiong, Z. Y. (2010). Study on the Application of Safety Assessment Model about Source of Hazardous Chemicals. *Advanced Materials Research*, *113-116*, 1925–1929. doi:10.4028/www.scientific.net/AMR.113-116.1925

Iannaccone, G., Marcucci, E., & Gatta, V. (2021). What young e-consumers want? Forecasting parcel lockers choice in Rome. *Logistics*, *5*(3), 57. doi:10.3390/logistics5030057

ILO. (2020). *The effects of COVID-19 on trade and global supply chains*. Research Brief.

ILO. (2020a). *ILO SCORE Global Covid-19 Enterprise Survey*. Retrieved from https://www.ilo.org/wcmsp5/groups/public/---ed_emp/---emp_ent/documents/presentation/wcms_745097.pdf

ILO. (2020b). *Working from Home: Estimating the worldwide potential*. International Labour Organization Policy Brief.

ILO. (2021a). *World Employment And Social Outlook: The role of digital labour platforms in transforming the world of work International*. International Labour Organization.

ILO. (2021b). *World Employment And Social Outlook: Trends 2021*. ILO.

Inoue, H., & Todo, Y. (2020). The Propagation of the Economic Impact through Supply Chains: The Case of a Mega-City Lockdown against the Spread of COVID-19. SSRN *Electronic Journal*. doi:10.2139/ssrn.3564898

International Labour Organization. (2020). *COVID-19 : Action in the Global Garment Industry*. Author.

International Textile Manufacturers Federation. (2020). *2nd ITMF-Survey about the Impact of the Corona-Pandemic on the Global Textile Industry*. ITMF Press Release.

IRU. (2021). *COVID-19 Impact on the Road Transport Industry*. Retrieved July 25, 2021, from https://www.iru.org/resources/iru-library/covid-19-impacts-road-transport-industry-executive-summary-update-june-2021

Irwin, N. (2012). Why Hurricane Katrina Should Make Us Optimistic About Economic Impact of Sandy. *Washington Post*.

Ivanov, D. (2020). Predicting the impacts of epidemic outbreaks on global supply chains: A simulation-based analysis on the coronavirus outbreak (COVID-19/SARS-CoV-2) case. *Transportation Research Part E, Logistics and Transportation Review*, *136*, 101922. doi:10.1016/j.tre.2020.101922 PMID:32288597

Ivanov, D., & Dolgui, A. (2021). OR-methods for coping with the ripple effect in supply chains during COVID-19 pandemic: Managerial insights and research implications. *International Journal of Production Economics*, *232*, 107921. doi:10.1016/j.ijpe.2020.107921 PMID:32952301

Ivanov, D., Sokolov, B., & Dolgui, A. (2014). The Ripple effect in supply chains: Trade-off 'efficiency-flexibility-resilience' in disruption management. *International Journal of Production Research*, *52*(7), 2154–2172. doi:10.1080/00207543.2013.858836

Compilation of References

Jabbour, A. B. L. de S., Jabbour, C. J. C., Latan, H., Teixeira, A. A., & de Oliveira, J. H. C. (2015). Reprint of "Quality management, environmental management maturity, green supply chain practices and green performance of Brazilian companies with ISO 14001 certification: Direct and indirect effects.". *Transportation Research Part E, Logistics and Transportation Review, 74*, 139–151. doi:10.1016/j.tre.2014.12.011

Jackson, J. L., & Judd, J. (2020). *The Supply Chain Ripple Effect: How COVID-19 is affecting garment workers and factories in Asia and the Pacific*. Academic Press.

Jaggernath, R., & Khan, Z. (2015). Green supply chain management. *World Journal of Entrepreneurship, Management and Sustainable Development, 11*(1), 37–47. doi:10.1108/WJEMSD-06-2014-0018

Jalalvand, F., Teimoury, E., Makui, A., Aryanezhad, M. B., & Jolai, F. (2011). A method to compare supply chains of an industry. *Supply Chain Management, 16*(2), 82–97. doi:10.1108/13598541111115347

Janakiraman, N., & Ordóñez, L. (2012). Effect of effort and deadlines on consumer product returns. *Journal of Consumer Psychology, 22*(2), 260–271. doi:10.1016/j.jcps.2011.05.002

Janakiraman, N., Syrdal, H. A., & Freling, R. (2016). The effect of return policy leniency on consumer purchase and return decisions: A meta-analytic review. *Journal of Retailing, 92*(2), 226–235. doi:10.1016/j.jretai.2015.11.002

Jaśkowski, P., Sobotka, A., & Czarnigowska, A. (2018). Decision model for planning material supply channels in construction. *Automation in Construction, 98*(15), 773–787. doi:10.1016/j.autcon.2018.02.026

Javaid, M., Haleem, A., Vaishya, R., Bahl, S., Suman, R., & Vaish, A. (2020). Industry 4.0 technologies and their applications in fighting COVID-19 pandemic. *Diabetes & Metabolic Syndrome, 14*(4), 419–422. doi:10.1016/j.dsx.2020.04.032 PMID:32344370

Jayaraman, V., & Luo, Y. (2007). Creating competitive advantages through new value creation: A reverse logistics perspective. *The Academy of Management Perspectives, 21*(2), 56–73. doi:10.5465/amp.2007.25356512

Jin, D., Caliskan-Demirag, O., Chen, F. Y., & Huang, M. (2020). Omnichannel retailers' return policy strategies in the presence of competition. *International Journal of Production Economics, 225*, 107595. doi:10.1016/j.ijpe.2019.107595

John, G. (2014). *Innovative Approaches to Supply Chain Risk (SCM World)*. Report.

Johnson, A., & McGinnis, L. (2011). Performance Measurement in The Warehousing Industry. *IIE Transactions, 43*(3), 220–230. doi:10.1080/0740817X.2010.491497

Jones, C., & Livingstone, N. (2018). The 'online high street' or the high street online? The implications for the urban retail hierarchy. *International Review of Retail, Distribution and Consumer Research, 28*(1), 47–63. doi:10.1080/09593969.2017.1393441

Jüttner, U., & Maklan, S. (2011). Supply chain resilience in the global financial crisis: An empirical study. *Supply Chain Management*, *16*(4), 246–259. Advance online publication. doi:10.1108/13598541111139062

Jüttner, U., Peck, H., & Christopher, M. (2003). Supply Chain Risk Management: Outlining an Agenda for Future Research. *International Journal of Logistics: Research and Applications*, *6*(4), 197–210. doi:10.1080/13675560310001627016

Kabir, G., & Sumi, R. S. (2015). Hazardous Waste Transportation Firm Selection Using Fuzzy Analytic Hierarchy and PROMETHEE Methods. *International Journal of Shipping and Transport Logistics*, *7*(2), 115. doi:10.1504/IJSTL.2015.067847

Karki, M. (2014). Green economy for sustainable development in Nepal: Role of forestry sector. *The Initiation*, *5*, 96–109. doi:10.3126/init.v5i0.10259

Katsikeas, C. S., & Leonidou, L. C. (1996). International Supplier Selection. *Journal of Global Marketing*, *9*(3), 23–45. doi:10.1300/J042v09n03_03

Keršuliene, V., Zavadskas, E. K., & Turskis, Z. (2010). Selection of Rational Dispute Resolution Method by Applying New Step-Wise Weight Assessment Ratio Analysis (SWARA). *Journal of Business Economics and Management*, *11*(2), 243–258. doi:10.3846/jbem.2010.12

Kobu, B. (2017). *Üretim Yönetimi*. İstanbul: Beta Basım Yayım Dağıtım A.Ş.

Koç, E. (2020). *Internet of Things (IoT) Applications for Enterprise Productivity*. IGI Global. doi:10.4018/978-1-7998-3175-4

Končar, J., Grubor, A., Marić, R., Vučenović, S., & Vukmirović, G. (2020). Setbacks to IoT implementation in the function of FMCG supply chain sustainability during COVID-19 pandemic. *Sustainability*, *12*(18), 7391. doi:10.3390u12187391

Koren, Y. (2010). *The Global Manufacturing Revolution: Product-Process-Business Integration and Reconfigurable Systems*. John Wiley & Sons. doi:10.1002/9780470618813

Korpela, J., & Tuominen, M. (1996). A decision aid in warehouse site selection. *International Journal of Production Economics*, *45*(1-3), 169–180. doi:10.1016/0925-5273(95)00135-2

Korucuk, S. (2018). *Tehlikeli Madde Taşımacılığında Çok Kriterli Karar Verme Yöntemlerinin Kullanımına İlişkin Literatür Taraması*. SOSCON Congress, Antalya.

Korucuk, S., & Erdal, H. (2018). AHP-VIKOR Bütünleşik Yaklaşımıyla Lojistik Risk Faktörlerinin ve Risk Yönetimi Araçlarının Sıralanması: Samsun İli Örneği. *İşletme Araştırmaları Dergisi*, *10*(3), 282-305.

Korucuk, S., Memiş, S., & Karamaşa, Ç. (2021). *Gıda İşletmelerinde Tedarik Zinciri Dinamiklerinde Meydana Gelen Karışıklıkların Derecelendirilmesi: Giresun İli Örneği*. International Academician Studies Congress 2021 Spring, Mersin.

Compilation of References

Korucuk, S. (2018). ÇKKV Yöntemleri İle İmalat İşletmelerinde TZY Performans Faktörlerinin Önem Derecelerinin Belirlenmesi ve En İdeal Rekabet Stratejisi Seçimi: Ordu İli Örneği. *Dokuz Eylül Üniversitesi İktisadi ve İdari Bilimler Fakültesi Dergisi, 33*(2), 569–593. doi:10.24988/deuiibf.2018332782

Korucuk, S. (2021). Ordu Ve Giresun İllerinde Kentsel Lojistik Performans Unsurlarına Yönelik Karşılaştırmalı Bir Analiz. *Dicle Üniversitesi Sosyal Bilimler Enstitüsü Dergisi, 13*(26), 141–155.

Korucuk, S., & Memiş, S. (2018). Tedarik Zinciri Yönetimindeki Risk Faktörlerinin AHP İle Ölçülmesi: Erzurum İli Örneği. *Bitlis Eren Üniversitesi Sosyal Bilimler Enstitüsü Dergisi, 7*(2), 1036–1051.

Korucuk, S., & Memiş, S. (2018). Tedarik Zinciri Yönetimindeki Risk Faktörlerinin AHP ile Ölçülmesi: Erzurum İli Örneği. *Bitlis Eren Üniversitesi Sosyal Bilimler Dergisi, 7*(2), 1036–1051.

Kouchaksaraeı, R. H., Zolfanı, S. H., & Golabchı, M. (2015). Glasshouse Locating Based On SWARA-COPRAS Approach. *International Journal of Strategic Property Management, 19*(2), 111–122. doi:10.3846/1648715X.2015.1004565

Krajewski, L. J., Malhotra, M. K. & Ritzman, L. P. (2016). *Operations Management Processes and Supply Chains.* Pearson.

Kraude, R., Narayanan, S., Talluri, S., Singh, P., & Kajiwara, T. (2018). Cultural Challenges in Mitigating International Supply Chain Disruptions. *IEEE Engineering Management Review, 46*(1), 98–105. Advance online publication. doi:10.1109/EMR.2018.2809910

Kroupenev, A. (2020). What Will Manufacturing's New Normal Be After COVID-19? *Industry Week*, 1–12.

Kumar, A., Luthra, S., Mangla, S. K., & Kazançoğlu, Y. (2020). COVID-19 impact on sustainable production and operations management. *Sustainable Operations and Computers, 1*(July), 1–7. doi:10.1016/j.susoc.2020.06.001

Kumar, S., Raut, R. D., Narwane, V. S., & Narkhede, D. B. E. (2020). Applications of industry 4. 0 to overcome the COVID-19 operational challenges. *Diabetes & Metabolic Syndrome, 14*(January), 1283–1289. doi:10.1016/j.dsx.2020.07.010 PMID:32755822

Kunovjanek, M., & Wankmüller, C. (2020). An analysis of the global additive manufacturing response to the Covid-19 pandemic. *Journal of Manufacturing Technology Management, 32*(9), 75–100. doi:10.1108/JMTM-07-2020-0263

Lahdelma, R., Salminen, R. P., & Hokkanen, J. (2002). Locating a waste treatment facility by using stochastic multicriteria acceptability analysis with ordinal criteria. *European Journal of Operational Research, 142*(2), 345–356. doi:10.1016/S0377-2217(01)00303-4

Large, R. O., & Thomsen, C. G. (2011). Drivers of green supply management performance: Evidence from Germany. *Journal of Purchasing and Supply Management, 17*(3), 176–184. doi:10.1016/j.pursup.2011.04.006

Lazar, R. E., Dumitrescu, M., & Stefanescu, I. (2001). Risk Assessment Of Hazardous Waste Transport. Perspectives of GIS Application, 808.1-808.8.

Lee, J., Krishnan, V., & Shin, H. (2020). Business models for technology-intensive supply chains. *Management Science*, *66*(5), 2120–2139. doi:10.1287/mnsc.2019.3306

Leonard, M. (2020). *What procurement managers should expect from a 'bullwhip on crack.* Retrieved from https://www.supplychaindive.com/

Lepthien, A., & Clement, M. (2019). Shipping fee schedules and return behavior. *Marketing Letters*, *30*(2), 151–165. doi:10.100711002-019-09486-8

Levary, R. R. (2007). Ranking foreign suppliers based on supply risk. *Supply Chain Management*, *12*(6), 392–394. doi:10.1108/13598540710826317

Li, G., Li, L., Sethi, S. P., & Guan, X. (2019). Return strategy and pricing in a dual-channel supply chain. *International Journal of Production Economics*, *215*, 153–164. doi:10.1016/j.ijpe.2017.06.031

Lim, S. F. W. T., & Srai, J. S. (2018). Examining the anatomy of last-mile distribution in e-commerce omnichannel retailing: A supply network configuration approach. *International Journal of Operations & Production Management*, *38*(9), 1735–1764. doi:10.1108/IJOPM-12-2016-0733

Lin, C. T., Chiu, H., Chu, P. Y., & Lou, P. (2006). Agility Index In The Supply Chain. *International Journal of Production Economics*, *100*(2), 285–289. doi:10.1016/j.ijpe.2004.11.013

Lin, R. J., Chen, R. H., & Nguyen, T. H. (2011). Green supply chain management performance in automobile manufacturing industry under uncertainty. *Procedia: Social and Behavioral Sciences*, *25*, 233–245. doi:10.1016/j.sbspro.2011.10.544

Liu, J. J., Xu, X. H., & Xu, K. (2005). Discussion and analysis of dangerous cargo's road transport. *Journal of Safety Science and Technology*, *1*(1), 74–77.

Li, X., Ma, B., & Chu, H. (2021). The impact of online reviews on product returns. *Asia Pacific Journal of Marketing and Logistics*, *33*(8), 1814–1828. Advance online publication. doi:10.1108/APJML-02-2020-0074

Li, X., Zhuang, Y., Fu, Y., & He, X. (2019). A trust-aware random walk model for return propensity estimation and consumer anomaly scoring in online shopping. *Science China. Information Sciences*, *62*(5), 52101. doi:10.100711432-018-9511-1

Loree, N., & Aros-Vera, F. (2018). Points of distribution location and inventory management model for postdisaster humanitarian logistics. *Transportation Research Part E, Logistics and Transportation Review*, *116*, 1–24. doi:10.1016/j.tre.2018.05.003

Lummus, R. R., Vokurka, R. J., & Duclos, L. K. (2005). Delphi Study on Supply Chain Flexibility. *International Journal of Production Research*, *43*(13), 2687–2708. doi:10.1080/00207540500056102

Compilation of References

Lyons, A. C., & Ma'aram, A. (2014). An Examination of Multi-tier Supply Chain Strategy Alignment in the Food Industry. *International Journal of Production Research*, *52*(7), 1911–1925. doi:10.1080/00207543.2013.787172

Malik, A. A., Masood, T., & Kousar, R. (2020). Reconfiguring and ramping-up ventilator production in the face of COVID-19: Can robots help? *Journal of Manufacturing Systems*, (June). Advance online publication. doi:10.1016/j.jmsy.2020.09.008 PMID:33082617

Maliszewska, M., Mattoo, A., & Van Der Mensbrugghe, D. (2020). *The Potential Impact of COVID-19 on GDP and Trade: A Preliminary Assessment*. World Bank Policy Research Working Paper.

Mandal, P., Basu, P., & Saha, K. (2021). Forays into omnichannel: An online retailer's strategies for managing product returns. *European Journal of Operational Research*, *292*(2), 633–651. doi:10.1016/j.ejor.2020.10.042

Manero, A., Smith, P., Koontz, A., Dombrowski, M., Sparkman, J., Courbin, D., & Chi, A. (2020). Leveraging 3D printing capacity in times of crisis: Recommendations for Covid-19 distributed manufacturing for medical equipment rapid response. *International Journal of Environmental Research and Public Health*, *17*(13), 4634. doi:10.3390/ijerph17134634 PMID:32605098

Manuj, I., & Şahin, F. (2011). A model of supply chain and supply chain decision-making complexity. *International Journal of Physical Distribution & Logistics Management*, *41*(5), 511–549. doi:10.1108/09600031111138844

Marcus, A. A., & Fremeth, A. R. (2009). Green management matters regardless. *The Academy of Management Perspectives*, *23*(3), 17–26. doi:10.5465/amp.2009.43479261

Mareschal, B. (2013). *Visual PROMETHEE manual*. Academic Press.

Mareschal, B. (2018). *Preference functions and thresholds*. Academic Press.

Masudin, I., Ramadhani, A., Restuputri, D. P., & Amallynda, I. (2021). The effect of traceability system and managerial initiative on Indonesian food cold chain performance: A Covid-19 Pandemic perspective. *Global Journal of Flexible Systems Management*. doi:10.1007/s40171-021-00281-x

Mathiyazhagan, K., Govindan, K., NoorulHaq, A., & Geng, Y. (2013). An ISM approach for the barrier analysis in implementing green supply chain management. *Journal of Cleaner Production*, *47*, 283–297. doi:10.1016/j.jclepro.2012.10.042

Memiş, S., Demir, E., Karamaşa, Ç., & Korucuk, S. (2020). Prioritization Of Road Transportation Risks: An Application in Giresun Province. *Operational Research in Engineering Sciences: Theory and Applications*, *3*(2), 111–126.

Mete, H. O., & Zabinsky, Z. B. (2010). Stochastic optimization of medical supply location and distribution in disaster management. *International Journal of Production Economics*, *126*(1), 76–84. doi:10.1016/j.ijpe.2009.10.004

Milgate, M. (2001). Supply chain complexity and delivery performance: An international exploratory study. *Supply Chain Management, 6*(3), 106–118. doi:10.1108/13598540110399110

Ministry of Transportation. (2008, June 15). Tehlikeli Maddelerin Karayoluyla Taşınması Hakkında Yönetmelik. *Sayılı Resmi Gazete*.

Minnema, A., Bijmolt, T. H., Petersen, J. A., & Shulman, J. D. (2018). Managing product returns within the customer value framework. In R. W. Palmatier, V. Kumar, & C. M. Harmeling (Eds.), *Customer engagement marketing* (pp. 95–118). Palgrave Macmillan. doi:10.1007/978-3-319-61985-9_5

MMH. (2020). *Other Voices: Pop-up distribution centers help overcome outbound logistics delivery obstacles*. Retrieved May 25, 2021, from https://www.mmh.com/article/other_voices_pop_up_distribution_centers_help_overcome_last_mile_delivery_o

Mollenkopf, D. A., Frankel, R., & Russo, I. (2011). Creating value through returns management: Exploring the marketing–operations interface. *Journal of Operations Management, 29*(5), 391–403. doi:10.1016/j.jom.2010.11.004

Mollenkopf, D. A., Rabinovich, E., Laseter, T. M., & Boyer, K. K. (2007). Managing internet product returns: A focus on effective service operations. *Decision Sciences, 38*(2), 215–250. doi:10.1111/j.1540-5915.2007.00157.x

Moorthy, S., & Srinivasan, K. (1995). Signaling quality with a money-back guarantee: The role of transaction costs. *Marketing Science, 14*(4), 442–466. doi:10.1287/mksc.14.4.442

Morais, D. C., & de Almeida, A. T. (2006). Modelo de decisão em grupo para gerenciar perdas de água. *Pesquisa Operacional, 26*(3), 567–584. doi:10.1590/S0101-74382006000300007

NAM. (2020). *Manufacturers' Survey Reveals Current Industry Impact of COVID-19*. Retrieved May 20, 2021, from https://www.nam.org/manufacturers-survey-reveals-current-industry-impact-of-covid-19-7411/?stream=series-press-releases

National Association of Manufacturers. (2018). *NAM Manufacturers' Outlook Survey*. https://www.nam.org/wp-content/uploads/2019/05/NAM-Q4-2018-Manufacturers-Outlook-Survey.pdf

Obricovic, S., & Milaradov, M. (2016). Multi-Criteria Selection of Municipal Waste Treatment System Using VIKOR Method. *International Journal of Environment and Waste Management, 18*(1), 43. doi:10.1504/IJEWM.2016.080261

OEC. (2020). *Exports of textiles for selected countries*. Author.

OECD. (2020). *International trade — OECD Statistics on International Trade in Services Publication*. OECD.

Ofek, E., Katona, Z., & Sarvary, M. (2011). "Bricks and clicks": The impact of product returns on the strategies of multichannel retailers. *Marketing Science, 30*(1), 42–60. doi:10.1287/mksc.1100.0588

Compilation of References

Oggero, A., Darbra, R. M., Munoz, M., Planas, E., & Casal, J. (2006). A survey of accidents occurring during the transport of hazardous substances by road and rail. *Journal of Hazardous Materials*, *133*(1), 1–7. doi:10.1016/j.jhazmat.2005.05.053 PMID:16298045

OIT. (2019). *Promoting decent work in garment sector global supply chains: Highlights and insights from the ILO project*. OIT.

OIT. (2020a). *A COVID-19 e a indústria automóvel*. Retrieved from https://www.ilo.org/lisbon/publicações/WCMS_754378/lang--pt/index.htm

Opricovic, S., & Tzeng, G. H. (2007). Extended VIKOR Method in Comparison with Outranking Methods. *European Journal of Operational Research*, *178*(2), 514–529. doi:10.1016/j.ejor.2006.01.020

Oral, N., Yumuşak, R., & Eren, T. (2021). AHP ve ANP yöntemleri kullanılarak tehlikeli madde depo yeri seçimi: Kırıkkale ilinde bir uygulama. *NOHU J. Eng. Sci.*, *10*(1), 115–124.

Özbekler, T. M., & Akgül, A. K. (2020). An Ex-Ante Assessment of City Distribution Alternatives Based on Multi Actor Multi Criteria Framework. *Business & Management Studies: An International Journal*, *8*(5), 4241–4272. doi:10.15295/bmij.v8i5.1650

Özbekler, T. M., & Öztürkoğlu, Y. (2020). Analysing the importance of sustainability-oriented service quality in competition environment. *Business Strategy and the Environment*, *29*(3), 1504–1516. doi:10.1002/bse.2449

Özçakar, N., & Demir, H. (2011). Bulanık TOPSIS Yöntemiyle Tedarikçi Seçimi. *Yönetim Dergisi.*, *69*, 25–44.

Özder, E. H., Özcan, E., & Eren, T. (2019). Staff task-based shift scheduling solution with an ANP and goal programming method in a natural gas combined cycle power plant. *Mathematics*, *7*(2), 192–218. doi:10.3390/math7020192

Özkır, V., & Başlıgil, H. (2013). Multi-objective optimization of closed-loop supply chains in uncertain environment. *Journal of Cleaner Production*, *41*, 114–125. doi:10.1016/j.jclepro.2012.10.013

Özyağcı, S. (2008). *Tehlikeli Maddelerin Karayolu İle Taşınması* (Unpublished Master Thesis). İstanbul Technical University Graduate School of Science.

Paddeu, D., Parkhurst, G., Fancello, G., Fadda, P., & Ricci, M. (2018). Multi-stakeholder collaboration in urban freight consolidation schemes: Drivers and barriers to implementation. *Transport*, *33*(4), 913–929. doi:10.3846/transport.2018.6593

Palomares, G. (2006). *Relaciones internacionales en el siglo XXI*. Tecnos.

Perçin, S. (2006). An application of the integrated AHP-PGP model in supplier selection. *Measuring Business Excellence*, *10*(4), 34–49. doi:10.1108/13683040610719263

Perona, M., & Miraglıotta, G. (2004). Complexity management and supply chain performance assessment: A field study and a conceptual framework. *International Journal of Production Economics*, *90*(1), 103–115. doi:10.1016/S0925-5273(02)00482-6

Petersen, J. A., & Kumar, V. (2009). Are product returns a necessary evil? Antecedents and consequences. *Journal of Marketing*, *73*(3), 35–51. doi:10.1509/jmkg.73.3.035

Petersen, J. A., & Kumar, V. (2010). Can product returns make you money? *MIT Sloan Management Review*, *51*(3), 85–89.

Phua, M. H., & Minowa, M. (2005). A GIS-Based Multi-Criteria Decision Making Approach To Forest Conservation Planning At A Landscape Scale: A Case Study In The Kinabalu Area, Sabah, Malaysia. *Landscape and Urban Planning*, *71*(2-4), 207–222. doi:10.1016/j.landurbplan.2004.03.004

Pınarbaşı, F. (2020). Sharing Economy and Applications: Business and Marketing Perspective. In Networked Business Models in the Circular Economy (pp. 82-102). IGI Global.

Pinho, R. R., & Lopes, A. P. (2020). *Multicriteria Decision Support Model for Selection of Tinplate Suppliers*. doi:10.4018/978-1-7998-2216-5.ch006

Piotrowicz, W., & Cuthbertson, R. (2014). Introduction to the special issue information technology in retail: Toward omnichannel retailing. *International Journal of Electronic Commerce*, *18*(4), 5–16. doi:10.2753/JEC1086-4415180400

Piron, F., & Young, M. (2000). Retail borrowing: Insights and implications on returning used merchandise. *International Journal of Retail & Distribution Management*, *28*(1), 27–36. doi:10.1108/09590550010306755

Piroth, P., Rüger-Muck, E., & Bruwer, J. (2020). Digitalisation in grocery retailing in Germany: An exploratory study. *International Review of Retail, Distribution and Consumer Research*, *30*(5), 479–497. doi:10.1080/09593969.2020.1738260

Pisuchpen, R. (2012). Integration of JIT Flexible Manufacturing, Assembly and Disassembly Using a Simulation Approach. *Emerald Insight*, *32*(1), 51–61. doi:10.1108/01445151211198719

PMI. (2020). *Turkey: PMI falls to 48.1 due to COVID-19 outbreak*. Retrieved May 20, 2021, from https://www.aa.com.tr/en/economy/turkey-pmi-falls-to-481-due-to-covid-19-outbreak/1787549

Podvezko, V. (2009). Application of AHP technique. *Journal of Business Economics and Management*, *10*(2), 181–189. doi:10.3846/1611-1699.2009.10.181-189

Polyviou, M., Croxton, K. L., & Knemeyer, A. M. (2019). Resilience of medium-sized firms to supply chain disruptions: The role of internal social capital. *International Journal of Operations & Production Management*, *40*(1), 68–91. doi:10.1108/IJOPM-09-2017-0530

Ponomarov, S. Y. (2012). *Antecedents and consequences of supply chain resilience: a dynamic capabilities perspective*. Doctoral Dissertations University.

Compilation of References

Ponomarov, S. Y., & Holcomb, M. C. (2009, May 22). Understanding the concept of supply chain resilience. *International Journal of Logistics Management, 20*(1), 124–143. Advance online publication. doi:10.1108/09574090910954873

Popek, M. (2019). Factors influencing on the environment during hazardous goods transportation by the sea. *IOP Conf. Series: Earth and Environmental Science, 214*, 1-8.

Power, D. J., Sohal, A. S., & Rahman, S. U. (2001). Criticial Success Factors In Agile Supply Chain Management – Emprical Study. *International Journal of Physical Distribution & Logistics Management, 31*(4), 247–265. doi:10.1108/09600030110394923

Powers, T. L., & Jack, E. P. (2015). Understanding the causes of retail product returns. *International Journal of Retail & Distribution Management, 43*(12), 1182–1202. doi:10.1108/IJRDM-02-2014-0023

Prem, K., Liu, Y., Russell, T. W., Kucharski, A. J., Eggo, R. M., Davies, N., & Abbott, S. (2020). The effect of control strategies to reduce social mixing on outcomes of the COVID-19 epidemic in Wuhan, China: A modelling study. *The Lancet. Public Health, 5*(5), e261–e270. doi:10.1016/S2468-2667(20)30073-6 PMID:32220655

Pritchard, A. (1969). Statistical bibliography or bibliometrics. *The Journal of Documentation, 25*(4), 348–349.

PSFK Research. (2020). *Building consumer confidence in retail's new virtual world.* https://www.psfk.com/2020/08/consumer-confidence-virtual-retail.html

Rae, E. (2020). *COVID-19 and impacts on global wind supply chain.* Retrieved from https://gwec.net/covid-19-and-impacts-on-global-wind-supply-chains/

Rafiei, M., Mohammadi, M., & Torabi, S. (2013). Reliable multi period multi product supply chain design with facility disruption. *Decision Science Letters, 2*(2), 81–94. doi:10.5267/j.dsl.2013.02.002

Rao, S., Lee, K. B., Connelly, B., & Iyengar, D. (2018). Return time leniency in online retail: A signaling theory perspective on buying outcomes. *Decision Sciences, 49*(2), 275–305. doi:10.1111/deci.12275

Rao, S., Rabinovich, E., & Raju, D. (2014). The role of physical distribution services as determinants of product returns in Internet retailing. *Journal of Operations Management, 32*(6), 295–312. doi:10.1016/j.jom.2014.06.005

Ribeiro, J. P., & Barbosa-Povoa, A. (2018). Supply Chain Resilience: Definitions and quantitative modelling approaches–A literature review. *Computers & Industrial Engineering, 115*, 109–122. doi:10.1016/j.cie.2017.11.006

Rice, J. B., & Caniato, F. (2003). Building a secure and resilient supply network. *Supply Chain Management Review, 7*(5), 22–30.

Roberts, M. (2020). *A global manufacturing recession.* https://www.cadtm.org/A-global-manufacturing-recession

Robertson, T. S., Hamilton, R., & Jap, S. D. (2020). Many (un) happy Returns? The changing nature of retail product returns and future research directions. *Journal of Retailing, 96*(2), 172–177. doi:10.1016/j.jretai.2020.04.001

Rodríguez-Espíndola, O., Albores, P., & Brewster, C. (2018). Disaster preparedness in humanitarian logistics: A collaborative approach for resource management in floods. *European Journal of Operational Research, 264*(3), 978–993. doi:10.1016/j.ejor.2017.01.021

Rodrik, D. (2000). How far will international economic integration go? *Journal of Economic Perspective, 14*(1), 177-186.

Rodrik, D. (2007). *One Economics Many Recipes, Globalization, Institutions and Economic Growth.* Princeton University Press. doi:10.1515/9781400829354

Röllecke, F. J., Huchzermeier, A., & Schröder, D. (2018). Returning customers: The hidden strategic opportunity of returns management. *California Management Review, 60*(2), 176–203. doi:10.1177/0008125617741125

Rostamzadeh, R., Govindan, K., Esmaeili, A., & Sabaghi, M. (2015). Application of fuzzy VIKOR for evaluation of green supply chain management practices. *Ecological Indicators, 49*, 188–203. doi:10.1016/j.ecolind.2014.09.045

Rozar, N. M., Mahmood, W. H. W., Ibrahim, A., & Razik, M. A. (2015). A study of success factors in green supply chain management in manufacturing industries in Malaysia. *J Econ Bus Manag, 3*(2), 287–291. doi:10.7763/JOEBM.2015.V3.196

Ruzgys, A., Volvačiovas, R., Ignatavičius, Č., & Turskis, Z. (2014). *Integrated Evaluation of External Wall Insulation in Residential Buildings Using SWARA-TODIM MCDM.* Academic Press.

Ryan, T. (2020). *Has COVID-19 exacerbated online return challenges?* https://www.retailwire.com/discussion/has-covid-19-exacerbated-online-return-challenges/

Saarijärvi, H., Sutinen, U. M., & Harris, L. C. (2017). Uncovering consumers' returning behaviour: A study of fashion e-commerce. *International Review of Retail, Distribution and Consumer Research, 27*(3), 284–299. doi:10.1080/09593969.2017.1314863

Saaty, T. L. (1990). The analytic hierarchy process in conflict management. *International Journal of Conflict Management, 1*(1), 47–68. doi:10.1108/eb022672

Sadler, I. (2007). *Logistics and Supply Chain Integration.* Sage Publications Ltd.

Sahoo, N., Dellarocas, C., & Srinivasan, S. (2018). The impact of online product reviews on product returns. *Information Systems Research, 29*(3), 723–738. doi:10.1287/isre.2017.0736

Compilation of References

Sá, M. M. D., Miguel, P. L. D. S., Brito, R. P. D., & Pereira, S. C. F. (2019). Supply chain resilience: The whole is not the sum of the parts. *International Journal of Operations & Production Management*, *40*(1), 92–115. doi:10.1108/IJOPM-09-2017-0510

Samuelson, P. A., & Northaus, W. D. (1988). Economia (12th ed.). New York: McGraw-Hill.

Šaparauskas, J., Zavadskas, E. K., & Turskis, Z. (2011). Selection of Facade's Alternatives of Commercial and Public Buildings Based on Multiple Criteria. *International Journal of Strategic Property Management*, *15*(2), 189203. doi:10.3846/1648715X.2011.586532

Sapir, J. (2016). Jacques Sapir: Donald Trump, président de la démondialisation? *Le Figaro*. Available on web: https://www.lefigaro.fr/vox/monde/2016/11/10/31002-20161110ARTFIG00233-jacques-sapir-donald-trump-president-de-la-demondialisation.php

Sapir, J. (2011). *La demondialisation*. Seuil.

Sawik, T. (2013). Integrated selection of suppliers and scheduling of customer orders in the presence of supply chain disruption risks. *International Journal of Production Research*, *51*(23-24), 7006–7022. doi:10.1080/00207543.2013.852702

Schleiden, V., & Neiberger, C. (2020). Does sustainability matter? A structural equation model for cross-border online purchasing behaviour. *International Review of Retail, Distribution and Consumer Research*, *30*(1), 46–67. doi:10.1080/09593969.2019.1635907

Schmitt, A. J., & Singh, M. (2012). A quantitative analysis of disruption risk in a multi-echelon supply chain. *International Journal of Production Economics*, *139*(1), 23–32. doi:10.1016/j.ijpe.2012.01.004

Scholten, K., & Schilder, S. (2015). The role of collaboration in supply chain resilience. *Supply Chain Management*, *20*(4), 471–484. doi:10.1108/SCM-11-2014-0386

Scholten, K., Scott, P. S., & Fynes, B. (2014). Mitigation processes-antecedents for building supply chain resilience. *Supply Chain Management*, *19*(2), 211–228. doi:10.1108/SCM-06-2013-0191

Scholten, K., Stevenson, M., & van Donk, D. P. (2019). Dealing with the unpredictable: Supply chain resilience. *International Journal of Operations & Production Management*, *40*(1), 1–10. doi:10.1108/IJOPM-01-2020-789

Seeger, M. K., Kemper, J., & Brettel, M. (2019). How information processing and mobile channel choice influence product returns: An empirical analysis. *Psychology and Marketing*, *36*(3), 198–213. doi:10.1002/mar.21170

Sellitto, M. A., Pereira, G. M., Borchardt, M., Da Silva, R. I., & Viegas, C. V. (2015). A SCOR-based model for supply chain performance measurement: Application in the footwear industry. *International Journal of Production Research*, *53*(16), 4917–4926. doi:10.1080/00207543.2015.1005251

Şenses, O. (2019). *İşletme Açısından Kapasite*. http://disticaret.besikduzumyo.trabzon.edu.tr/Files/ckFiles/disticaret-besikduzumyo-trabzon-edu-tr/Orhan%20%C5%9Eenses/Genel%20%C4%B0%C5%9Fletme/b%C3%B6l%C3%BCm%207-%20%C4%B0%C5%9ELETMELER%20A%C3%87ISINDAN%20%20KAPAS%C4%B0TE%20pdf.pdf

Serdarasan, S. (2013). A review of supply chain complexity drivers. *Computers & Industrial Engineering*, 66(3), 533–540. doi:10.1016/j.cie.2012.12.008

Sert, M., & Kesen, S. E. (2019). Tam Zamanında Üretim Felsefine Dayalı Bir Seri Üretim Hattının Simülasyon Tekniğiyle Performans Analizi. *Selçuk Üniversitesi Mühendislik, Bilim Ve Teknoloji Dergisi*, 7(1), 115–134. doi:10.15317/Scitech.2019.186

Sethi, A. K., & Sethi, S. P. (1990). Flexibility in Manufacturing : A Survey. *International Journal of Flexible Manufacturing Systems*, 2(4), 289–328. doi:10.1007/BF00186471

Sezen, B., & Çankaya, S. Y. (2013). Effects of green manufacturing and eco-innovation on sustainability performance. *Procedia: Social and Behavioral Sciences*, 99, 154–163. doi:10.1016/j.sbspro.2013.10.481

Shang, H., Dong, D., Wang, X. & Wu, X. (2008). The Risk Evaluation for Hazardous Materials Transportation. *Service Operations and Logistics, and Informatics*, 1553 – 1558.

Shang, G., Ferguson, M. E., & Galbreth, M. R. (2019). Where should I focus my return reduction efforts? Empirical guidance for retailers. *Decision Sciences*, 50(4), 877–909. doi:10.1111/deci.12344

Shang, G., Pekgün, P., Ferguson, M., & Galbreth, M. (2017). How much do online consumers really value free product returns? Evidence from eBay. *Journal of Operations Management*, 53(1), 45–62. doi:10.1016/j.jom.2017.07.001

Shcherbakov, V., & Silkina, G. (2021). Supply Chain Management Open Innovation: Virtual Integration in the Network Logistics System. *Journal of Open Innovation*, 7(1), 54. doi:10.3390/joitmc7010054

Sheffi, Y., & Rice, J. B. (2005). A supply chain view of the resilient enterprise. *MIT Sloan Management Review*.

Sherman, E. (2020). *94% of the Fortune 1000 are seeing coronavirus supply chain disruptions: Report*. Fortune.

Shi, X., Dong, C., & Cheng, T. C. E. (2018). Does the buy-online-and-pick-up-in-store strategy with pre-orders benefit a retailer with the consideration of returns? *International Journal of Production Economics*, 206, 134–145. doi:10.1016/j.ijpe.2018.09.030

Shokrani, A., Loukaides, E. G., Elias, E., & Lunt, A. J. (2020). Exploration of alternative supply chains and distributed manufacturing in response to COVID-19; a case study of medical face shields. *Materials & Design*, 192, 108749. doi:10.1016/j.matdes.2020.108749 PMID:32341616

Shrestha, S. S. (2017). Strengthening supply chains for a sustainable housing sector in Nepal : Factors influencing the organization, management, relationships and the adoption and use of green practices, products and services. *International Journal of Managing Value and Supply Chains*, *8*(1), 1–22. doi:10.5121/ijmvsc.2017.8101

Shulman, J. D., Coughlan, A. T., & Savaskan, R. C. (2011). Managing consumer returns in a competitive environment. *Management Science*, *57*(2), 347–362. doi:10.1287/mnsc.1100.1274

Skibińska, W., & Kott, I. (2015). Green management in companies policies and activities. In *WEI International Academic Conference Proceedings* (pp. 220-226). WEI.

Smarter C. X. Team. (2020). *8 retail innovations reshaping your shopping experience*. https://smartercx.com/8-retail-innovations-reshaping-your-shopping-experience/

Sorkun, M. F. (2019). The impact of product variety on LSQ in e-marketplaces. *International Journal of Physical Distribution & Logistics Management*, *49*(7), 749–766. doi:10.1108/IJPDLM-06-2018-0223

Sorkun, M. F., & Onay, M. (2018). The effects of companies' reverse logistics motivations on their reverse logistics networks. In H. Dinçer, Ü. Hacıoglu, & S. Yüksel (Eds.), *Strategic design and innovative thinking in business operations* (pp. 3–21). Springer. doi:10.1007/978-3-319-77622-4_1

Sorkun, M. F., Yumurtacı Hüseyinoğlu, I. Ö., & Börühan, G. (2020). Omni-channel capability and customer satisfaction: Mediating roles of flexibility and operational logistics service quality. *International Journal of Retail & Distribution Management*, *48*(6), 629–648. doi:10.1108/IJRDM-07-2019-0235

Stanujkic, D., Karabasevic, D., & Zavadskas, E. K. (2015). A Framework For The Selection of A Packaging Design Based on The SWARA Method, *Inzinerine Ekonomika-. The Engineering Economist*, *26*(2), 181–187.

Stefan Kühn, C. V. (2020). *A COVID-19 e as cadeias globais de abastecimento: Como a crise no emprego se propaga além-fronteiras*. Academic Press.

Steinberg, F. (2005). *Cooperación y Conflicto en el Sistema Comercial Multilateral: La Organización Mundial de Comercio como Institución de Gobernanza Económica Global* (Tesis Doctoral). Presentada en el Departamento de Análisis Económico: Teoría Económica e Historia Económica de la Facultada de Ciencias Económicas y Empresariales de la Universidad Autónoma de Madrid, España.

Stock, J. R. (2001). Reverse logistics in the supply chain. *Revista Transport & Logistics*, 44-48.

Stock, J., Speh, T., & Shear, H. (2006). Managing product returns for competitive advantage. *MIT Sloan Management Review*, *48*(1), 57–62.

Stone, J., & Rahimifard, S. (2018). Resilience in agri-food supply chains: A critical analysis of the literature and synthesis of the novel framework. *Supply Chain Management*, *23*(3), 207–238. doi:10.1108/SCM-06-2017-0201

Suguna, M., Shah, B., Raj, S. K., & Suresh, M. (2021). *A study on the influential factors of the last mile delivery projects during Covid-19 era*. Operations Management Research., doi:10.100712063-021-00214-y

Sujatha, R., & Karthikeyan, M. S. (2021). Investigating green supply chain management practices and performance among apparel manufacturing firms. *International Journal of Integrated Supply Management*, *14*(3), 271–290. doi:10.1504/IJISM.2021.117239

Supeekit, T., Somboonwiwat, T., & Kritchanchai, D. (2016). DEMATEL-modified ANP to evaluate internal hospital supply chain performance. *Computers & Industrial Engineering*, *102*, 318–330. doi:10.1016/j.cie.2016.07.019

Suryanto, T., Haseeb, M., & Hartani, N. H. (2018). The correlates of developing green supply chain management practices: Firms level analysis in Malaysia. *International Journal of Supply Chain Management*, *7*(5), 316.

Su, X. (2009). Consumer returns policies and supply chain performance. *Manufacturing & Service Operations Management*, *11*(4), 595–612. doi:10.1287/msom.1080.0240

Swami, S., & Shah, J. (2013). Channel coordination in green supply chain management. *The Journal of the Operational Research Society*, *64*(3), 336–351. doi:10.1057/jors.2012.44

Swant, M. (2020). *From near death with chatbots to new life in e-commerce, Octane AI raises $4.25 million*. https://www.forbes.com/sites/martyswant/2020/08/21/from-celebrity-chatbots-to-new-life-in-e-commerce-octane-ai-raises-425-million/#540a3c474795

Swierczek, A. (2020). Investigating the role of demand planning as a higher-order construct in mitigating disruptions in the European supply chains. *International Journal of Logistics Management*, *31*(3), 665–696. doi:10.1108/IJLM-08-2019-0218

Szeto, W. Y., Farahani, R. Z., & Sumalee, A. (2017). Linkbased multi-class hazmat routing-scheduling problem: A multiple demon approach. *European Journal of Operational Research*, *261*(1), 337–354. doi:10.1016/j.ejor.2017.01.048

Tan, W. J., & Enderwick, P. (2006). Managing threats in the Global Era: The impact and response to SARS. *Thunderbird International Business Review*, *48*(4), 515–536. Advance online publication. doi:10.1002/tie.20107

Tardivo, A., Carrillo Zanuy, A., & Sánchez Martín, C. (2021). COVID-19 Impact on Transport: A Paper from the Railways' Systems Research Perspective. *Transportation Research Record: Journal of the Transportation Research Board*, *2675*(1), 12. doi:10.1177/0361198121990674

Taylor, S. R. (1992). Green management: The next competitive weapon. *Futures*, *24*(7), 669–680. doi:10.1016/0016-3287(92)90075-Q

Taymaz, E. (2020). *Covid-19 tedbirlerinin Türkiye ekonomisine etkisi ve çözüm önerileri*. Retrieved May 20, 2021, from https://sarkac.org/2020/04/covid19-tedbirlerinin-turkiye-ekonomisine-etkisi-cozum-onerileri/

Thomasson, E. (2020). *Brands See an Uptick in Online Sales During the Covid-19 Crisis.* Retrieved from https://www.businessoffashion.com/articles/retail/brands-see-an-uptick-in-online-sales-during-the-covid-19-crisis

Thun, J. H., & Müller, A. (2010). An empirical analysis of green supply chain management in the German automotive industry. *Business Strategy and the Environment, 19*(2), 119–132.

Tisdell, C. A. (2020). Economic, social and political issues raised by the COVID-19 pandemic. *Economic Analysis and Policy, 68,* 17–28. doi:10.1016/j.eap.2020.08.002 PMID:32843816

Tukamuhabwa, B. R., Stevenson, M., Busby, J., & Zorzini, M. (2015). Supply chain resilience: Definition, review and theoretical foundations for further study. *International Journal of Production Research, 53*(18), 5592–5623. doi:10.1080/00207543.2015.1037934

Tummala, R., & Schoenherr, T. (2011). Assessing and managing risks using the Supply Chain Risk Management Process (SCRMP). *Supply Chain Management, 16*(6), 474–483. Advance online publication. doi:10.1108/13598541111171165

Tumpa, T. J., Ali, S. M., Rahman, M. H., Paul, S. K., Chowdhury, P., & Khan, S. A. R. (2019). Barriers to green supply chain management: An emerging economy context. *Journal of Cleaner Production, 236,* 117617. doi:10.1016/j.jclepro.2019.117617

Turkey, K. M. P. G. (2020). *Perakende COVID-19 Sınavında.* Retrieved May 25, 2021, from https://home.kpmg/tr/tr/home/medya/press-releases/2020/03/perakende-covid-19-sinavinda.html

Twinn, I., Qureshi, N., Conde, M. L., Guinea, C. G., Rojas, D. P., Luo, J., & Gupta, H. (2020). *The Impact of COVID-19 on Logistics.* International Finance Corporation (IFC).

U.S. Bureau of Labor Statistics. (2020). *Economic News Release.* https://www.bls.gov/news.release/archives/prod2_08142020.htm

Um, J., & Han, N. (2020). Understanding the relationships between global supply chain risk and supply chain resilience: The role of mitigating strategies. *Supply Chain Management, 26*(2), 240–255. doi:10.1108/SCM-06-2020-0248

United Nations. (2021). *Trade trends under the COVID-19 pandemic.* Retrieved June 15, 2021, from https://unctad.org/webflyer/key-statistics-and-trends-international-trade-2020

UPS. (2019). *UPS Pulse of the online shopper: A customer experience study.* https://solutions.ups.com/rs/935-KKE-240/images/UPS-Pulse-of-the-Online-Shopper-Report.pdf

Ustasüleyman, T., & Perçin, S. (2007). Analitik ağ süreci yaklaşımıyla kuruluş yeri seçimi. *Gazi Üniversitesi İktisadi ve İdari Bilimler Fakültesi Dergisi, 9*(3), 37–55.

Ustasüleyman, T., & Perçin, S. (2015). Tedarik Zinciri Karmaşıklığının İşletme Performansına Etkisinin Belirlenmesine Yönelik Yapısal Model Önerisi. *Global Journal of Economics and Business Studies, 3*(6), 1–12.

Uta Lojistik Magazine. (2020). *Lojistik Sektörünün Koronavirüs Envanteri*. Retrieved April 15, 2021, from https://lojistikhatti.com/images/pdf/UTA_LOJISTIK_DERGISI_NISAN_2020_SAYISI.pdf

UTİKAD. (2020). *COVID-19 Dolayısıyla Taşımacılık Faaliyetlerinde Alınan Önlemler*. Retrieved June 15, 2021, from https://www.utikad.org.tr/Covid-19

Vachon, S., & Klassen, R. D. (2002). An Exploratory Investigation of the Effects of Supply Chain Complexity on Delivery Performance. *IEEE Transactions on Engineering Management, 49*(3), 218–230. doi:10.1109/TEM.2002.803387

Vahdani, B., Zandieh, M., & Roshanaei, V. (2011). A hybrid multi-stage predictive model for supply chain network collapse recovery analysis: A practical framework for effective supply chain network continuity management. *International Journal of Production Research, 49*(7), 2035–2060. doi:10.1080/00207540903289748

Vakulenko, Y., Shams, P., Hellström, D., & Hjort, K. (2019). Online retail experience and customer satisfaction: The mediating role of last mile delivery. *International Review of Retail, Distribution and Consumer Research, 29*(3), 306–320. doi:10.1080/09593969.2019.1598466

Van der Vegt, G., Essens, P., Wahlstrom, M., & George, G. (2015). Managing risk and resilience: From the editors. *Academy of Management Journal, 58*(4), 971–980. doi:10.5465/amj.2015.4004

Vanpoucke, E., & Ellis, S. C. (2020). Building supply-side resilience – a behavioural view. *International Journal of Operations & Production Management, 40*(1), 11–33. doi:10.1108/IJOPM-09-2017-0562

Verhoef, P. C., Kannan, P. K., & Inman, J. J. (2015). From multi-channel retailing to omni-channel retailing: Introduction to the special issue on multi-channel retailing. *Journal of Retailing, 91*(2), 174–181. doi:10.1016/j.jretai.2015.02.005

Walsh, G., Albrecht, A. K., Kunz, W., & Hofacker, C. F. (2016). Relationship between online retailers' reputation and product returns. *British Journal of Management, 27*(1), 3–20. doi:10.1111/1467-8551.12120

Walsh, G., & Möhring, M. (2017). Effectiveness of product return-prevention instruments: Empirical evidence. *Electronic Markets, 27*(4), 341–350. doi:10.100712525-017-0259-0

Wang, D., Hu, B., Hu, C., Zhu, F., Liu, X., Zhang, J., Wang, B., Xiang, H., Cheng, Z., Xiong, Y., Zhao, Y., Li, Y., Wang, X., & Peng, Z. (2020). Clinical Characteristics of 138 Hospitalized Patients with 2019 Novel Coronavirus-Infected Pneumonia in Wuhan, China. *Journal of the American Medical Association, 323*(11), 1061. Advance online publication. doi:10.1001/jama.2020.1585 PMID:32031570

Wang, Y. F., Chen, S. P., Lee, Y. C., & Tsai, C. T. (2013). Developing green management standards for restaurants: An application of green supply chain management. *International Journal of Hospitality Management, 34*(1), 263–273. doi:10.1016/j.ijhm.2013.04.001

Wang, Y. M., & Luo, Y. (2010). Integration of Correlations with Standard Deviations for Determining Attribute Weights in Multiple Attribute Decision Making. *Mathematical and Computer Modelling*, *51*(1-2), 1–12. doi:10.1016/j.mcm.2009.07.016

Ward, D. (2020). *4 ways to reduce e-commerce returns during Covid-19.* https://www.threekit.com/blog/4-ways-to-reduce-ecomm-product-returns

Webster, T. (2020). *Covid-19: Policies and protocol for returns and exchanges.* https://downtownfrederick.org/wp-content/uploads/COVID-19-Policies-and-Protocol-for-Returns-and-Exchanges1.pdf

Wells, J. (2020). *Amazon's Woodland Hills supermarket is now a dark store.* Retrieved June 15, 2021, from https://www.grocerydive.com/news/amazons-woodland-hills-supermarket-is-now-a-dark-store/575953/

WHO. (2010). The world health report: health systems financing: The path to universal coverage. WHO Library,

Wieland, A., & Wallenburg, C. M. (2012). Dealing With Supply Chain Risks: Linking Risk Management Practices and Strategies to Performance. *International Journal of Physical Distribution & Logistics Management*, *42*(10), 887–905. doi:10.1108/09600031211281411

Wieland, A., & Wallenburg, C. M. (2013). The influence of relational competencies on supply chain resilience: A relational view. *International Journal of Physical Distribution & Logistics Management*, *43*(4), 300–320. doi:10.1108/IJPDLM-08-2012-0243

Wieser, H., Tröger, N., & Hübner, R. (2015). The consumers' desired and expected product lifetimes. Plate Conference, 1-6.

Wong, C. W. Y., Lai, K. H., Shang, K. C., Lu, C. S., & Leung, T. K. P. (2012). Green operations and the moderating role of environmental management capability of suppliers on manufacturing firm performance. *International Journal of Production Economics*, *140*(1), 283–294. doi:10.1016/j.ijpe.2011.08.031

Wood, S. L. (2001). Remote purchase environments: The influence of return policy leniency on two-stage decision processes. *JMR, Journal of Marketing Research*, *38*(2), 157–169. doi:10.1509/jmkr.38.2.157.18847

World Bank. (2016). *World Bank Data.* http://data.worldbank.org/?display=default

World Economic Forum. (2020). *How to rebound stronger from Covid-19 Resilience in manufacturing and supply systems.* WEF White Paper. https://www3.weforum.org/docs/WEF_GVC_the_impact_of_COVID_19_Report.pdf

World Health Organization. (2020). *Coronavirus disease 2019 (COVID-19). Situation Report, 32.* WHO.

World Health Organization. (2020). *Coronavirus disease 2019 (COVID-19): Situation report 72.* WHO.

Xin, C., Cui, Y., & Zhao, J. (2007). Research on Some Problems in The Exploration of Project Logistics. *China Water Transport*, *5*, 206–208.

Xu, Z., Elomri, A., Kerbache, L., & El Omri, A. (2020). Impacts of COVID-19 on global supply chains: Facts and perspectives. *IEEE Engineering Management Review*, *48*(3), 153–166. doi:10.1109/EMR.2020.3018420

Yang, S., & Xiong, G. (2019). Try it on! Contingency effects of virtual fitting rooms. *Journal of Management Information Systems*, *36*(3), 789–822. doi:10.1080/07421222.2019.1628894

Yıldırım, A., & Şimşek, H. (2005). *Sosyal Bilimlerde Nitel Araştırma Yöntemleri*. Seçkin Yayıncılık.

Yu, Y., & Kim, H. S. (2019). Online retailers' return policy and prefactual thinking: An exploratory study of USA and China e-commerce markets. *Journal of Fashion Marketing and Management*, *23*(4), 504–518. doi:10.1108/JFMM-01-2019-0010

Zavadskas, E. K., Antucheviciene, J., Saparauskas, J., & Turskıs, Z. (2013a). MCDM Methods WASPAS and MULTIMOORA: Verification Of Robustness Of Methods When Assessing Alternative Solutions. *Economic Computation and Economic Cybernetics Studies and Research*, *47*(2), 1–5.

Zavadskas, E. K., Antucheviciene, J., Šaparauskas, J., & Turskis, Z. (2013b). Multi-Criteria Assessment of Facades' Alternatives: Peculiarities of Ranking Methodology. *Procedia Engineering*, *57*, 107–112. doi:10.1016/j.proeng.2013.04.016

Zhidong, Y., Xitang, Z. & Xiang, Y. (2012), Research on the Safety Evaluation of Oil-gas Storage and Transportation Systems Based on AHP. *Guangdong Chemical Industry*, 14.

Zhou, H., Benton, W. C. Jr, Schilling, D. A., & Milligan, G. W. (2011). Supply chain integration and the SCOR model. *Journal of Business Logistics*, *32*(4), 332–344. doi:10.1111/j.0000-0000.2011.01029.x

Zhu, Q., Krikke, H., & Caniels, M. (2016). Collaborate or not? A system dynamics study on disruption recovery. *Industrial Management & Data Systems*, *116*(2), 271–290. doi:10.1108/IMDS-05-2015-0209

Zhu, Q., & Sarkis, J. (2004). Relationships between operational practices and performance among early adopters of green supply chain management practices in Chinese manufacturing enterprises. *Journal of Operations Management*, *22*(3), 265–289. doi:10.1016/j.jom.2004.01.005

About the Contributors

Ana Paula Lopes is Professor at the Mathematics Department of the Porto Accounting and Business School (ISCAP) of the Polytechnic Institute of Porto (P.PORTO), Portugal, since 2000. She teaches subjects like Mathematics, Applied Mathematics, Financial Mathematics, Statistics, Simulation and Decision Models, Sampling Methods among others. She has a PhD in Mathematics (2006), in the field of Numerical Linear Algebra. Author and co-author of several peer-reviewed publications on teaching and learning methodologies and innovations on educational technology. She has coordinated several projects related to the Use of Technology and Pedagogical Innovation in Distance Education since '07 and received many awards over the years, namely: 3rd e-learning Excellence Awards (Award of Merit) for the case history "MatActiva Project – A Mathematical Dynamic Environment to engage Students in the Learning Process" ('17); the Honorable Mention of the Internationalization and Mobility Best Practices Award (BPIM) regarding the MatActiva Project (Math Connections, '16); the Award for Pedagogical Innovation in Distance Education ('15). She has been Member of Scientific Committee of several International Conferences, Member of the Scientific Board and Associate Editor of some Journals, serves as a regular reviewer of the program committee for several International Conferences and Journals, researcher at CEOS.PP - Centre for Organisational and Social Studies of P. Porto and at the Research Centre for the Study of Population, Economics and Society. She has spent teaching periods abroad, within the framework of Erasmus+ STT (Šiauliai -Lithuania, Prishtina - Kosovo, Maribor - Slovenia, Ourense - Spain, Split - Croatia, Warsaw - Poland, Málaga - Spain, Siedlce - Poland, Vilniaus - Lithuania, Hyvinkää - Finland, Bursa -Turkey, Prague - Czech Republic) and is actively developing new co-operations with partners and improving research contacts. Her main research interests are LMS supports platforms, ICT in education, b/ e-learning, teaching/learning education paradigm, Learning Analytics, E-Assessment, Multi-Criteria Decision Making, Applied Mathematics, Supply Chain Management, Logistics and Financial Mathematics.

* * *

About the Contributors

Ezgi Demir was born in Istanbul, Turkey. After completing her primary and secondary school education in Istanbul, she graduated from Yıldız Technical University from the department of Mathematical Engineering in 2014. She completed her master's degree in Marmara University, Department of Operational Research in 2016 with her studies in Artificial Intelligence and Game Theory. In 2020, she completed her PhD. studies in the same department with her studies on data mining and deep learning techniques in production planning and control processes. In 2019, she worked in the fields of "Applications of Artificial Intelligence for Healthcare Informatics" at Eindhoven Technical University. In addition to papers, articles and book chapters in the fields of "Artificial/Deep Learning", "Data Mining" and "Multi-Criteria Decision Making" in various journals and books; She has been working as a researcher in various national and international projects. She provides consultancy services in the sector within the scope of R&D, artificial intelligence, data science, strategy and feasibility studies. She gives lectures on Big Data Analytics, Database Management and Data Security at Piri Reis University and Kyrenia University. In addition to studying on an international project on route planning and artificial intelligence studies in UAVs at Lancaster University, she also has been working as an Assistant Proffessor at Gebze Technical University.

Niranjan Devkota is an economist with the special focus on cross border activities and climate change related issues focusing adaptation. He has over 10 years of experience in the field of economics related research with varietal dynamics. His recent research focuses ranges from development economics especially in cross-border activities and agriculture. He received his PhD degree from Tribhuvan University Nepal. He has experience in impact analysis and model building. He has worked in terms to prepare strategic and implementation plans of several economic issues as a research associates. He has received high level training and capacity building workshop on international co-operation, natural resource management and trade related activities from several international agencies like SANDEE (ICIMOD), NDRC (China), Hi-Aware (ICIMOD), SANEM (Bangladesh) and from esteemed organizations and universities (online mode). He has command over STATA and basic knowledge of R.

Çağlar Karamaşa was graduated from the Department of Business Administration at Anadolu University, Eskişehir, Turkey, in 2008. He finished his master degree in Quantitative Methods at Anadolu University in 2012. Following that he completed PhD degree in Quantitative Methods at the same university in 2018. He has been working as an Ass. Prof. in the Department of Business Administration at Anadolu University since 2014. His research interests include integer programming and applications, semi definite programming, dynamic programming, decision

About the Contributors

support systems, fuzzy sets, MCDM, data mining, information technologies and e-commerce applications.

Erdinç Koç received his BSc degree from the Department of Business Administration in Çankaya University, his master's and PhD degree from the Department of Business Administration in Ankara University. Currently he is an Assistant Professor at the Department of Business Administration in Bingol University. His research interest includes production management, productivity, supply chain management and technology management.

Selcuk Korucuk is an Associate Professor Operations Management at Giresun University, Turkey. He received his BS in Business Administration from Inonu University, MS in Business Administration from Gumushane University and PhD in Business Administration from Ataturk University. He teaches courses in Operations Management and Operations Research. His research interests are focused on, process management, logistics, fuzzy logic, and decision-making. Korucuk has several publications in national refereed journals and international conference proceedings.

Salih Memiş currently works at the Giresun University. Salih does research in Business Administration, Supply Chain Management, Innovation and Marketing.

Seeprata Parajuli is a Research Assistant at Quest Research Management Cell, Quest International College, Pokhara University, Gwarko, Lalitpur.

Udaya Raj Paudel is a principal at Quest International College.

Sharad Rajbhandari is an MBA Graduate at Quest International College.

Sashi Rana Magar is an MBA graduate from Quest International College.

Celina Rodrigues is a Master's degree student from Logistics Master Degree at Porto Accounting and Business School, Polytechnic of Porto.

Ruby Shrestha is an MBA Graduates at Quest International College.

Metehan Feridun Sorkun is an Associate Professor of Operations Management at Izmir University of Economics. His recent research interests cover topics in the fields of product returns, modularity, logistics service quality, reverse logistics, and waste management. He has publications in the leading academic journals, such as Industrial Marketing Management, Waste Management, and International Journal of Physical Distribution & Logistics Management. He earned his bachelor's degrees in Logistics Management and International Trade & Finance from Izmir University of Economics in 2010. He was a Visiting Scholar at the University of Greenwich in 2014. He completed the Ph.D. program in management, in 2016, jointly organized by Ca'Foscari University of Venice, the University of Padua, and the University of Verona.

José G. Vargas-Hernández, M.B.A., Ph.D., Member of the National System of Researchers of Mexico and a research professor at Posgraduate and Research Department, Tecnológico Mario Molina, Unidad Zapopan. Professor Vargas-Hernández has a Ph. D. in Public Administration and a Ph.D. in Organizational Economics. He has undertaken studies in Organisational Behaviour and has a Master of Business Administration, published four books and more than 200 papers in international journals and reviews (some translated to English, French, German, Portuguese, Farsi, Chinese, etc.) and more than 300 essays in national journals and reviews. He has obtained several international Awards and recognition.

Index

A

AHP 58, 119, 122, 129-130, 132, 142-145, 168-170, 173-174, 179, 182-184

B

bibliometrics 93-94, 115

C

co-citation analysis 96-97, 102
collaboration 70-73, 75, 79, 81-82, 84, 94, 108, 150, 160
collaborative network design 62, 74-75, 77-78
commercial product returns 86-89, 91-97, 99, 102, 104-105, 107-108, 112, 118
consumer returns 86, 104, 109-110, 116-117
corporate sustainability 74-78, 85
COVID-19 1-10, 13-20, 30, 39, 42, 62-69, 72, 76-77, 79-84, 86, 88-89, 107-110, 113-115, 117, 120-121, 145, 167, 180, 183-186, 190-193, 195, 197-202
co-word analysis 86, 98

D

dangerous goods 164-169, 175-176, 179-180
dangerous goods transportation 164, 167-169, 175-176, 179
deglobalization 21-23, 25-34, 36-38
digital-intensive business models 62

E

enterprises 14, 18, 23, 28, 42-43, 52-55, 120, 148, 163, 185, 195
environment 22, 27, 40, 43, 54, 58, 70, 75, 81, 86, 109, 114, 116, 146, 148-149, 160, 162, 164-168, 175, 180, 183, 197

F

flexibility 1, 3, 6, 14, 17-18, 20, 23, 43-44, 56-57, 59, 63, 68, 70-71, 73, 116, 121, 123-124, 134, 166, 179, 197-198
Food Businesses 39

G

global supply chains 9, 19, 21, 28-34, 80, 84, 186, 191-192, 197, 201-202
green supply management chain 146-147

K

Kathmandu valley 146, 150-152, 155-156

L

logistics 1, 3, 10-11, 16-18, 20, 28, 30-31, 33-34, 57-61, 65-67, 69, 71-81, 83-84, 86-87, 90, 93-94, 98, 101-104, 107-113, 116-118, 144, 160-161, 166, 168-169, 175, 181-184, 199-201

M

manufacturing 1-20, 24, 27, 29, 33-34, 46, 56-57, 62, 65, 67-68, 71, 83, 111, 113, 117, 120, 144, 146-153, 155-156, 159-163, 167, 183, 193, 195
manufacturing industries 146-150, 152-153, 155-156, 159-161

N

Nepal 146-148, 151, 159-162
NETWORK ANALYSIS 86, 96

O

omni-channel 86, 98, 101, 104-105, 108-110, 116-118
omni-channel returns 86, 104-105, 108-109
online shopping 69, 86, 90, 98, 101-103, 106-108, 113
operational efficiency 75, 85, 149, 155, 198

P

picture fuzzy sets 168, 170, 173, 179-181
production chain 29, 38, 71
production chains 21, 29-30, 33-34
PROMETHEE-GAIA 119
protectionism 21-28, 31, 37-38
protectionist policies 21-22, 29, 37

R

relocation of production 21-22, 27, 34-36, 38
resilience 20, 62, 65, 69-72, 76-78, 80, 82-84, 144, 185-186, 188-189, 196-201
resilient supply chain 65, 74, 77, 79, 85, 196, 199
return policy 90, 94, 98, 101-104, 109, 112-113, 118
reverse logistics 86, 93-94, 98, 101-104, 107-110, 112, 116-118, 160
risk management 43, 56-58, 61, 63-65, 69-70, 75, 80-81, 85, 165, 186-190, 196-198, 200, 202

S

Spatial Separation 98, 118
Strategic Returns 91, 118
supplier selection 45, 71, 119-120, 122-123, 129-130, 144-145
supply chain disruptions 62-63, 65, 68, 72, 76, 80, 82, 108, 190, 199-201
supply chain dynamics 39-42, 46, 52-55
supply chain resilience 62, 65, 70-72, 76, 78, 82-84, 198, 200-201
Supply Chain Risk Management Strategies 64, 85
sustainability 23, 31, 40-41, 45, 62, 65-68, 74-78, 85, 98, 102-103, 107, 113, 116, 148, 156, 160-161, 166
SWARA 39, 42, 45-46, 52-53, 55-56, 58, 60
systematic literature review 78

T

technology level 1, 3, 7, 9, 14-15, 17-18
Temporal Separation 107, 118
TOPSIS 59, 168, 170, 174, 178-179

V

value chains 3, 21-22, 28-34, 38, 197-198

W

warehouse location selection 164, 167-168, 176, 181
WASPAS 39, 42, 46, 49, 52-53, 55-57, 61

Recommended Reference Books

IGI Global's reference books can now be purchased from three unique pricing formats:
Print Only, E-Book Only, or Print + E-Book.
Shipping fees may apply.

www.igi-global.com

ISBN: 978-1-7998-1048-3
EISBN: 978-1-7998-1049-0
© 2020; 605 pp.
List Price: US$ 285

ISBN: 978-1-5225-8933-4
EISBN: 978-1-5225-8934-1
© 2020; 667 pp.
List Price: US$ 295

ISBN: 978-1-7998-0357-7
EISBN: 978-1-7998-0359-1
© 2020; 451 pp.
List Price: US$ 235

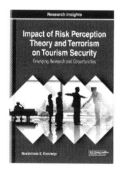

ISBN: 978-1-7998-0070-5
EISBN: 978-1-7998-0071-2
© 2020; 144 pp.
List Price: US$ 175

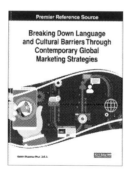

ISBN: 978-1-5225-6980-0
EISBN: 978-1-5225-6981-7
© 2019; 339 pp.
List Price: US$ 235

ISBN: 978-1-5225-5390-8
EISBN: 978-1-5225-5391-5
© 2018; 125 pp.
List Price: US$ 165

Do you want to stay current on the latest research trends, product announcements, news, and special offers?
Join IGI Global's mailing list to receive customized recommendations, exclusive discounts, and more.
Sign up at: **www.igi-global.com/newsletters**.

Publisher of Peer-Reviewed, Timely, and Innovative Academic Research

www.igi-global.com   Sign up at www.igi-global.com/newsletters   facebook.com/igiglobal   twitter.com/igiglobal

Ensure Quality Research is Introduced to the Academic Community

Become an Evaluator for IGI Global Authored Book Projects

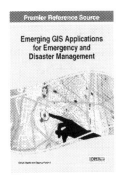 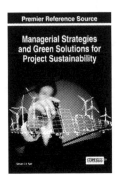  

The overall success of an authored book project is dependent on quality and timely manuscript evaluations.

Applications and Inquiries may be sent to:
development@igi-global.com

Applicants must have a doctorate (or equivalent degree) as well as publishing, research, and reviewing experience. Authored Book Evaluators are appointed for one-year terms and are expected to complete at least three evaluations per term. Upon successful completion of this term, evaluators can be considered for an additional term.

If you have a colleague that may be interested in this opportunity, we encourage you to share this information with them.

IGI Global Author Services

Providing a high-quality, affordable, and expeditious service, IGI Global's Author Services enable authors to streamline their publishing process, increase chance of acceptance, and adhere to IGI Global's publication standards.

Benefits of Author Services:

- **Professional Service:** All our editors, designers, and translators are experts in their field with years of experience and professional certifications.
- **Quality Guarantee & Certificate:** Each order is returned with a quality guarantee and certificate of professional completion.
- **Timeliness:** All editorial orders have a guaranteed return timeframe of 3-5 business days and translation orders are guaranteed in 7-10 business days.
- **Affordable Pricing:** IGI Global Author Services are competitively priced compared to other industry service providers.
- **APC Reimbursement:** IGI Global authors publishing Open Access (OA) will be able to deduct the cost of editing and other IGI Global author services from their OA APC publishing fee.

Author Services Offered:

English Language Copy Editing
Professional, native English language copy editors improve your manuscript's grammar, spelling, punctuation, terminology, semantics, consistency, flow, formatting, and more.

Scientific & Scholarly Editing
A Ph.D. level review for qualities such as originality and significance, interest to researchers, level of methodology and analysis, coverage of literature, organization, quality of writing, and strengths and weaknesses.

Figure, Table, Chart & Equation Conversions
Work with IGI Global's graphic designers before submission to enhance and design all figures and charts to IGI Global's specific standards for clarity.

Translation
Providing 70 language options, including Simplified and Traditional Chinese, Spanish, Arabic, German, French, and more.

Hear What the Experts Are Saying About IGI Global's Author Services

"Publishing with IGI Global has been an amazing experience for me for sharing my research. The strong academic production support ensures quality and timely completion." – **Prof. Margaret Niess, Oregon State University, USA**

"The service was very fast, very thorough, and very helpful in ensuring our chapter meets the criteria and requirements of the book's editors. I was quite impressed and happy with your service." – **Prof. Tom Brinthaupt, Middle Tennessee State University, USA**

Learn More or Get Started Here:

For Questions, Contact IGI Global's Customer Service Team at cust@igi-global.com or 717-533-8845

Celebrating Over 30 Years of Scholarly Knowledge Creation & Dissemination

www.igi-global.com

InfoSci®-Books

A Database of Nearly 6,000 Reference Books Containing Over 105,000+ Chapters Focusing on Emerging Research

GAIN ACCESS TO **THOUSANDS** OF REFERENCE BOOKS AT **A FRACTION** OF THEIR INDIVIDUAL LIST **PRICE**.

InfoSci®-Books Database

The **InfoSci®-Books** is a database of nearly 6,000 IGI Global single and multi-volume reference books, handbooks of research, and encyclopedias, encompassing groundbreaking research from prominent experts worldwide that spans over 350+ topics in 11 core subject areas including business, computer science, education, science and engineering, social sciences, and more.

Open Access Fee Waiver (Read & Publish) Initiative

For any library that invests in IGI Global's InfoSci-Books and/or InfoSci-Journals (175+ scholarly journals) databases, IGI Global will match the library's investment with a fund of equal value to go toward **subsidizing the OA article processing charges (APCs) for their students, faculty, and staff** at that institution when their work is submitted and accepted under OA into an IGI Global journal.*

INFOSCI® PLATFORM FEATURES

- Unlimited Simultaneous Access
- No DRM
- No Set-Up or Maintenance Fees
- A Guarantee of No More Than a 5% Annual Increase for Subscriptions
- Full-Text HTML and PDF Viewing Options
- Downloadable MARC Records
- COUNTER 5 Compliant Reports
- Formatted Citations With Ability to Export to RefWorks and EasyBib
- No Embargo of Content (Research is Available Months in Advance of the Print Release)

*The fund will be offered on an annual basis and expire at the end of the subscription period. The fund would renew as the subscription is renewed for each year thereafter. The open access fees will be waived after the student, faculty, or staff's paper has been vetted and accepted into an IGI Global journal and the fund can only be used toward publishing OA in an IGI Global journal. Libraries in developing countries will have the match on their investment doubled.

To Recommend or Request a Free Trial:
www.igi-global.com/infosci-books

eresources@igi-global.com • Toll Free: 1-866-342-6657 ext. 100 • Phone: 717-533-8845 x100

www.igi-global.com

Publisher of Peer-Reviewed, Timely, and Innovative Academic Research Since 1988

IGI Global's Transformative Open Access (OA) Model:
How to Turn Your University Library's Database Acquisitions Into a Source of OA Funding

Well in advance of Plan S, IGI Global unveiled their OA Fee Waiver (Read & Publish) Initiative. Under this initiative, librarians who invest in IGI Global's InfoSci-Books and/or InfoSci-Journals databases will be able to subsidize their patrons' OA article processing charges (APCs) when their work is submitted and accepted (after the peer review process) into an IGI Global journal.

How Does it Work?

Step 1: **Library Invests in the InfoSci-Databases:** A library perpetually purchases or subscribes to the InfoSci-Books, InfoSci-Journals, or discipline/subject databases.

Step 2: **IGI Global Matches the Library Investment with OA Subsidies Fund:** IGI Global provides a fund to go towards subsidizing the OA APCs for the library's patrons.

Step 3: **Patron of the Library is Accepted into IGI Global Journal (After Peer Review):** When a patron's paper is accepted into an IGI Global journal, they option to have their paper published under a traditional publishing model or as OA.

Step 4: **IGI Global Will Deduct APC Cost from OA Subsidies Fund:** If the author decides to publish under OA, the OA APC fee will be deducted from the OA subsidies fund.

Step 5: **Author's Work Becomes Freely Available:** The patron's work will be freely available under CC BY copyright license, enabling them to share it freely with the academic community.

Note: This fund will be offered on an annual basis and will renew as the subscription is renewed for each year thereafter. IGI Global will manage the fund and award the APC waivers unless the librarian has a preference as to how the funds should be managed.

Hear From the Experts on This Initiative:

"I'm very happy to have been able to make one of my recent research contributions *freely available* along with having access to the *valuable resources* found within IGI Global's InfoSci-Journals database."

– **Prof. Stuart Palmer**, Deakin University, Australia

"Receiving the support from IGI Global's OA Fee Waiver Initiative *encourages me to continue my research work without any hesitation*."

– **Prof. Wenlong Liu**, College of Economics and Management at Nanjing University of Aeronautics & Astronautics, China

For More Information, Scan the QR Code or Contact: IGI Global's Digital Resources Team at eresources@igi-global.com